Decoding the Socio-Economic Approach to Management

Results of the Second SEAM Conference in the United States

A volume in
Research in Management Consulting
Anthony F. Buono, *Series Editor*

Decoding the Socio-Economic Approach to Management

Results of the Second SEAM Conference in the United States

edited by

John Conbere
University of St. Thomas

Henri Savall
University Jean Moulin Lyon 3 and ISEOR

Alla Heorhiadi
University of St. Thomas

INFORMATION AGE PUBLISHING, INC.
Charlotte, NC • www.infoagepub.com

Library of Congress Cataloging-in-Publication Data

A CIP record for this book is available from the Library of Congress
http://www.loc.gov

ISBN: 978-1-68123-251-5 (Paperback)
       978-1-68123-252-2 (Hardcover)
       978-1-68123-253-9 (ebook)

Printed in the United States of America

CONTENTS

v

PART II

ORGANIZATIONAL EXPERIENCES USING SEAM

PART III

FURTHER REFLECTIONS ON SEAM

PREFACE

Anthony F. Buono

This book is part of an ongoing collaboration between (a) the Research in Management Consulting (RMC) series, (b) Henri Savall, Véronique Zardet, and their team from the Socio-Economic Institute for Firms and Organizations (ISEOR) in Ecully, France, and (c) John Conbere and Alla Heorhiadi from St. Thomas University in Minneapolis. Our endeavor is to bring the Socio-Economic Approach to Management (SEAM) to life in the United States. In November 2012 Conbere and Heorhiadi hosted Savall and his team of intervener-researchers for the first conference devoted to SEAM in the United States, a gathering that was captured in Savall, Conbere, Heorhiadi, Cristallini, and Buono (2014). That volume attempted to capture the papers, critiques, and exchanges that were presented and took place at the 2012 meeting. This book continues that exploration, delving further into the application of SEAM based on the outcomes from a second conference in May 2014.

For those not familiar with the work of ISEOR or the 2012 breakthrough conference on SEAM in the United States, a bit of background is in order. The Socio-Economic Approach to Management (SEAM) is an integrative intervention model that encompasses the qualitative, quantitative, and financial dimensions of organizational life. Emerging from Savall's seminal work on organizational intervention (e.g., Savall, 1975; Savall & Zardet, 1987, 2004), SEAM is a scientific approach to consultancy that focuses on uncovering the *dysfunctions* and *hidden costs* that exist in organizations,

Decoding the Socio-Economic Approach to Management, pages ix–xi
Copyright © 2016 by Information Age Publishing
All rights of reproduction in any form reserved.

"hidden" in the sense that they are not captured by traditional accounting methods and financial analyses. Through focused intervention that encompasses the entire organization—what the ISEOR team refers to as the HORIVERT approach (combining horizontal and vertical intervention)—the underlying goal is to enhance organizational performance by attacking the "TFW virus." According to Savall and his colleagues, this virus, which is a vestige of the early work by Frederick Taylor, Henri Fayol, and Max Weber (hence the TFW acronym), has sufficiently infiltrated our thinking about management and organization to the point where we are falling well short of our own potential. The resultant *dysfunctions* this virus unleashes creates *hidden costs* that lead to the *noncreation of potential,* readily destroying a firm's *value-added* possibilities.

Similar to my own experience in being captivated by SEAM, after being exposed to this work while visiting ISEOR, Conbere and Heorhiadi became sufficiently intrigued by the SEAM approach that they worked diligently to become "SEAM practitioners." Following their participation in a number of ISEOR conferences and training sessions, they continued to explore and reflect on the cultural differences and nuances that raised knowledge transfer-related challenges in bringing SEAM to the United States. As a way of further developing and testing their understanding and expertise with the SEAM approach, they integrated the framework in their classrooms, working with the next generation of intervener-researchers in ISEOR's ongoing internationalization and entry in the United States—providing the impetus for the initial 2012 conference.

The results of that first undertaking—*Facilitating the Socio-Economic Approach to Management* (Savall et al., 2014)—captured the ideas exchanged during the meeting. The volume attempted to draw the reader into the conference itself as the different chapters included the contributors' comments at the meeting ("Chapter Prologue: Conference Remarks"), their revised conference papers, and the question and answer dialogue for the session. This volume builds on that earlier work and is based on the second U.S. conference dedicated to SEAM, held once again on the St. Thomas University campus in Minneapolis in May 2014.

As you read through the volume, you will gain more insight into the destructive nature of the TFW virus, and the ways we can intervene to unleash the human potential that exists in our organizations. In addition to the emphasis on SEAM within a U.S. context, the volume also explores the potential of the approach in Belgium, Lebanon, and Ukraine, in a variety of different contexts, including the relationship of SEAM with other intervention frameworks (Lean, Six Sigma) and the challenge of creating agile organizations (Worley, Williams, & Lawler, 2014) that regularly outperform other firms in the same industry.

I would like to, once again, add my personal thanks to my ISEOR and University of St. Thomas colleagues, as well as all the conference participants and chapter co-authors, for their contribution to a core objective of the RMC series—to capture the true blending of theory and practice as we continually strive to improve our ability to successfully intervene in today's complex and ever-changing organizations.

REFERENCES

Savall, H. (1975). *Enrichir le travail humain: L'évaluation économique* [Job enrichment: An economic evaluation]. Paris, France: Dunod.

Savall, H., Conbere, J., Heorhiadi, A., Cristallini, V., & Buono, A.F. (2014). *Facilitating the socio-economic approach to management: Results of the first SEAM conference in North America.* Charlotte, NC: Information Age Publishing.

Savall, H. & Zardet, V. (1987). *Maîtriser les coûts et les performances cachés: Le contrat d'activité périodiquement négociables* [Mastering hidden costs and performance: The periodically negotiable activity contract]. Paris, France: Economica.

Savall, H. & Zardet, V. (2004). *Recherche en sciences de gestion: Approche qualimétrique – Observer l'objet complexe.* [Research in management sciences: The qualimetric approach—Observing the complex object]. Paris, France: Economica.

Worley, C., Williams, T., & Lawler, E. E., III. (2014). *The agility factor: Building adaptable organizations for superior performance.* San Francisco, CA: Jossey-Bass.

INTRODUCTION

John Conbere and Alla Heorhiadi

We were introduced to the Socio-Economic Approach to Management (SEAM) at the ISEOR-Academy of Management conference in Lyon in 2006. We sensed then that SEAM had tremendous potential—and our experience since has confirmed our hunch. We are practitioners and academics, teaching Organization Development on the masters and doctoral level and consulting about organizational change in the United States and Europe. We believe SEAM is the best organizational change approach of which we know.

Why? There are several reasons. SEAM begins with the right values. SEAM is intentionally a whole system intervention. SEAM actively challenges the destructive managerial fantasies that are predominant in most organizations, and which Henri Savall and his colleagues have spelled out as the TFW (Taylorism-Fayolism-Weberism) virus . (See Chapters 9 and 10 and Henri Savall's brief history for more on the virus). SEAM has the most extensive research base of any organizational change approach—over 40 years of detailed assessment of SEAM interventions. SEAM recognizes that standard accounting misses around 40% of what happens in organizations, and teases out these hidden costs. More than anything else, we have chosen to use SEAM because SEAM works. That is an important criterion since many change efforts fail. "Even with dozens of change models developed and countless changes implemented, in a study of 210 North American businesses . . . 75 percent of initiatives fail to make an impact" (Raelin & Cataldo, 2011, p. 482).

Decoding the Socio-Economic Approach to Management, pages xiii–xvi
Copyright © 2016 by Information Age Publishing
All rights of reproduction in any form reserved.

There are two aspects of SEAM that we want to address in this introduction, analysis and respect. In the SEAM experience, interventions are most often carried out through the whole organization, beginning with leaders and including all employees. This is the participatory inclusion that according to Rensis Likert, was shown to be most effective, yet is not practiced often enough in the United States. Underneath the idea of inclusion of all is respect for the rights and needs of every individual. Henri Savall and the ISEOR team use the sociological term "actors" to describe employees, be they CEOs or janitors. All are actors in the workplace drama. All are essential. All are included.

This is not to say that each actor has the same role. Managers' primary task is steering the organization. If managers are not steering, they are failing the organization. One of the SEAM management tools involves assessing how managers use time. This tool discloses how much time is spent on doing everyday mundane work, responding to dysfunctions, or steering people. Most time assessment tools measure what people do, but none of those tools aim at analysis of how much time is spent on dealing with dysfunction versus steering people and developing people's potential.

In SEAM, analysis is constant. In the Mirror Effect, Hidden Costs, and Expert Opinion, the researcher-interveners analyze the whole organization. In the Piloting Logbook, managers are encouraged to assess progress on efforts to reduce dysfunctions and increase potential. The management tools allow managers to analyze how time, resources, and effort are used, and the extent to which these enable or reduce dysfunctions.

There is a radical concept underpinning the analysis. This is the belief that actors do the best they can. If they are not effective, the fault is probably that of the organization. Too often when problems are found in the workplace, the response is to figure out who should be blamed. This is the opposite of respect. The penchant for blaming is a result of the TFW virus, the mental model in which if people are obedient, then everything will work well, and so if there is a problem, some people were not doing their part—They were not obedient. SEAM challenges the very idea of obedience and begins with respecting all actors in the organization.

The respect for all persons has other ramifications. In SEAM there is emphasis on negotiation. There will always be differences between the needs and desires of employees and employer, between managers and the people who report to them. Usually people are blind to these, since the modern business is based on a mental model, in which an employee must be obedient as a condition of employment. However, employees cannot be not obedient, as they are not automatons. When employees' needs are not met, they can get angry, or sulk, or quit, or slow down, or even sabotage. When employees are not respected, the organization loses some of their effort. In SEAM language, the organization fails to make use of their full human potential. So the SEAM task is recognizing when there are differences, and then using these differences as opportunities to negotiate a situation that would work for all who are involved.

Probably it is hard to realize how radical the process of negotiation in the workplace is. The insistence on negotiation is certainly counter-cultural in organizations in western society. Someone may disagree and bring the example of unions. Yes, a union can bargain for the rights of the group of workers, but never for the needs of the individual to be effective. And the goal of negotiation from the SEAM perspective is to achieve a high effectiveness of work, while having satisfaction from this work. Three of the six SEAM management tools foster negotiation. In the Competency Grid, all of the knowledge and skills that are needed for doing the work, and for developing new work opportunities, are spelled out. Each person's abilities are assessed, and one has a holistic picture of the state of the department, or division, or whatever unit is being assessed. The Competency Grid is then used to start negotiations with each employee. What does the employee need to learn, where would the employee like to develop? Two factors are considered, the needs of the employee and the needs of the organization. The outcome is negotiated.

With the Priority Action Plan the specific goals for the next six months are detailed, and each manager has to create, and negotiate, her own Priority Action Plan. As the planning cascades down through the levels of managers, the actors' efforts are aligned. But it is a negotiation, not an imposition by fiat. This negotiation approach allows the actors to avoid magical thinking, when employees are given more tasks every day without removing any tasks, with the expectation of maintaining the quality and efficiency of their work. We have a student who used the concept of negotiation at work. Each time her boss gave her a new task, she would say, "I am working as hard as I can, so when I take on this task what should I give up?" Then they would talk about where she would apply her efforts. After a while the manager came to expect her question. By negotiating she trained her manager to give up magical thinking.

Such negotiation cannot happen if the employee is not respected. The temptation to revert to the mental model in which employees should be obedient is very strong, and we suspect that it is respect that helps managers overcome the illusion of employee obedience.

Having praised SEAM, we acknowledge that it is not easy to learn SEAM. There are several reasons. SEAM appears to be complex at first. There is new jargon, a series of prescribed steps, the mystery of digging out and calculating hidden costs, the puzzle of how one actually does increase human potential, and the challenge of changing deep beliefs and values. We have taught SEAM for some years before creating a certificate and master's programs in which people could learn the art of SEAM interventions.

Most students of the certificate program were either OD doctoral graduates or working on their OD dissertations—a smart and experienced crew. Yet even after 5 classes, many of them found it difficult to do the first SEAM intervention.

The French all along have apprenticed SEAM intervener-researchers, and we can see the value of modeling with apprentices before asking people to do the work themselves. We think that this is true, in part, because some of the work of SEAM develops in response to the need of the organization. At this point, however, we have not developed enough to be able to supply a steady series of apprenticeships.

The hardest thing about learning SEAM is that a person has to be willing to try to live the SEAM values, and to nurture this in the managers of the client organization. The learning calls for self-analysis, internal change, and then examination of the ways one helps managers learn SEAM. Without this internal change, SEAM efforts will remain on the surface, and will shrink or disappear with the next change in organizational top management.

What we wanted to do in the SEAM conferences is bring people together with knowledge and experience of SEAM. Partly this is so English speaking people in North America can talk with each other and the European founders and practitioners of SEAM. This is not the same as apprenticing, but unless one can spend a serious amount of time in Lyon, France, these conferences may be an important way to transmit both the knowledge of the founders of SEAM and the experience of intervener-researchers on both sides of the Atlantic.

The readers may find the materials in the book to be rich and informative with one caveat. The reader will not get the experience of Henri Savall quietly asking if he might add something, and then jumping to the board and illustrating a subtle point, his body taut and his eyes flashing with excitement. For that you have to attend the conference. To counterbalance this visual deficit, we have both the presentations and discussions that took place after presentations in this book. This may help to partially convey the atmosphere of the conference and create a sense of "live" knowledge.

REFERENCE

Raelin, J. D. & Cataldo, C. G. (2011). Whither Middle Management? Empowering Interface and the Failure of Organizational Change. *Journal of Change Management, 11*(4), 481–507.

TFW VIRUS CONCEPT HISTORY

Henri Savall

The "TFW virus" is a concept developed in the socio-economic theory created by Henri Savall. It is a criticism of Taylor, Fayol, and Weber's theories which are classical organizational models considered by socio-economic theory as generating ineffectiveness, inefficiency, and human frustration.

Actually, the maximal division of labor, the dichotomy between conception, decision, and realization of activities (Taylor, 1911; Fayol, 1916), as well as the depersonalization of jobs and prominence of impersonal rules (Weber, 1947) were advised to achieve performance. It could be a viable assumption in the old context. But, today, an organizational model and a way of thinking based on them would not allow anymore creating value-added. However, they are still thriving in contemporary organizations.

For the first time, these criticisms were put forward by Henri Savall in 1974 in his second PhD dissertation at the University Paris–Dauphine named *Enrichir le travail humain: L'évaluation* économique [Job enrichment: An economic evaluation], which was fully published in 1975 with former president of European Communities, Jacques Delors's preface; and translated into Spanish, *Por un trabajo más humano* (1977); and English, *Work and People: An Economic Evaluation of Job-Enrichment* (1981) with Ansoff's preface. Through many intervention-research projects, Henri Savall and Véronique Zardet noticed many impacts due to these theories and tried to

Decoding the Socio-Economic Approach to Management, pages xvii–xx
Copyright © 2016 by Information Age Publishing
All rights of reproduction in any form reserved.

attenuate them. As they learned how to proceed when implementing SEAM within organizations, they created a vaccine named "socio-economic management." The present name "TFW virus" was created by Henri Savall and Véronique Zardet and first taught to the ISEOR's scholars and researchers. Then, they disseminated this concept in their courses at the University Jean Moulin Lyon 3 master and PhD programs. The "TFW virus" concept appeared as such in 2006, 2009, and 2010 in French and Mexican conference proceedings and books published by French and Belgian publishers and further publications.

Nowadays, the socio-economic theory is fitting in the corporate social responsibility (CSR) and sustainable development trend, which is going full steam. So, the "TFW virus" concept can be easily known and keeps being diffused in many conferences, as other authors continue to publish on this concept, particularly Alla Heorhiadi, John Conbere and Chato Hazelbaker (2014), and Alanna Kennedy (2014).

REFERENCES

Fayol, H. (1916). *Administration industrielle et générale* [*General and industrial management*]. Paris, France: Dunod.

Heorhiadi, A., Conbere, J., & Hazelbaker, C. (2014). Virtue vs. Virus: Can OD Overcome the Heritage of Scientific Management? *Organization Development Practitioner, 46* (3) 27–31.

Kennedy, A. G. (2014). Taylor's illusion: An historical account of the progression of the "TFW" virus. In H. Savall, J. P. Conbere, A. Heorhiadi, V. Cristallini, & A. F. Buono (Eds.), *Facilitating the socio-economic approach to management: Results of the first SEAM conference in North America* (pp. 19–32). Charlotte, NC: Information Age.

FOR FURTHER READING

Savall, H. (1974). *Enrichir le travail humain: l'évaluation* économique [Job enrichment: An economic evaluation] (Doctoral dissertation). University Paris–Dauphine. Text fully published by Dunod editions, 1975, with former president of European Communities, Jacques Delors's preface. Translated in Spanish in 1977, *Por un trabajo más humano* (Tecniban editions, Madrid). Translated in English in 1981, *Work and people—An Economic Evaluation of Job-Enrichment* (Oxford University Press editions, New York), with H. I. Ansoff's preface (republished in 2010, Charlotte, NC: IAP).

Savall, H., & Zardet, V. (2006, April). *Théorie socio-économique des organisations: Impacts sur quelques concepts dominants dans les théories et pratiques managériales [Socio-economic theory: Impacts on some mainstream concepts in management theories and pratices]*. Paper present at the Academy of Management (ODC Division) & ISEOR Conference, Lyon, France, 267–302.

Savall, H., & Zardet, V. (2006, November). *Émergence des micro-théories psychoso-ciologiques cachées dans la théorie socio-économique des organisations [Emergence of psycho-sociological micro-theories hidden in SEAM]*. Paper presented at the IPM Conference proceedings, Lyon, France, 323:340.

Savall, H., & Zardet, V. (2009, June). *Mesure et pilotage de la responsabilité sociale et so-ciétale de l'entreprise: Résultats de recherches longitudinales [Measuring and piloting corporate social responsibility: Results from longitudinal research]*. Paper presented at the International conference proceedings and doctoral consortium, partnership between the Academy of Management (AOM) and ISEOR, Lyon, France.

Savall, H. & Zardet, V. (2009, July), *Responsabilidad social y societal de la empresa: indicadores para dialogar con las partes interesadas [The corporate social responsibility: Indicators to converse with stakeholders]*. Paper presented at the ACACIA's Conference proceedings, Mexico City, México.

Savall, H. & Zardet, V. (2009, September). *Los indicadores de pilotaje de la responsabilidad social y societal de la empresa resultados de experimentación [Piloting indicators of the corporate social responsibility—results of experiments]*. Paper presented at the 11th International Conference on Costs Management proceedings, Trelew, Argentina.

Savall, H., & Zardet, V. (2010, March). *Le management de la responsabilité sociale de l'entreprise par les indicateurs [Corporate social responsibility management through indicators]*. Paper presented at the International Conference proceedings on Corporate Social Responsibility, Descartes, Paris.

Savall, H., & Zardet, V. (2010). Le non-dit dans la théorie socio-économique des organisations: Situations de management et pièces de théâtre [Unvoiced comment in the socio-economic theory of organizations: Management situations and theatrics]. In Rodolphe OCLER (Ed.), *Fantasmes, mythes, non-dits et quiproquo: Analyse de discours et organisation [Fantasy, myths, unvoiced and misunderstanding: Analysis of speech and organization]* (pp. 9–35). Paris, France: L'Harmattan.

Savall, H., & Zardet, V. (2010, April). *Inversión en desarrollo cualitativo del potencial humano: Mejorar la responsabilidad social de la empresa y la rentabilidad [Investment in qualitative development in human potential: Improve corporate social responsibility and profitability]*. Paper presented at the ACACIA's Conference proceedings, Monterrey, Mexico.

Savall, H. & Zardet, V. (2010, June). *La métamorphose des services publics: Résultats qualimétriques d'amélioration de l'efficience, de l'efficacité et de la qualité des services aux usagers [Public services metamorphosis: Qualimetrics results of improvement of efficiency, effectivenes,s and quality of services to users]*. Paper presented at the 2nd Transatlantic Conference on Auditing, Mangement Control, and Costs proceedings, sponsored by American Accounting Association (AAA)-International Institute of Costs (IIC) & ISEOR, Lyon, France.

Savall, H., Zardet, V., & Bonnet , M. (2010, March). *RSE et développement durable, fondements de la théorie socio-économique des organisations [CSR and sustainable development, basis of socio-economic theory]*. Paper presented at the ADERSE Conference proceedings. La Rochelle, France. Published in Nicole Barthe

& J-Jacques Rosé (Eds.), RSE et développement durable [CSR between globalization and sustainable development] (pp. 3–36). Brussels, Belgium: De Boeck.

Savall, H. (2011, March). *Petite lecture épistemologique sans prétention de la responsabilité sociale de l'entreprise* [Little epistemological reading without arrogance of corporate social responsibility]. Keynote speaker at the ADERSE 2011 Conference proceedings, on CSR and global governance, Paris, France. Published in A. Le Flanchec, O. Uzan, & M. Doucin (Eds.), RSE et gouvernance mondiale [CSR and global governance] (pp. 3–22). (2012). Paris, France: Economica.

Taylor, F.W. (1911). *The principles of scientific management.* New York, NY: Harper & Brothers.

Weber, M. (1947). *Theory of social and economic organization.* Translated by A. Henderson & T. Parsons. New York, NY: Free Press.

PART I

THE SOCIO-ECONOMIC APPROACH
TO MANAGEMENT: THEORETICAL PERSPECTIVES

CHAPTER 1

HUMAN POTENTIAL AT THE CORE OF SOCIO-ECONOMIC THEORY (SEAM)

Henri Savall, Michel Péron, and Véronique Zardet

CONFERENCE REMARKS:
Chapter Prologue

The socio-economic approach to management led ISEOR, as a center of research and consulting company, to consider business as an exploration area suitable for both experimentation and clear-cut conceptualization, and prohibiting all our researchers to escape the abstract and abstruse ratiocinations. If the smooth running of a business depends on the creativity and initiative of the individuals that compose it, it seems obvious that focusing on human potential and its development is crucial.

The cornerstone that imparts strength and durability to our method is precisely the particular importance we attach to human potential whose consideration is vital in all areas of activity regardless of type and size of an enterprise, an organization, a city, a region, or a nation. It is around this concept that our analysis of the very core of our work will hinge.

Decoding the Socio-Economic Approach to Management, pages 3–26
Copyright © 2016 by Information Age Publishing
All rights of reproduction in any form reserved.

A BIRD'S EYE-VIEW OF HUMAN POTENTIAL

We are far from being the first to take an interest in human potential. Jean Bodin already argued in 1576 in a book entitled *The Six Books of the Commonwealth* that there was neither wealth nor power than men. Human resources are highlighted today in mission statements or statements of beliefs of many American companies. Human potential is, besides, part and parcel of the traditional values of Puritanism as it is closely connected to the concepts of individualism (i.e., personal responsibility with a strong desire to move forward). It also reminds us of the pyramid of needs of Abraham Maslow (1954) which culminates with personal fulfillment.

The concept of human potential (or human potentialities) would become very important and widespread with the New Wave movement (between 1960 and 1980). The latter will invite people to escape the prevailing materialistic and utilitarian trend in favor of a more spiritual vision marked, apart from the evocation of individual Karma, by the seals of Hinduism and Buddhism which it rejuvenates in a westernized version supplemented by meditation techniques and yoga sessions. This approach is supposed to bring meaning to the absurd existence of the individual who does not hold the truth alone. Such a philosophy aims at a collective transformation of ways of being and not that of the isolated individual.

The New Agers believed in the possibility of creating a new age of love, joy, peace, abundance, and harmony. The purpose of human existence would be to learn about one's own qualities in order to evince them in one's daily activities. The sphere of business was gradually invaded by consultants claiming such an approach to encourage behavioral change at all levels of the company. They offer, as is done today around the world but generally in a purely incantatory way, to rethink the decision-making process in companies and organizations and to introduce dialog as the mainspring of communication and pivotal element in intra-company and inter-company cooperation.

While searching on the web what the concept of human potential is connected with, we realized that the spiritual approach occupies center stage, without having to refer to the Church of Scientology which tries to maximize human potential by supervising the activity of organizations that provide training to employees of companies in Human Potential Seminars. They are sometimes considered psychologically dangerous and accused of traumatic experiences leading to brainwashing.

In the United States, a Human Potential Movement, born in the mid-1960s within the counter-culture stream, referred to Maslow's (1954) about the theory of human motivation which raised its pyramid of needs with self-actualization at its top. This movement aimed to foster happiness, creativity, and individual fulfillment. In 1962, the Ensalen Institute invited its trainees tempted by introspection, to sessions of psychotherapy on the lookout for untapped psychological and spiritual resources. Through specialized seminars, these sessions, have since been largely opened to the world of business. In 1986 a Human Potential Center opened in Austin (Texas) for people eager to learn and grow.

But the title of a book by Christopher Lasch, *The Culture of Narcissism: American life in an age of diminishing expectations* (1979), expresses the difference between the essentially contemplative approach of New Agers and our collective mobilization of human potentials essential to ensure the survival and development of companies. We should not, however, fail to mention the "Human Potential Project" of Chris Majer, outlined in his book *The Power to Transform* (2009), which led to developing (for twenty years) a commitment based management at a time when, he says, coordination will supplant supervision in the business world. Hence the need for companies to count on leaders and managers able to develop their potential.

It sounds like advice given by experts of recruitment agencies on the lookout for high potential personnel as the saying goes—or like questions put forward by future employers on candidates' personality, adaptability, listening skills, curiosity, versatility. But to say "your people determine your success or failure" is a truism, everything rests on the most effective and most efficient method to mobilize them. Commitment based management provides a list of qualities that leaders must demonstrate on the one hand and managers on the other hand in a relatively academic approach. ISEOR is interested in misused or unemployed human potential in the company where its researchers were called in. Indeed, hidden costs arise from conflicting relationships within companies and organizations between the individual (or team) and the direction of the company. Although it has some similarities with the concept of human potential as evidenced by the above remarks, our theory of human potential makes this concept the pivotal factor, in a pro-active approach to business. Of course the self-fulfillment of the employees at every level of the enterprise, is an indispensable step forward increasing the firm's performance. They have to be made more responsible, motivated, implicated, and empowered but their objective as part of a team is to achieve interpersonal effectiveness.

When we talk about human potential theory, it is not an abstract discourse on the subject, but a structured set of identified elements and interrelationships between them all. It is a way to redeploy active factors, the active units of François Perroux, and to distinguish inert factors, even passive ones. Our theory is somehow evidence-based, experimented and experienced, materialized by a set of concepts immediately and systematically organized. It is the result of a research work carried out with the field's cooperation for nearly 40 years whose results had been tested *in vivo*.

In management, contrary to what happens in the social sciences that take into account individual drives, the concept of human potential cannot be applied to each actor of the company individually. Because, apart from the case of one-person companies, any form of organization is by its very nature inter-individual, inter-tram, even inter-company. The socio-economic theory distinguishes between the visible structure of the company and "the intangible and hidden infrastructure based on human potential."

The active unit of Perroux (1975) should be understood as the individual and his environment, in line with our definition of human potential which is: the resources which are latent in an individual or a group of people, which has the capacity for production, innovation, creation, development and transformation of the environment. Company actors are not doomed to be subjected to their environment. Far from being passive contemplators of the evolution of their enterprises, they have the ability to fight against the exogenous determination of their fate in so far as they are not considered as hired-hands (labor) but as full members of an organization whose interests converge with theirs.

There is a key idea that sums up the innermost objective of the socio-economic methodology. The survival and development of enterprises rests on having a better change strategy that includes intangible investments in the development of human potential (Savall & Zardet, 2008). This consideration does not appear, in general, in the balance sheets bottom-line of companies and organizations. The socio-economic method aims to see beyond this line by adding the studied factors in great breadth and detail of the creation of value added generated by a stronger involvement of human potential. The concept is also mentioned in the book of Tad Tuleja, *Beyond the Bottom Line* (1987), where the author questions the values of companies. But, it is a caring about strategy rather than a working with one, concerned with commitment to the individual rather than to development of people.

A single individual cannot bear alone on his/her environment. The signatories of the Mayflower Compact had realized this when highlighting the community nature of their enterprise, committing themselves to reach agreement for the proper ordering, maintaining, and furthering of the goals of their mission. Everyone's potential is put at the service of all. It is the only active factor in value added creation, technical and financial capital being undoubtedly a valuable tool but a sterile one, when it is not activated by human potential. They are trying to convince us that to deal with difficulties in a competitive environment, it would be sufficient to consider the personnel as an adjustment variable and to resort to material investments in the form of new machines, new technologies much more efficient than those of our competitors. But the socio-economic theory demonstrates that machine, even in the humanoid era, does not spark off productivity or prosperity. Man who created the machine is the only one able to make it work. To maintain that the purchase and the installation of a more powerful machine will save a company from bankruptcy is a sham if the human potential as the active factor is eliminated. That is why the socio-economic approach to companies does not allow labor cutback except in exceptional cases, as it aims to increase the level of intangible investment in human potential. If during what is euphemistically called a restructuring we believe to reduce costs, we forget that at the same time we deprive the company of the value brought in by laid-off individuals. The capital of the company is, of course, a valuable tool in terms of human potential productivity but only if we consider the two factors as complementary rather than opposed, as it is the case with the decision to resort to massive layoffs. Cost accounting should actually consider not only the costs of activities, but incorporate the value carried by human potential. The socio-economic theory considers both elements as inseparable and invites from now on to speak about costs-values of activities in companies and organizations.

There exists in every individual alone a potential source of conflict that teamwork and collective interaction integrate into a collaborative quest of solutions, shifting it from a factor status to that of dynamic factor in discussion: The company performance is directly related to the control of the individualism of individuals. Under the direction of a bandmaster, musicians will produce a symphony, but leaving them free to play their respective partitions cannot but lead to a cacophony. Human potential can be defined ultimately as the cooperation and interaction ability of companies and organizations' actors and their capacity to create value. In mainstream models, this cooperation is poorly organized. The socio-economic theory has developed 3 principles that entail a greater openness to conflicting issues and facilitates the collective achievement of a compromise. This is the contradictory inter-subjectivity, cognitive interactivity, and generic contingency principles.

The principle of contradictory inter-subjectivity is to explicitly compare the different actors with their respective views and analyses to identify convergences and specificities and enable a collaborative use of the information obtained. These interactions between actors are the only possibility to lead to a limited convergence without wasting constructive potentialities. So as to avoid the difficulties entailed by subjectivity in organizational operations, the contradictory inter-subjectivity principle consists in building up some common ground for, or hard core of generic knowledge, which the company actors are in a position to recognize, share, and take over, starting from the subjective and contrary statements collected during the intervention-research.

At all levels of the company, conflicts or tensions can take place in teams, which is positive because the controversy eventually is a source of knowledge. Diversity in the teams' composition can contribute to the enrichment of intra-company dialogue and strengthens the cognitive interactivity resulting from the clash of ideas, from the permanent confrontation of points of view. An individual does not create alone a genuine dysfunction. Dysfunction is, in truth, a concatenation of mini-dysfunctions. The wrongdoer causes dysfunctions which effect others and himself. This is one of the elements that explains how we move from the individual to the team or from the individual to the collective. Moreover the cognitive interactivity principle implies that knowledge is not carried by one given actor, but results from the interaction between two or more actors. What one actor brings positively or critically constitutes a contribution to knowledge creation.

This adversarial position provides a series of data and thus allows us to build information and extract a set of knowledge: Multiple dysfunctions allow identifying patterns that provide key dysfunction insights that lead, after a cumulative research, to a basis of key generic ideas. So, each intervention carries both specific, contingent knowledge, and generic knowledge. The generic contingency principle consists in the assumption that any social community is run by some invariant rules.

Traditional methods emphasize the need for companies to have at their top, individualities able to boost them. But, in our view, it would be a waste of time if the transition did not occur between individual creativity and potential collective creativity that still exists but often form an untapped energy and know-how reservoir. The socio-economic approach is not focused on the personal will of a company actor but on his/her ability to lead a team, in other words to communicate, to cooperate and to negotiate with other energies that represent the entire human potential with which the value creation should be shared. The main problem of an organization is to create a performance that can only be achieved through cooperation between individuals or teams.

The emphasis on human potential as the sole active ingredient in the corporate world is the central factor of a collective commitment culture. That is why an unused potential represents a significant hidden cost because it is a source of psychological dissatisfaction and frustration. On the other hand, the use of this potential could avoid some dysfunctions resulting in loss of economic resources. A greater attention given to company human resources has led us to develop our socio-economic approach with a hyphen, which represents and symbolizes the link that we established between social and economic, between satisfaction and performance. This major contribution of our method stems from observations made during our interventions: Taking into account the hidden human potential, not mobilized by traditional methods, is often the most effective way to put a failing firm back on an even keel.

Consequently, ISEOR has made available to its researchers a number of tools aimed, inter alia, at supporting human potential mobilization. If we prefer human potential to human resources, it is to better bring out all unrealized performance elements undiagnosed during job interviews, the unexplored face of the resource person. That is why ISEOR keeps on wondering how to develop a management method that would allow social and economic performance through the pivotal role attributed to human potential materialized by tools instrumental in its implementation. The implementation of communication, coordination, and cooperation tools is the method we advocate to achieve cohesion and consistency throughout the workplace and ensure proper and constructive interplay and interaction across the board.

The periodically negotiable activity contract (PNAC) concluded between each company employee and his line manager is truly at the heart of a strategy aimed at making better use of the potential of each. Indeed, it aims to achieve that the employee agrees to a more efficient and productive behavior, improving his/her immediate results and subsequently a greater contribution to collective potential, in exchange of better material conditions, for more appropriate specific means, not to mention an increase in their compensation self-financed by saving permitted by their own contribution to reducing dysfunctions and therefore hidden costs. It is also a tool for personal development, a factor whose importance we have already stressed. The competency grid also plays a key role in updating and tracking skills; that is to say in the potential activation of each and his/her promotion within the company, or the need to improve some points. They highlight in a synoptic form unemployed know-how at all stages of the company and enable to develop the versatility of members of the various teams and can lead to their increased empowerment. They help to measure the potential of each as a team member with respect to all stakeholders and to seek ways to channel it with a view to leading to a creative and productive collective energy. The grid will gradually improve over time. It is a fully-fledged system. The socio-economic management type goes, indeed, further than other approaches of the human factor because, apart from problems related to time management and treated in a self-analysis of time grid, it leads teams and actors themselves to integrate the concept of measuring performance through the use of qualimetrics.

The socio-economic approach suggests that intangible investment in qualitative development of human potential (IIQDHP) turns out to be much more profitable than any technology investment. It comes down, in a public or private organization, to devote time to the implementation of a truly integrated training for all staff while raising awareness of the less qualified, within innovation projects groups impelled by participatory proximity management. Our concept of integrated training corresponds to an internal and external adaptation training as it seeks to respond correctly to the assessment of both the company's business and the new market needs, which is not systematically offered by vocational training which does not capitalize on the expertise gained through experience. The latter result in an accumulation of knowledge to which we prefer greater latitude given to actors to achieve their potential for themselves on the field defined (and not only in terms of research) as the first locus of knowledge production but also as a place of learning. We therefore do not equate our integrated training with some form of on the job training (learning by doing). It is not limited, indeed, to the acquisition of technical knowledge but is based on a transformative approach that involves the active participation of employees to the evolution of the field. This is when developing a priority action plan, designed collectively, that appears the training needs and proposals are made for a better use of existing skills. This type of training requires a prerequisite, that is, not to neglect the ins and outs of intangible investment in programs offered if we want to deal in depth and not just from a purely accounting point of view with value added creation and potential creation. It must be accompanied by a stronger motivation to change. This approach is part of the strategic management of human potential. Integrated training is, in this sense, a real development factor for both the individual and the organization, leading to a more participatory form of management with at the key a manual of integrated training capitalizing on learning knowledge. This last point is the basis of our conception of learning which we define as "a structured assimilation of learning knowledge in the real execution of professional activity and reusable later"—an acquisition mode of human potential in some way, and a method of enrichment of the latter at the level of an individual and a group.

Companies and organizations going through a bad patch have to choose between changing or withering away. Human potential, considered both emotionally and rationally, is the prime mover behind any endogenous type of development. People have to reach beyond their objectives and responsibilities, beyond what was specified in job interviews. Flexibility is the key word. To that effect company actors should be given opportunities of broadening their capacities with a view to achieving new common goals. Relationships within companies depend upon a spirit of cooperation to be fostered and mutual understanding to be reinforced among individuals and groups.

But all this would remain a piece of wishful thinking were it not for the SEAM methodological approach we have just sketched out and are now going to consider in further details.

MAJOR CHARACTERISTICS OF THE SEAM MODEL

The three basic assumptions of the socio-economic theory, first concerns the primary and prominent role of the human potential, sole creator of value. Then, the imperfections of the conventional accounting model can be reduced to improve the decision-making relevance. Finally, traditional modes of organization (TFW virus) are the main cause of the economic activity ineffectiveness and inefficiency.

Economic Performance of Organizations and Societal Prosperity

Macro-Economic Foundations of Socio-Economic Theory

The socio-economic theory has its roots in our macro-economic research findings (Savall, 1973/1975) about the theory of crises and that of under-employment. The main conclusions were that the macro-economic analysis is not adequate to understand value creation. An approach alternating the macro and micro economic analyses had to be adopted by using an "elevator" for observing the different levels of activities that contribute to the creation of economic value: the individual, the team, the company, the sector, local, regional, national, and international territories, Linking these different levels allows us to understand how value is generated through the interactions between these different levels of analysis.

We had to create appropriate methodologies so as to reach an in-depth and reliable observation process as compared with statistical analyses of macro-economic aggregates. Thus, we conceived, developed, and tested the qualimetric research-intervention method, combining qualitative, quantitative, and financial observations (Savall, 1975; Savall & Zardet 2004, 2011).

Back and Forth Itineraries Between Macroeconomic and Micro-Economic Analyses Within Organizations

The socio-economic theory stems from our transdisciplinary research itinerary focusing on economic and social well-being. The three results of our initial research in macroeconomics, in history of economic and social thought, as well as in underemployment and crises analysis were completed in 1973. In the tradition of the heterodox economic theories of Germán Bernácer (1922, 1955) and of François Perroux (1974, 1975), as well as in attempts to go beyond the neoclassical and Marxian theories, the hypothesis about crisis (Savall, 1975) is that human potential is the only actual factor of real sustainable value creation, while capital and technology are only complementary factors. Putting the emphasis on the isolated analyses of financial flows, of labor and innovation values; as well as the fact to consider that the two factors of production, capital, and labor are of an equivalent nature, as the macro-economy does; has been considered a conceptual error. Labor is an active factor in the creation of economic value while capital is an inert and passive factor, a simple and indeed valuable tool but only helps increase the human labor productivity and economic and social progress. Thus, these factors are highly complementary and not systematically interchangeable, unlike what some brutal decisions of downsizing would like to show. We had to remedy to this conceptual error by differentiating factors related to the superstructure, that is, the visible or apparent part of the economic phenomena (capital, labor, technological innovation), and the intangible and hidden infrastructure based on human potential and its ability to spend energy, creativity, and to drive innovative projects. Indeed, econometrics shed light on an important residual factor which accounts for half of the growth level of national economies (Carré, Dubois, & Malinvaud, 1972; Perroux, 1973). This refutation of the theory of equivalence of the two factors marks the starting point of the socio-economic theory construction. It proposes to consider that the residual factor in the production function could be made clearer by the concept of hidden cost-performance in order to better understand the "black hole" of the performance theories. The multilevel model we propose is based on an assumption of isomorphism in value creation from the societal to the individual levels; through the organization and the working team.

The observation of the professional practices within organizations showed that only human activity is intelligent and pro-active: adapting to its environment, creating products—goods or services—commercial and noncommercial, detecting new and innovative needs. The so-called intelligent machines were designed, used, and maintained by humans who have incorporated some of the knowledge that only humans are able to create, produce, reproduce, disseminate, transform, improve, and question. The variable, financial, and material capital is therefore a valuable tool developed, built up or destroyed, exploited, or on the contrary, wasted by human potential.

Criticism and Transcendence of the Value of Work: The Socio-Economic Concept of Value-Activity

Various theories put labor value in the heart of the economic activity, particularly the heterodox or Marxist economists. By contrast, François Perroux (1973) made a critical analysis, aware that labor itself and the labor accumulation were not unconditionally value creator. Thus, he thought that creativity or collective creation value were above labor value. We have adopted a similar position in the socio-economic theory. We called human potential the primary factor in the economic value creation, in order to differentiate it from the traditional concept of labor used in different streams of economic thought. This amounts to substitute the socio-economic concept of value-activity to the labor value one.

Socio-Economic Theory of Value Creation

The socio-economic theory of value creation can be briefly summarized as follows. Every organization has a spontaneous tendency to produce hidden costs-performances due to endogenous or exogenous dysfunctions of their accumulation and fluctuation. Human productivity is individual and collective. It is highly elastic, as evinced by more or less hidden costs high level. The performance creation requires it to be contractualized between stakeholders. It allows converting part of hidden costs into value-added creation. The IIQDHP—compared to tangible investments, a traditional source of productivity—has a much higher level of profitability, between 200% and 4,000% (Savall & Zardet, 2008). The most effective counterparties have a hybrid characteristic and consist in improving work conditions (health, satisfaction) and increasing the purchasing power. Sustainable economic performance has two components: the short-term measurable immediate results and the creation of potential, consisting of material and intangible investment. The creation of potential is self-financed by the organization and will positively impact its future economic performance.

Social Corporate Responsibility and Sustainable Development of the Socio-Economic Performance of Organizations

A proactive strategy based on the resources is characterized by the emphasis put in strategic choices to the enhancement and the development of the different resources of the company beyond the only financial ones. Human potential is the core of such strategy and its activation is essential for the business development stimulation. Thus, any individual in the company can be considered as a strategist because he/she has a more or less conscious personal project and helps realize with more or less involvement the strategic actions of the company.

Indeed, human potential creativity sparks off the innovations of products, of market relations, of technology, and of organization. It founds the dynamics of organizations and of the entire economic and social system. A sustainable development of enterprises and jobs, fueling the demand in the real economy market, requires a strategy that favors investment in qualitative development of human potential (changing skills and behavior) and then creates new jobs. Indeed, if the company wants to face the natural aging of its employees and the mutation of professional skills, it must regularly invest part of its resources to involve its employees and to maintain their level of commitment as well as their re-professionalizing and, thus maintain its level of competitiveness.

The sustainable socio-economic performance approach implies the expansion of an organization scope across the border, which traditionally separates it from its environment, as suggested by the concept of corporate social responsibility (CSR), integrated in the socio-economic theory construction since its birth. Indeed, taking into account the different stakeholders in the development and management of the company strategy is a source of value and competitiveness.

Our longitudinal researches based on *in vivo* experiments highlighted that the internal and external company flexibility, agility, ease of remodeling its structures and its behaviors in a medium and long term horizon; as well as its pro-activity degree, based on its human potential energy activation and its capacity for creating and innovating product–market–technology–organization; are determinants factors of sustainable competitiveness, development, and growth.

Internal Structure of Human Potential: The Energy–Behavior–Skill Triptych

The basic assumption of the socio-economic theory is that human potential is the only active factor in value-added creation. Technical and/or financial capital is a valuable but sterile tool when it is not activated by the energy, the behavior, and the skill of the company human potential. Thus, qualitative development, that is, the quality of behaviors and the skills development of the human potential, is a primordial IIQDHP. It generates a high level of value-added and a competitive advantage for the company that is hard to imitate on the market since it is conceived by the company itself with its internal resources.

The human potential level and intensity of an organization is based on three main components: human energy, actors' behavior in the workplace, and their skills. The combination of these three factors gives the level of sustainable economic performance of an organization. It is measured by its value added.

The Individual and Collective Energy of the Active Unit

We can draw an analogy with the theory of the active units as designed by François Perroux (1975). He stated that an economic agent is an active unit when he/she is able to change his/her environment rather than, simply, endure it. Thus, individuals, members of an organization bear an endogenous energy they more or less activate in their professional sphere.

The energy level that is used depends on the degree of compatibility between the project of each individual and the collective strategy of the organization (Savall & Zardet, 1995). The higher the compatibility is, the higher the individual is committed to business practices that create value-added to be distributed among the organization stakeholders. Conversely, when compatibility is low, the individual is less involved in his/her professional activity and generates, in interaction with his/her business partners, more dysfunctions and hidden costs by searching how to apply his/her excess energy in the extra-professional sphere.

The role of management and leadership is to accompany actors, individually and in teams, to stimulate them in the deployment of their creative energy, to synchronize their actions, and to periodically clean up the dysfunctions that naturally reappear and thus steer the socio-economic performance of team and organization.

The socio-economic theory considers that the root causes of dysfunctions and hidden costs are related to the lack of consideration of the human potential and its ability to evolve. Indeed, conflicts of objectives between individuals and between teams are often overlooked. The conflict-cooperation dynamics is at the heart of the economic value creation mechanism. One of the natural characteristics is trying to capture, sometimes unconsciously, the value-added created by others. Such predation of value is a deviance from a fair and ethical functioning of the organization, where each person is recognized in his/her collective utility, obtaining multifaceted and deserved rewards. The hidden nature of these deviances reveals an atrophy of the contracting between the stakeholders, often due to failures of management and leadership quality.

Behavior Instability

Professional behaviors play a central role in the socio-economic theory. The research-interventions of ISEOR showed that the observable human behaviors have major impacts on social and economic performance of the organization. They also showed that the needs of the actor in a professional situation are multifaceted: physiological (comfort and quality of life); psychological and sociological (emotion, affect, personal, and professional development); and economic (purchasing power). Unlike Maslow's (1954) theory, they must be satisfied simultaneously, not according to the hierarchy of needs that this author offers. The activation of professional behaviors depends on factors such as recognition, development, career development, qualitative, and monetary remuneration.

During their research-interventions, ISEOR intervener-researchers observed the importance of the conceptual couple of conflict-cooperation, which is central to the analysis of François Perroux (1979) and to the socio-economic theory. Our analysis showed some dialectics that explain actors' individual and collective fluctuating behaviors: involvement versus avoidance, commitment versus disobedience, creation versus value destruction, and teamwork versus selfish competition.

Behaviors are influenced by the work environment conditions. The socio-economic theory has identified six categories of conditions: working conditions, work organization, communication–coordination–cooperation, time management, integrated training (training-employment adequacy), and strategic implementation. These segments of the working environment are characterized by their organizational, managerial, and social dimensions and permit to classify the dysfunctions generated by the organization operation. These dysfunctions cause economic resources destruction that are not assessed in monetary terms in common information systems nor in financial and management accounting (see Figure 1.1). These hidden costs are calculated through five indicators: absenteeism, work accidents and occupational injuries, staff turnover, non-quality, and direct productivity gap.

Formal and Informal Powers of All the Stakeholders

The existence of these hidden costs at all levels of the company (top management, middle management, down the line employees) led the socio-economic theory to balance the concept of power used by many theories of organizations. It highlights the high level of individuals and groups' informal powers in the organization, approximately measured through hidden costs. The socio-economic theory of power states that no actor, regardless of his/her place in the organization, is devoid of powers and responsibilities. Formal powers are organized and prioritized, while informal powers are spread throughout the company and present in small or low-skilled positions.

Unlike some theories of organizations that oppose the actions of human development focusing on qualitative benefits as an incentive means (e.g., job content, working conditions, recognition, promotion) from approaches that emphasize quantitative monetary benefits (e.g., wage evolution, target-based bonuses, employee ownership), the socio-economic management believes that these two types of advantages are inseparable.

Nowadays, the professional behavior criteria tend to become more discriminating in the management of human potential than the professional skills criteria. Indeed, changing the professional skills seems easier than changing behaviors. However, professional skills are actually used only if the actors have the will to and adopt pro-active behaviors.

TFW Virus (Taylorism–Fayolism–Weberism)

The TFW virus metaphor refers to the anachronistic survival of some organization principles of the classical schools, put forward by Taylor (1911), Fayol (1916), and Weber (1924). They contributed to the economic and social progress in their time. However, it is regrettable that a century later,

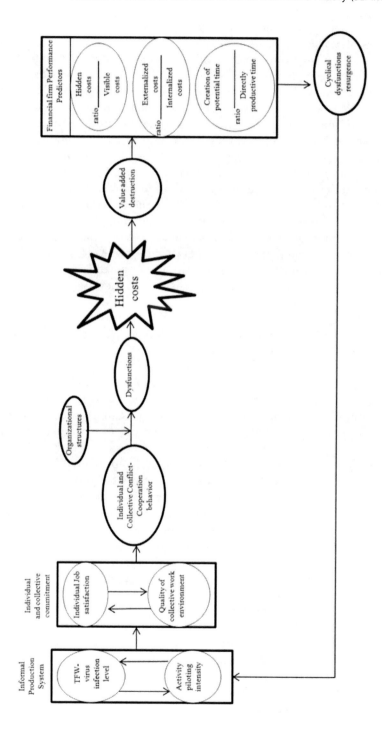

Figure 1.1 General presentation of the hidden costs socioeconomic theory.

theorists, experts, and practitioners keep on propagating three obsolete principles: the maximal division of labor, the dichotomy between conception, decision and realization of activities, as well as the depersonalization of jobs, organization charts, processes, methods, and rules (Lussato, 1977; Montmollin, 1981). These factors do not contribute any more to the sustainable global performance, considering the behavior, skills, social environment, and national and international policies evolutions (Savall, 1974, 2010). The combined models of these three authors have generated extensive literature on job analysis, recruitment, and organization theory.

A virus is defined as a small infectious agent, formed by a group of submicroscopic entities reproducing themselves inside animal, human, or plant cells. Most viruses are pathogenic. The TFW virus infection degree of the organizational modes and of the dominant managerial practices refers to a more or less important cooperation deficiency between participants in an activity, between individuals in a team, between the same organization sites, subsidiaries, or departments. A critique would not be addressed to Taylor, Fayol, or Weber themselves but to their successors; theorists, experts, and practitioners as applicants of obsolete theories in an environment which had been faced by numerous and in-depth mutations. Indeed, the human, social, and geopolitical contexts as well as the level of education of the labor force have considerably evolved in the past century.

The Individual and Collective Skills Constant Regeneration

The professional skills level results from knowledge mobilization in order to help completing company activities. The socio-economic theory differentiates two types of knowledge: the current and reactive living knowledge activated by individuals, in thought and action, versus the inert knowledge, issued from the past, preserved, formalized, and represented by symbols and signs (letters and numbers) on written memory supports. This knowledge is mobilized through the cognitive interactivity mechanism, notably thanks to interpersonal exchange. Professional skills are used when cognitive interactivity produces its effects—activities then assigned to individuals mobilizing their knowledge acquired through experience. We understand the negative impact of the TFW virus (Taylorism–Fayolism–Weberism), which severely limits the range of activities that a person could be left to perform. The latter quickly loses the acquired knowledge (skills) that returns to an inert state if not implemented in his/her current occupation. The obsolescence of knowledge and skills, that we had frequently observed, is a major source of chronic dysfunctions within organizations.

Skills acquisition is mostly realized through individual and collective learning. Cognitive psychology has addressed the issue of individual knowledge acquisition, especially Jean Piaget. Collective learning still requires extensive researches, considering it does not boil down to the sum of individual learnings. A major issue that the 2000 socio-economic diagnoses of ISEOR had revealed is the quality of cooperation between individual learning within a team or an organization.

Organization observation has brought into light that human potential undergoes a life cycle phenomenon; its components are subject to a permanent evolution in time. Thus, energy has a propensity to wear away. It requires maintenance; otherwise it deteriorates over time through entropy phenomenon. Behaviors change very frequently according to how things go with nations—professional or non-professional events. It requires from the management a lot of attention to keep listening, promoting dialogue, and very frequently contracting performance with employees. Skills are also subject to erosion and deterioration. This phenomenon requires preventive and maintenance actions with regard to skills potential in order to ensure their availability for the organization activities.

The socio-economic diagnoses methodology, designed by the ISEOR team (Savall & Zardet, 1987, 2004, 2011; Savall, Zardet, & Bonnet, 2008b), has an ethical and democratic dimension. Indeed, the dysfunctions and productivity pools detection is made by witnesses. They are the company employees who are suffering from or generating dysfunctions in interaction with their collaborators. The desire for an increased well-being encourages these actors to reveal the dysfunctions that disrupt their activity and deteriorate their life conditions at work. They express legitimately their perception of these dysfunctions and their impacts throughout semi-structured interviews.

SEAM Implementation as Both an Organization Development (OD) and a Change Management Method

SEAM concept has attracted more than 1310 organizations, belonging to 72 sectors in 37 countries on four continents. SEAM implementation process has been developed along with many intervention-researches through the years. These interventions allowed to create, not a management model itself, but a socio-economic intervention process in change management related to the epistemological principle of generic contingency. Each case of company or organization is specific, both in terms of diagnosis and implementation of improvement solutions. However, generic rules for carrying out effective, efficient, and sustainable change have been brought out from these many intervention-researches. Those rules concern the mechanism for mobilizing actors in a change action (an horizontal and vertical architecture called HORI-VERT), the tools for contracting performance, and the qualimetric method to evaluate results of the change dynamic, especially the demonstration of the high profitability of a qualitative development investment in human potential. Those are the resources involved in the implementation of SEAM.

Mobilizing All the Company Actors Through the HORIVERT Architecture

SEAM implementation process respects the organization chart. During the first months of the change process, it mobilizes primarily the line managers at all levels, leadership, senior, and middle management, including supervisors. This horizontal action is deployed on the entire perimeter of the organization and enables the creation of a common language around the dynamic of change, around the implementation of simple socio-economic tools that stimulate and harmonize common practices. The main effect of this horizontal action on the entire management team is to sensitize managers to the numerous dysfunctions that affect the social and economic performance of the organization. It also aims to assess, with their participation, the economic impacts of the dysfunctions on value added destruction, appearing as hidden-cost. It allows, thus, to discover potential economic resources to self-finance the survival and development of the organization.

In a second step, and in at least two areas of the organization, a vertical action is carried out by the sector managers. It allows the inclusion of all the concerned sector staff in the diagnoses process and in the improvement projects. It enhances the employees satisfaction, a better functioning, and a conversion of hidden costs into value-added (see Savall & Zardet, 2008b, on Horivert architecture). One of the important effects of this vertical action is to improve relations between the managers and the shop floor through integrated training methods that enhance managers' role and provides an opportunity for the employees to reveal and develop their creative and innovative potential.

SEAM intervention process proposes to improve the organization integral quality (both internal and external) and the sustainable economic and social performance piloting through three axes:

- A methodology of problem solving and change management that allows improving the quality of products (goods and services), business operations and team management thanks to the simultaneous development of structures and behaviors quality. This method consists of four steps: a dysfunctions diagnosis, an improvement project, the implementation of solutions and an assessment of the results in terms of satisfaction, quality and economic performance improvement;
- The implementation of 6 socio-economic management (SEAM) tools;

- The socio-economic management (SEAM) method, which allows targeting the human potential, improving management analysis as well as the relevance of strategic decisions and empowering all managers and employees.

Socio-Economic Performance Contracting

Human potential, wieldy consciously or not, has formal and informal powers which contribute positively and in harmony in value creation. In other cases, human potential participates, in interaction with others, to value destruction materialized by hidden costs. Then, it is logical to consider that value creation results from a contracting process between actors involved in the activity. The socio-economic theory states that the level of performance of an organization depends on its ability to organize synchronization of the performance contracts. Individuals and teams need to regularly contract the latter for a sustainable social and economic performance. Those performances do not depend only on the amount of technical capital and the number of labor force but merely on the ability to organize the complementary action between human potential and material and financial resources. It can be realized thanks to permanent practices of contracting.

Trust Factor
The socio-economic theory postulates a certain confidence in the individual's potential ability to change and to make their inter-individual relationships evolve for a better collective efficacy-effectiveness. It also postulates on the one hand, that the worker has the ability to act locally on working structures so as to transform or adapt them, and, on the other hand that the organization has capacity to achieve sustainable and healthy economic developments, without relying on external and uncertain financing.

One of the levers that regenerate trust within teams and organizations is the periodic performance contracting. It allows to adjust in the objectives of the partners the potentialities of each other through a periodically renewed negotiation accompanied by an assessment of trust regeneration and performance level.

Socio-Economic Management Tools
SEAM six main tools are: the self-analysis of time grid, the competency grid, the strategic and operational piloting logbook, the internal/external strategic action plan, the priority action plan, and the semi-annual periodically negotiable activity contract. They improve priorities management, a better use of available skills, an increased visibility through piloting indicators of activity and of dysfunctions and hidden costs prevention, and

a better anticipation of medium and long term changes in the business environment.

In terms of contracting, the most powerful socio-economic tool is the periodically negotiable activity contract (PNAC). It is made of personalized objectives and means that combine the collective goals of the organization, of the team, and of the individual in exchange for an additional remuneration. It is accompanied by a semi-annual meeting to spark off dialogue, discussion, and mutual resolutions between every employee and his/her direct hierarchic supervisor. PNAC requires bilateral trust relations, both in the hierarchical and transversal lines. PNAC has been implemented for 30 years in an important number of companies or organization from the top management team to the shop floor. Numerous cases of PNAC implementation show that it is a strategic management and human potential management tool. Its characteristics of management by objective for every actor, of the employees assessment, and of stimulating wages policy, allow to make a positive statement on the ability of the PNAC to foster an innovative and ambitious human potential management. Those cases shed light on the extraordinary ability of the individuals to change their practices, to release their latent energy, and to convert hidden costs into individual and collective, social, and economic performance.

Intangible Investment in Qualitative Development of Human Potential (IIQDHP) Profitability

SEAM implementation in numerous cases, up to 1,310 organizations, shows that the increase of the efficacy, the efficiency, and the company competitiveness mainly depends on the increase of the IIQDHP level. This investment consists in enhancing the entire company employees' competencies, energy, implication, synchronization, and employability. It includes leaders, executives, supervisors, technicians, employees, and shop-floor workers. The word investment, instead of the word expense is used in its economic meaning. An investment is any resource that produces recurring effects beyond the cost realization period. This investment, aimed at enhancing qualitatively human potential from a preventive approach of dysfunctions, is basically intangible but can also include some material components such as equipment renewal.

The socio-economic change dynamics in the organization leads to hidden-costs conversion into value-added creation. This process allows increasing sustainable economic performance. ISEOR database shows that the rate of hidden costs conversion into value-added (i.e., the ratio of hidden costs recouped either through lower charges or, as is often the case, in revenue increases in the accounting sense) hovers between 35% and 55% of the hidden cost amount calculated throughout the diagnosis phase. It allows forecasting in the organizations that implement SEAM. The intangible investment cost for obtaining those results has a high profitability rate hovering between 210% and 4,014%. Each euro or dollar invested in developing human potential in a SEAM intervention process can thus be said to yield between 2 and 40 euros or dollars in investment return (ROI).

Socio-economic intervention-researches demonstrated that all the organizations, regardless of their size, their sector, their legal status or their location, have the capacity to self-finance a significant part of their survival-development without depending on outside financing. Indeed, the hidden-cost sizeable pool constitutes resources, which can be re-used for financing innovative actions, releasing time, and resources that are to be affected into endogenous proactive strategy. Thus, any company can, without added external funding, self-finance its investments in developing human potential and its internal cohesion, a tangible source of sustainable performance.

CONCLUSION

The research conducted in compliance with the socio-economic theory demonstrated that the diversity of the companies and organizations does not significantly impact the nature of the dysfunctions that affect human potential. Regardless of the country, the sector and industry, the size, the legal status (public, private, associative), the purpose (profit or non-profit), or the financial situation (prosperity or difficulty), the observed organizations show similar organizational issues. Those problems affect the individual and collective energy, behaviors, and skills that are the primary components of human potential within companies and organizations. There are three categories of problems: human potential management; organization, methods, and work conditions; communication, involvement of, and cooperation between employees.

The explanatory assumption is that the root-causes of the dysfunctions and the hidden costs are related to the lack of consideration of human potential. Indeed, conflicts of objectives are often overlooked in the conflict-cooperation dynamics that is at the heart of the economic value creation mechanism, both because of ignorance and because one of the human nature characteristics is to try capturing the value-added created by others according to a predation logics. It is a deviance form with regard to a fair functioning of the organization, where each person or economic actor is useful and recognized by obtaining multifaceted and deserved rewards. The hidden nature of these deviances reveals an atrophy of the contracting process between stakeholders, due to management deficiency regarding both organizations and other economic actors.

Every professional or extraprofessional organization has a spontaneous tendency to produce hidden costs-performance due to endogenous or exogenous dysfunctions and their fluctuation.

Human productivity is individual and collective. It is highly elastic, as testified by a more or less high level of hidden costs. It means that an organization is able to increase its production with headcount at the same level, without increasing the weekly hours worked if it is able to reduce its dysfunctions. This ability is acquired through organizational learning effect focused on the actors' behaviors and their interactions with the organizational structures.

The dysfunctions effects impact the employees' satisfaction degree at work and the performance level of the company. Indeed, the value-added destruction average order of magnitude is €29,100 of hidden costs per person and per year. It represents a 60% evaporation of resources of the company's payroll. Other studies have shown that 35% to 55% of these hidden costs are recoverable into value added (Savall & Zardet, 2008a), through change processes such as SEAM interventions. The quasi-universality of the human potential issues, in spite of the cultural, ethical, and geopolitical diversity of the organizations can astonish. The organizational biology metaphor considers dysfunctions as non-specific organizational pathologies. In the human biology area, beyond the obvious diversity of the individuals, the universality of pathologies has allowed significant progresses in curative and preventive medicine. It is what we can wish for, by analogy, for improving the companies and organizations health and for preserving employment.

REFERENCES

Bernácer, G. (1922). *La teoría de las disponibilidades como interpretación de las crisis y del problema social* [Availability theory as an interpetation of the crisis and the social problem]. Madrid, Spain: Revista nacional de economía.

Bernácer, G. (1955). *Una economía libre, sin crisis y sin paro* [A free economy without crisis and without arrest]. Madrid, Spain: Aguilar.

Bodin, J. (1576). *Les six livres de la République [The six books of the Commonwealth]*. Lyon, France: Gabriel Cartier.

Carré, J. J., Dubois, P., & Malinvaud, E. (1972). *La croissance française* (Vol. 1) [The French growth]. Paris, France: Seuil.

Fayol, H. (1916). *Administration générale et industrielle* [General and Industrial Administration]. Paris, France: Gauthiers Villars.

Lasch, C. (1979). *The culture of narcissism: American life in an age of diminishing expectations.* New York, NY: W. W. Norton and Company.

Lussato, B. (1977). *Introduction critique aux théories d'organisation: Modèles cybernétiques, hommes, entreprises* [Critical introduction to the oganizational theories: Cybernetic, people, companies models]. Paris, France: Dunod.

Majer, C. (2009). *The Power to Transform—Passion, power, and purpose in daily life.* Emmaus, PA: Rodale Press.

Maslow, A. (1954). *Motivation and Personality.* New York, NY: Harper.

Montmollin, M. (1981). *Le taylorisme à visage humain* [The human face of Taylorism]. Paris, France: Presses universitaires de France.

Perroux, F. (1973). *Pouvoir et économie* [Power and economy]. Paris, France: Dunod.

Perroux, F. (1974). Économie de la ressource humaine [Economy of human resources]. *Revue Mondes en développement. ISMEA,* 15–81.

Perroux, F. (1975). *Unités actives et mathématiques nouvelles—Révision de la théorie de l'équilibre économique général* [Active units and new math: Revision of the theory of general economic equilibrium]. Paris, France: Dunod.

Savall, H. (1973). *G. Bernácer: l'hétérodoxie en science économique* [G.Bernácer: Heterodoxy in economics]. PhD dissertation, University of Paris-Sobonne, Dalloz, Collection Les Grands Économistes.

Savall, H. (1974). Avant Keynes et au-delà: Germán Bernácer, économiste espagnol [Before and beyond Keynes: Germán Bernáce, a Spanish economist]. *Revue Mondes en développement, 5,* 255–261.

Savall, H. (2010). *Work and People: An economic evaluation of job enrichment,* 2nd edition. Charlotte, NC: Information Age. (Originally published 1981)

Savall, H., & Zardet, V. (1987). *Maîtriser les coûts-performances cachés* [Mastering hidden costs and performance]. Paris, France: Economica.

Savall, H., & Zardet, V. (1995). *Ingénierie stratégique du roseau* [Strategic engineering of the reed]. Paris, France: Economica.

Savall, H., & Zardet, V. (2004). *Recherche en Sciences de Gestion: Approche Qualimétrique: Observer l'objet complexe* [Research in management sciences: The qualimetric approach: Observing the complex object]. Préface de David Boje. Paris, France: Economica.

Savall, H., & Zardet, V. (2005). *Tétranormalisation: Défis et dynamiques* [The dynamics and challenges of tetranormalization]. Paris, France : Economica.

Savall, H., & Zardet, V. (2008a). Le concept de coût-valeur des activités. Contribution de la théorie socio-économique des organisations [The concept of cost-value activities: A contribution to the socio-economic organization theory]. *Revue Sciences de Gestion-Management Sciences-Ciencias de Gestión, 64,* 61–90.

Savall, H., & Zardet, V. (2008b). *Mastering hidden costs and socio-economic performance.* Charlotte, NC: Information Age.

Savall, H., & Zardet, V. (2011). *The Qualimetrics approach, observing the complex object.* Charlotte, NC: Information Age.

Savall, H., Zardet, V., Bonnet M., (2008a). *Libérer les performances cachées des entreprises par un management socio-économique* [Releasing the untapped potential of enterprises through socio-economic management]. Geneve, Switzerland: BIT.

Savall, H., Zardet, V., & Bonnet, M. (2008b). *Management socio-économique: Une approche innovante* [Socioeconomic management: An innovative approach]. Paris, France: Economica.

Savall, H., Zardet, V., & Bonnet, M. (2008c). *Releasing the Untapped Potential of Enterprises Through Socio-Economic Management,* Geneve, Switzerland: ILO-BIT.

Taylor, F. (1911). *Principes d'organisation scientifique des usines* [Principles of scientific organization of factories]. Paris, France: Dunod.

Tuleja, T. (1987). *Beyond the Bottom Line.* Penguin Books: Harmondsworth, G. B.

Weber, M. (1924). *The theory of social and economic organization.* Translated by Talcott Parsons & A.M Henderson. New York, NY: The Free Press.

CHAPTER 2

VALUES, BELIEFS, AND CONCEPTUALIZATION OF COSTS

Susan Quint

CONFERENCE REMARKS:
Chapter Prologue

The SEAM conceptualization of visible and hidden costs is based on a set of values and beliefs that is different than the values and beliefs that underlie traditional accounting measures. As Henri Savall outlined in his presentation, there are three key tenets of SEAM. Number one, human potential is the sole active factor in creating added value. Second, technical and financial capital are inert inner tools. Three, capital and labor are complementary sources of value, as opposed to interchangeable sources of value. These three tenets of SEAM are quite profound because they re-conceptualize and expand prevailing definitions of costs. The expanded view of costs can inspire new perspectives on organization performance and change. For organization development practitioners, it is also important to consider that values and beliefs about costs are important factors that may affect the organization change process, and even the perception of business leaders about the relative success of organizational interventions.

Decoding the Socio-Economic Approach to Management, pages 27–45
Copyright © 2016 by Information Age Publishing
All rights of reproduction in any form reserved.

The SEAM paradigm is based on a different view of cost and cost control.

- The SEAM process of reducing hidden costs is not just another way to cut costs; instead, SEAM re-conceptualizes and expands prevailing definitions of costs.
- The SEAM conceptualization of visible and hidden costs is based on a set of values and beliefs that is different than the values and beliefs that underlie traditional accounting measures.
- The expanded view of costs can inspire new perspectives on organization performance and change; however, not all organizational actors are prepared to make the shift.
- Values and beliefs about costs are important factors that may affect the organization change process, or even the perception of business leaders about the success of organizational interventions.

THE DEVELOPMENT OF THE CONCEPT OF HIDDEN COSTS

Decades of French management research conducted by the Socio-Economic Institute of Firms and Organizations (ISEOR) has recently become accessible in the United States. The ISEOR research shows that there are inevitable gaps in performance as people interact with organizational structures—whether those structures are technological, demographic, structural, or even behavioral. These gaps in performance can create a very costly drag on the economic performance of an organization, and yet those costs may remain hidden because the cause is so difficult to isolate. Even the best financial reporting is often too aggregated for business leaders to see the true reasons that the organization is not performing in a way that is consistent with expectations or strategic plans. The Socio-Economic Approach to Management (SEAM) differentiates between *visible* costs reported within accounting systems and *hidden costs*, which are not specifically reported. By working with business leaders to consider visible and hidden costs, SEAM intervener-researchers show how resources can be freed up to focus on the strategic aims and objectives of the organization where there is the most strategic value.

At a time when the United States economy is still reeling from cost cutting and job layoffs resulting from the global economic crisis, the SEAM emphasis on both social and economic factors as drivers of organizational performance has perhaps never been more relevant. Organizations continue to look for new sources of competitive advantage and market opportunities. Very often, business leaders frame these opportunities as related to the need to reduce costs in order to increase market share. This focus on costs can encompass a broad scope of items, including salaries and benefits, technology, equipment, materials, or fees charged by vendors. A variety of organization development approaches may also be employed, which emphasize improvements in the efficiency of operations by reducing the number of hand-offs, consolidating work effort, or accelerating processes through focused application of technology and analytics.

While the cost-cutting measures may have achieved desired savings in the short term, the long-term impact of changes on the organization may not be fully understood or even assessed. Even if organizations are financially successful in cutting costs by cutting people, the socio-economic view is that this approach is only a short-term solution. Savall, Zardet, and Bonnet (2008) argued that even if layoffs enable an enterprise to reduce some visible costs, there are side effects such as loss of know-how, disorganization, and a decrease in confidence in the organization. Savall and Zardet (2008a) explained that they published the book Mastering Hidden Costs and Socio-economic Performance as a way to save businesses and jobs:

> Most business strategies were quite alarming, based on downsizing, labor shedding, and cuts and withdrawal—in a word, based on defensiveness. Today, while the context may have changed in an era of globalization and hyper-competition, such defensive strategies are still all too commonplace. Such strategic helplessness may result from errors in strategic analysis and misunderstandings of the underlying sources of economic performance. (p. xvii)

Rensis Likert, a pioneer in the field of organization development, found that traditional accounting measures, which show only a composite view of earnings and productivity, had obscured the true impact of the changes. The most productive organizations, he wrote, "apparently require an appreciable period of time before the impact of the change is fully manifest in corresponding improvement" (1967, p. 81). Likert also pointed to research that showed the positive impact of a shift in managerial behavior to achieve higher productivity and reduce costs. In organizations where only economic needs were considered, he found that cost-reduction had involved a tightening of hierarchical controls and increased pressure to increase productivity. There was also pressure to lower costs through personnel limitations, budget cuts, and the introduction or tightening of work standards. Citing numerous studies that had been conducted to evaluate the impact of cost-cutting in organizations, Likert wrote:

> When the unfavorable trends in productivity, waste, costs, and labor relations caused by the usual cost-reduction procedures finally become evident, there are no measurements which point to the true causes of the adverse shifts. As a con-

sequence, a wrong diagnosis is commonly made; the wrong causes are blamed, and the corrective steps are often focused on the wrong variables. (p. 84)

Although Likert wrote about cost cutting in the 1960s, his findings seem especially relevant in more contemporary contexts.

Of course, SEAM intervener-researchers would be the first to acknowledge that traditional measures of costs used in accounting are of critical importance to business leaders. The cost measures are based on a set of standards that are highly regulated and audited, and there are a multitude of requirements that are very prescriptive about how costs should be accounted for and defined. Although the traditional measures of costs are of critical importance to the financial operations of the organization, they may not be adequate for other more in-depth analyses used in decision making, assessments of the need for capability building within the organization, or evaluations of opportunities related to the long-term economic performance and sustainability of the organization.

While SEAM does focus on visible costs, this paper clarifies the idea that the SEAM process of identifying hidden costs is not just another way for business leaders to turn over another rock and uncover yet another way that costs can be cut. The differentiation between visible and hidden costs is not only an investigation of current expense vs. opportunity costs—though analysis of opportunity costs is certainly part of the SEAM process. Instead, SEAM re-conceptualizes and expands the definition of costs to include a broader set of social and economic factors that are of importance to the overall performance of the organization. These factors include the need for organizational change in response to market conditions, alignment of work with the strategic aims and objectives of the organization, a belief in the potential of people to create value, and an emphasis on the importance of the relationship between the organization and its stakeholders.

The SEAM conceptualization of costs is also based on a different set of values and beliefs than those that underlie traditional accounting measures. These differences in values and beliefs influence the way that organizational problems are framed, costs are conceptualized, measures are defined and developed, and results are interpreted. If this difference in values and beliefs is well understood by those working with the SEAM hidden cost measures, the expanded view of costs can also inspire new perspectives on organizational performance and change. However, not all organizational actors are prepared to make this shift in perspectives about costs. For that reason, it is important for SEAM intervener-researchers to consider that values and beliefs about costs are important factors that may affect the organization change process, or even the perception of business leaders about the success of organizational interventions.

VISIBLE VERSUS HIDDEN COSTS

Perhaps one of the most well-known aspects of SEAM theory is the concept of hidden costs. The socio-economic view takes the position that while accounting systems represent *visible costs* in the organization, there are also *hidden costs* that drive performance. The concept of hidden costs is based on ISEOR findings that there are, inevitably, gaps between expected performance and actual performance. Savall and Zardet (2008a) observed that business executives intuitively recognize this difference in expected vs. observed performance. For example, a business leader may notice that significant investments have been made without a noticeable improvement in operations or productivity. It may also be that reverse is true. Organizations may make strategic investments and succeed in lowering operating costs; however, the improvement in performance cannot be explained by an analysis of costs alone. Given the magnitude and importance of strategic investments, anecdotal explanations just do not provide enough perspective. In the SEAM view, these gaps in performance represent dysfunctions. Decades of ISEOR research has not only explored the dysfunctions in depth, but has also isolated the costs as part of organizational research and interventions all over the world.

SEAM intervener-researchers have also observed the impact of the mirror effect, where organizational actors are confronted with an estimate of the costs associated with organizational dysfunctions. In many cases, the dysfunctions are already well-known to people working within the organization—so much so that the dysfunctions themselves are part of the day-to-day operations and documented processes. The ISEOR research has pointed to similar patterns across all organizations, where issues associated with working conditions, the organization of work, time management, training, and strategic implementation create a drag on performance. Those problems are compounded when communications are poor, when work is not coordinated across organizational silos, or when people do not work cooperatively with each other. The interrelationships between all of these problems can be so overwhelming and complex that even business leaders with the best of intentions simply give up and focus on problems that are within their control. Yet the cost to the organization of these unproductive activities often remains hidden in organizations, in the sense that the cost of the dysfunctions has never been measured or quantified. ISEOR researchers have isolated the costs associated with many different kinds of dysfunctions and found that, in general, people spent as much as a third of their time on unproductive activities.

One key factor that motivates people to change is the cost associated with the dysfunctions. These costs can be embarrassing to business leaders who pride themselves on tight management of productivity and cost control. For many business leaders, the SEAM mirror effect and analysis of hidden costs is the first time that they have seen tangible information about the costs associated with problems that they may have routinely observed, ignored, or else ultimately accepted as "this is just the way it is here." These problems may also be a source of organizational debate and conflict that the business leaders acknowledged as part of the SEAM interview process. The reality of the hidden costs associated with maintaining the status quo is a call to action in a cost-conscious organization.

One reason that the costs associated with organizational dysfunctions are not well understood is that traditional accounting systems do not capture the reasons for variances in expected performance vs. actual performance. Accounting systems, according to Savall and Zardet (2008a), are usually limited to collecting information at the level of work units and departments. Savall and Zardet (2008a) pointed out that accounting systems tend to collect information about costs by their nature (e.g., personnel costs) and object (e.g., production department). In the socio-economic view, these reporting limitations create the need to differentiate between visible costs and hidden costs. Hidden costs may be included in accounting information, but dispersed across categories, or else diluted as part of aggregate totals.

Even when the reasons for variances in expected vs. actual performance are well understood, the complexity and depth of the problems faced by the organization are no less daunting or difficult to solve. SEAM interventions were developed so that people working within the organization can collaborate to address these inter-related problems. Reductions in hidden costs can become the driving force of organizational change, and a way to measure the progress that organizational actors are making. Yet traditional accounting is also limited for this new and important purpose. As business leaders begin to focus plans to reduce hidden costs, there is also a need to establish new measures of performance. While on the surface it may seem that analysis of hidden costs can be added to the set of accounting measures that is already in use within the organization, the hidden cost measures are not necessarily complementary. To see how this could be the case, it is important to explore the values and beliefs that underlie the SEAM conceptualization of costs, compared to the way that accounting measures are typically conceptualized and constructed.

VALUES, BELIEFS, AND CONCEPTUALIZATION OF COSTS

Three key tenets of the socio-economic approach to management are posted prominently on the ISEOR website:

- Human potential is the sole active factor in creating added value.
- Technical and financial capital are "inert" inner tools.

- Labor and capital are complementary sources of value, as opposed to interchangeable sources of value.

In Savall's view, the SEAM approach is not just another way to think about managing, but rather part of a larger set of moral, legal, ethical, and philanthropic responsibilities of the organization (Savall, 2010). Savall's book *Work and People* (2010) provides an in-depth exploration of these three tenets as it relates to a number of important management issues—most notably organizational development, strategic alignment, structural and behavioral characteristics of organizations, economic performance, job design, and factors affecting the productivity of people. As part of this larger framework, SEAM values and beliefs also frame the way that costs are conceptualized, assessed, and defined.

Human Potential Is the Sole Active Factor in Creating Added Value

The SEAM conceptualization of hidden costs is based on the belief that people have the ability to create value within an organization. On the other hand, people also have the ability to withhold their talents if they are not engaged. While the reasons may be varied, SEAM intervener-researchers take these many personal truths and perspectives into account, and move to those truths—as opposed to their own "expert" view of the truths as they work with the organization. SEAM intervener-researchers regard organizations as complex entities made up of structures and behaviors of people. In this view, organizational structures can take many forms, including physical, technological, organizational, demographic—and even mental, which would include factors such as the organizational mindset, management styles, and work atmosphere. Behaviors, according to the socio-economic view, are observed human actions that have an impact on the physical and social environment (Savall & Zardet, 2008a). Employees exercise their informal power to either slow down or speed up the pace of change. The interrelationship between behaviors and structures means that there is always a gap between planned and actual functions, which in turn results in unanticipated costs and sub-optimal performance (Savall, Zardet, & Bonnet, 2008). These gaps are considered dysfunctions, which are classified into six categories: working conditions, work organization, time management, communication-coordination-cooperation, integrated training, and strategic implementation (Savall & Zardet, 2008a).

While most business leaders are concerned with employee productivity and morale, the focus on productivity is generally related to how fast and efficiently people work. SEAM intervener-researchers view productivity differently, and conceptualize productivity as related to the economic value of the work that people are doing. SEAM intervener-researchers also link work to strategic priorities and help people see how their time could be used more effectively. While effective time management and prioritization of projects is nothing new to good managers, the association of work to the economic value is what makes the SEAM approach unique.

The Seen and Unseen, Visible and Hidden, and Tangible vs. Intangible Conceptualizations of Costs

To see the difference between the SEAM view—that people have the potential to create value—and the more traditional views about people that persist within organizations, it is important to understand the accounting of costs for people. As part of traditional accounting standards and methodology, people are accounted for as costs. The accounting view of people as costs includes consideration for not only salaries and benefits, but also the costs of organizational overhead related to people—such as facilities costs, workstations, phones, or even Internet connectivity. When executives say that people are the organization's greatest asset, the assessment is somewhat disingenuous because the salaries and benefits paid to people generally make up the majority of an organization's expenses. It is the knowledge, skills, and abilities that employees contribute that are seen by business leaders as assets. And yet the choice of the word "asset" can be misleading in the sense that the word asset might imply that people are accounted for as a benefit. Even in contemporary knowledge-based organizations, people are accounted for as costs, and traditional accounting draws only a very indirect link between the contributions of knowledge, skills, and abilities and the overall profitability of the organization.

The accounting terminology can also add to the confusion in SEAM interventions, because—like SEAM—traditional accounting also differentiates between costs that are visible and those that are hidden. In accounting vocabulary, costs and organizational assets are either *tangible* or *intangible*. At first glance, it would seem that the SEAM conceptualization of visible and hidden costs might be parallel with tangible and intangible costs. Both sets of words imply a distinction between what can be seen and what is unseen. However, the conceptualization of costs is quite different between traditional accounting and SEAM, and the differences are very meaningful.

In traditional accounting, *tangible assets* refer to those assets that have a physical form. Of course, people have a physical form, but in the accounting view tangible assets include consideration for items such as computer hardware, buildings, land, and equipment. Tangible assets also include financial capital and cash. Accounting standards for *intangible assets*, on the other hand, include a limited set of non-physical items, such as copyrights, patents, computer programs, or other rights that give an organization an exclusive or preferred position in the marketplace (Davidson, Stickney, & Weil, 1979).

Although these standards are still part of accepted practice, there is a large body of commentary in management literature about the need to expand the scope and change the definition of intangible assets to include human capital, organization capital, and customer capital. For knowledge-based organizations, management of tangible assets would mean that management would not only focus on the costs and overhead associated with people, but would also have a meaningful way to assess and measure the value of the work that people do. On that point, however, there is a lot of disagreement about whether or not the contributions of people can be measured or in any way quantified—especially since most people in knowledge-oriented organizations work as part of an interdisciplinary team. There are even epistemological debates about whether the enigmatic value of knowledge could ever be captured or attributed to a single individual. These arguments are even more relevant in technology-oriented businesses, where knowledge is easily copied, subsumed, and then transcended. Yet the need to manage differently persists in the literature about intangible assets, with some making a distinction between existing forms of organizational capital, as shown in Figure 2.1. On one hand, there is the need to continue to track financial capital, which includes the more traditional views of costs. On the other hand, there is a need to manage the value of the work of people, the value of organizational processes and technical platforms, and the value of relationships with customers. All of these items are now excluded from existing conceptualizations of intangible assets.

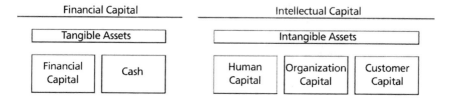

Figure 2.1 Schematic diagram of the concept of financial vs. intellectual capital. *Note:* Traditional accounting measures differentiate between tangible assets and intangible assets. Tangible assets include physical items such financial capital, plants and equipment, employee salaries and benefits, and cash. Intangible assets include nonphysical properties that are unique to the organization, such as copyrights and patent protections. There is longstanding debate about the need to expand the concept of intangible assets to include measures of the value of the knowledge and skills of people, the organization's capabilities, and customer relationships. Schematically, financial capital would be parallel in importance with intellectual capital.

Reductions in Hidden Costs

SEAM theory also holds that it is the responsibility of management to ensure that the knowledge and skills of people are applied appropriately to the needs of the organization. There are three key ways that SEAM intervener-researchers work with business leaders to create value. First, projects are developed to reduce hidden costs. Second, the organization invests in the development of employees, and third, business leaders work to align work with the strategic aims and objectives of the organization.

Hidden Costs Are Reduced

Once business leaders see the costs associated with organizational dysfunctions, they can be begin to address problems that might have otherwise been overlooked. These problems are typically too complex to solve within one business unit, so SEAM works both horizontally and vertically within the organization to both assess and address hidden costs. As dysfunctions are identified, the development of solutions is owned by interdisciplinary teams that are held accountable by the organization's top executives. As part of the focus on reducing hidden costs, participants also plan and prioritize projects that will reduce the costs associated with organizational dysfunctions.

In the SEAM view, reductions in hidden costs can free up people to focus on activities that will add more value to the organization. If, as ISEOR researchers found, 30 percent of employee time is spent on unproductive activities, then a shift to strategically-oriented projects will result in increased value to the organization. That value can take the form of new innovation, increased sales, new business models—any manner of work that creates potential for the organization. In the accounting view, a reduction in hidden costs does not necessarily translate to a reduction in tangible costs because the costs for the people involved are the same. The value is in the creation of potential that would have otherwise been lost. The potential value, though, is associated with the controversial set of issues associated with accounting for an expanded set of intangible assets, that is—as of now—a reconceptualization of the traditional accounting view.

The Organization Invests in the Development of the Employees

Investment in people is another important part of SEAM intervention and research. The idea of human potential is central to the discussion of the socio-economic view because people are regarded as the "the only active and creative factor of sustainable economic value" (Savall & Zardet, 2008b, p. 5). In the socio-economic view, investment in people means allowing for the time to study, train on new technologies, and apply what they learn in new ways that will benefit the organization. There are offsetting costs associated with these activities, of course, but new innovations may be regarded as an asset—though an intangible one. In other words, accounting systems do not recognize new capabilities of the organization as an asset, even though the new capabilities are really an outcome of the investments made.

Work is Aligned With the Strategic Aims and Objectives of the Organization

The key focus is on the value of projects to the organization, relative to other work that the employees are already doing. Alignment is not only a matter of agreeing on priorities, but also deciding the scope and depth of the work that will be done to serve those priorities. In an organization that has adopted SEAM management principles, the time spent on tasks would be reviewed through an analysis of the ways that people are utilizing their time. As part of the SEAM organizational intervention, the mix of tasks would not only be identified but also optimized through an effort to define projects, as part of the Periodically Negotiable Activity Projects assessment. Because of the focus on value as opposed to costs, it is up to management to ensure that people are focused on the right work relative to the needs of the organization. The SEAM principles emphasize that if people are not producing work of value, then that is the responsibility of management—and not the individual employee. Of course, knowing if people are adding value can be confounded by a multiplicity of factors, but in the socio-economic approach people also conduct their own time management assessment and they can see for themselves the amount of time spent on work that is important. SEAM researchers have found that when people analyze their own time, they are surprised to see the amount of time spent on work that is not considered important. Once they see the problem for themselves, they can usually find ways to increase time dedicated to value-added work.

Another important consideration in the process of aligning work to new areas of strategic value is in the SEAM assessment of opportunity costs. In the SEAM view, opportunity costs are a component of hidden costs. As with more traditional assessments of opportunity costs, alternative approaches or projects are weighed one against the other. Alignment of resources to value-add activities means that other work is de-prioritized or unaddressed.

Technical and Financial Capital are "Inert" Inner Tools

While Savall (2010) emphasizes the word "active" to convey the idea that it is people who have the capability to add value to the organization, he also uses the word "inert" to convey the idea that financial capital and technology cannot by themselves (without the contributions of people) produce value for the organization. Savall emphasized that technology and financial capital are only tools, and that it is people that leverage those tools to add value.

This second tenet of SEAM is especially relevant in organizational decision making processes, where the development of the business case for investments in new technology, systems, or infrastructure is often associated with major investments in funds. Given the need to control costs, these investments must stand up to intense scrutiny and must have the potential of generating significant cost savings, relative to the investment being made. Savall's (2010) reminder that the tools, systems, or other investments in plant or equipment are "inert" highlights the idea that the investments are only part of a larger picture of organizational capability building. Often the capability-building costs are left out of the business case analysis because reassignment of existing employees will not add to costs. Yet if the organization capability building aspects of investments get left out of the decision making process, there may not be sufficient focus on the need to consider the inter-relationships between the behaviors of people and new organizational structures. New investments without complementary investments in people may create dysfunctions in areas that are considered important for growth.

The Complementary Nature of Capital and Labor, as Opposed to Substitutability

When Savall (2010) described the active nature of people vs. the inert qualities of tools such as technology or financial capital, he advocated for an integration of perspectives. The third tenet of the SEAM paradigm emphasizes the complimentary relationship between labor and capital, as opposed to the idea of substitutability of labor and capital that is part of the industrial-era management mindset. "It is clear," he wrote, "that the purpose and meaning of work in the post-industrial society will be determined through a complex and subtle interplay of human, technological, and economic factors" (p. xii).

This third tenet highlights the problem that traditional accounting still treats the cost of people as units of production, as opposed to a source of value. This view results in situations where people continue to be subservient to machines. In other words, the cost for the salaries and benefits of people is lower than the cost to automate a process or to implement a new technology. In other contexts, however, people work as part of complex interdisciplinary processes where knowledge is essential. Some people work creatively with technology and can make a machine do work that it wasn't designed to do. Even the most technically-advanced applications involve people, the unaddressed variation in the inter-relationships between people and structures can also represent a dysfunction and source of hidden costs. Of course, technology is only one component of the complex interplay that Savall expressed—especially as the cost of people is weighed against other kinds of investments.

Evolving Ontological Perspectives

While on the surface it may appear that measurement of organization performance is best left to a company's finance professionals, it is important to consider that the debates about what to measure are, in part, ontological. The division between tangible and intangible assets may represent an ontological dividing line that differentiates between measures that are deemed objective vs. those that are subjective. Managers trained to think from a rational perspective may regard "tangible" assets as a knowable reality and "intangible" assets as invisible and therefore subjective. In the rationalist view, financial data and measurements do not require the same critical scrutiny as other forms of information.

Managers who view the nature of truth through a social constructionist lens, on the other hand, may be more comfortable with many forms of information—even the accounting measures. Presumably, those trained to manage rationally may be better equipped to critically evaluate the quality of the information, no matter what the source. Yet, ironically, many believe that the accounting measures should be accepted as facts, and that other measures should be dismissed as subjective. A schematic representation of this perspective is shown in Figure 2.2.

CONCLUSIONS

Different conceptualizations of costs may be important considerations for organization development practitioners. First, the implication is that in order

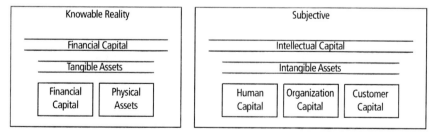

Figure 2.2 Objectivism and ontological perspectives about the meaning of financial performance measures. *Note:* The emphasis on rationalism in business management has influenced the perspective that some measures of financial performance can be accepted as truth, while other measures are subjective.

to effect change in organizations, practitioners must acknowledge the underlying values and beliefs that drive it. Second, and perhaps more important, the values and beliefs of business leaders may be different than the values and beliefs generally associated with the practice of organization development.

Organizational change initiatives related to the productivity of people or organizational capability building might be incompatible with the view that people are costs. For example, business leaders may appear to be in agreement as organization development practitioners talk about the importance of productivity and the value of people, but in reality the business leaders are working from a different set of values and beliefs about productivity and value. That is, business might mentally filter the concept of productivity gains as (a) reductions in the number of people and (b) a corresponding increase in net income. The organization development practitioner, in contrast, might be thinking that if employees can be freed up from existing tasks then the employees can take on new projects that will add more value. These differences in underlying beliefs may appear on the surface to be subtle, but in fact may ultimately affect the perceived success of organization change initiatives.

At the same time though, there is increasing recognition that cost-cutting in organizations—while associated with quick financial wins—has not necessarily produced desired results over the long term. In order to ensure the long-term sustainability of the organization, some organizations are applying collective brainpower to boost economic performance. Some of this new thinking about economic performance is not really new at all, but rather part of a long legacy of research in the field of organization development. The legacy of organization development research includes information about the ways that the economic performance of organizations could be improved. Many business leaders have been trained to manage costs, but have missed out on the significant body of organization development research related to economic performance. Given the legacy of the organization development profession, there is a new opportunity to return to a focus on economic performance—especially as it relates to the knowledge, skills and productivity of people.

APPENDIX:
Conference Dialogue

Henri Savall: From the beginning of the research on SEAM, I studied the concept of human capital and I thought it was an error conceptually, because the human capital is owned by individuals, it doesn't pertain to any organization. And the concept of human capital would be accurate when speaking of the individual, the owner of the human capital uses what he transfers to the organization is the result of the base potential. The base potential is low or high and what he brings to other people. Maybe low level or high level and that is the meaning of potential and we can't put on a balance sheet, in a sense human capital. When in mergers and acquisitions, the assessment of the enterprise is to estimate the value of human capital for the organization. Then the acquisition is made, it is done and then people leave, quit the organization. It is not a capital which belongs to the organization. It is a conceptual error. That is the meaning of human potential, not capital.

Conference Participant: May I follow up? First, you're bucking a very strong trend in economics. Since Becker won the Nobel Prize for his work, so I commend you for your boldness. One of the things that Becker talked about was who should pay for the investment in the individuals' potential and generally he said that when the skills were going to the firm, specifically, the firm should pay for it. And when the skills were transferrable to other firms, the individual should pay for it. Your research shows a huge payoff for investment in potential, in general. How have you dealt with that with your clients?

Henri Savall: I said there are two kinds of knowledge. Contingent knowledge and generic knowledge but we can't separate them. How can we manage that? Through contracting between the individual, the team, and the organization? Who pays? It's a contract.

Marc Bonnet: There's no mathematical formula.

Henri Savall: It's a signed agreement.

Conference Participant: It seems to me in today's world that line is increasingly fuzzy because skills are transferrable so easily that it's much harder sitting in the manufacturing environment 50 years ago to be able to do that. So, I think it's perhaps an easier sell for us today than it was earlier.

Henri Savall: The proposal is the cost of investment in intangible human potential to be amortized as machines or technology.

Conference Participant: This is perhaps a question for all of us. What companies are we aware of, perhaps some of you have worked with, who do the best job of adopting this mindset and this approach, who are seeing costs differently and practicing this? Here or in Europe.

Henri Savall: In Europe, in subsidiaries of Stanley Corporation and Manpower Corporation.

Gérard Desmaison: and of Nabisco and Carlson Companies.

Conference Participant: I'll tack on to what was said regarding the equation of the human capital investment, it could be something as simple as attending certification. Your organization will invest in it, right? Spend $4,000 or $5,000. They'd see the return on investment that's transferrable. If the individual leaves, they leave, so there is an economic and mathematical type of a cost to use and that's just the choice of the organization. That's absolutely transferrable.

Conference Participant: I have another question. How do intangible assets show up on a financial statement? I've never seen intangible assets on a financial statement. I know that a point of SEAM but if they were on a financial statement, what would that look like?

Henri Savall: For example, goodwill is an intangible investment. When you're thinking about finance, the mainstream CEOs admit it is an asset when speaking about working with the company.

Conference Participant: Is it feasible to analyze the benefits in an organization such as a public school where return on investment is notoriously difficult to measure? I'm personally interested in applying these concepts in secondary schools, universities. Is it feasible?

Henri Savall: 35% of our research work was in public services, non-profit organizations, and dysfunctions and hidden costs are generic. They are not specific and there no perfect operations.

Conference Participant: One of the great problems with that, though, is usually when people don't believe the results, they don't believe that there is a return. They don't believe that there is value because they are deemed as soft.

John Conbere: We saw that recently with the company we've been working with and the CEO simply will not accept anything that isn't cash has value and it's such a mental model, he's a finance guy, he can't break out of it.

Conference Participant: Has the research produced any kind of point of diminishing return study? There was interesting documentation that a dollar in equals two dollars to $4,000 out. One would think, well why not put in a million dollars per person. Obviously there's a point of diminishing returns. Where does that happen and is that intuitive or is that done through the contracting phase? How do we know when we've saturated the organization with the individual's potential?

Henri Savall: A major part of hidden cost is destruction of potential value added (i.e., opportunity cost), then there is no saturation point. We have an example of a company that started with 240 people. Now, for 30 years he has been applying SEAM model and there's no limit in its increasing performance [Henri explaining model on blackboard].

John Conbere: We talked with the head of Stanley Works in Lyon. Ten years ago, they invested a lot in SEAM. That intervention initially cost more. Their annual payment to ISEOR went down over the years, so they made the big initial investment. Their money paid to ISEOR actually shrinks so that it's another way of looking at your question. Once they get the change, they don't have to keep paying for it. It grows.

Henri Savall: It builds on itself, then. And then, another component to this is the government application of SEAM where you may have a stagnant factor where a city isn't growing, a county isn't growing. You're not really increasing your sales but you are responding ever more, trying to be more effective in your delivery of services, more flexible where you're not going to be able to see that kind of ratio in the government sector, I wouldn't think, because you're not really increasing sales. You're going to have to look at a different factor when it comes to investing in human potential. The return is going to look somewhat different.

Conference Participant: You get all the other value added pieces, dysfunctions are always going to exist and the return on investment is as long as the SEAM methodology is imbedded and you're investing in it, you're going to identify the dysfunctions. You'll be able to assess each one for its value.

Henri Savall: We compared 40 organizations, 20 non-profit and public organizations and 20 for profit companies and the results on the cost level where almost the same in both sectors.

Conference Participant: This is a really very basic question but do all humans have the potential to add value?

Henri Savall: All humans have it.

Conference Participant: What about incompetency?

Henri Savall: Incompetency means future competency. It doesn't exist.

John Conbere: So, a very simple example might be at one point people born with Down's Syndrome were seen as incompetent and now you find them working happily in many places.

Henri Savall: SEAM is a dynamic model. It's a formative and learning model. Things are not as they seem to be now as they are tomorrow. SEAM is a dynamic model.

Conference Participant: In your experience, you're talking about the transformation as changing the mental model not only of work, but of existence. How long does it take for people to get that? That's a huge thing.

Henri Savall: My answer will be politically incorrect. The higher the education, the higher the resistance.

Conference Participant: Taking competency development out of the equation, and just the identification of the dysfunctions, what are the one or two or three factors that stand out the most as far as maximizing human potential? With all the work that you've done and cases that you've found, what are the two or three things that have served to really make a difference? What is the largest dollar increase?

Henri Savall: Considering human potential at any moment, investing in it, cleaning up dysfunctions which grow back everyday and contracting performance at any moment between any part of the organization. In SEAM, contracting performance is the key factor

Conference Participant: I know this first developed for management but as I see it as a way of living, a way of life. You cannot separate this from your life, once you embrace it. How to apply it to everything you do with the community. I'm very involved with sport teams and children and other areas of the community. It's hard to separate them because you're going to see human potential. How can you just leave this at work and not in other areas of your life?

Henri Savall: In SEAM there is a "hidden theory" which is called "the broken person." It says that a person has three main status: he/she is a citizen, he/she is a consumer, and he/she is a producer. The person is "split" between being inside the organization or outside. People say happiness is a feeling. SEAM say happiness could be a feeling unless the organization would be splitting the person.

REFERENCES

Davidson, S., Stickney, C. P., & Weil, R. L. (1979). *Financial accounting: An introduction to concepts, methods and uses.* Hinsdale, IL: The Dryden Press.

Likert, R. (1967). *The human organization.* New York, NY: McGraw-Hill, Inc.

Savall, H. (2010). *Work and people: An economic evaluation of job-enrichment.* Charlotte, NC: Information Age Publishing. (1st French edition: Paris, France: Dunod, 1974).

Savall. H., & Zardet, V. (2007, June). L'importance stratégique de l'investissement incorporeal: Résultats qaulimétrics de cas d'enterprises [The strategic importance of intangible investment: Qualimetric results of case companies]. 1° Congrès transatlantique de comptabilité, audit, contrôle de gestion, gestion des coûts et mondialisation,–Institut International des Coûts (IIC)—American Accounting Association—ISEOR, Lyon.

Savall, H., & Zardet, V. (2008a). *Mastering hidden costs and socio-economic performance.* Charlotte, NC: Information Age Publishing. (Originally published in French in 1987).

Savall, H., & Zardet, V. (2008b, April). Le concept de coût-valeur des activités. Contribution de la théorie socio-économique des organisations [The concept of cost-value activities: A contribution to the socio-economic organization theory]. *Revue Sciences de Gestion-Management Sciences-Ciencias de Gestión, 64,* 61–90.

Savall, H., Zardet, V., & Bonnet, M. (2008). *Releasing the untapped potential of enterprises through socio-economic management.* Turin, Italy: International Training Centre of the ILO. 1st edition: 2000.

CHAPTER 3

SOCIO-ECONOMIC MANAGEMENT CONSULTING IN AMERICA

A Diffusion of Innovation Study

Mark E. Hillon, Yue Cai Hillon, and Collin Bunch

CONFERENCE REMARKS:
Chapter Prologue

Mark Hillon

I was noting questions from the earlier session that were so uniquely American that our French colleagues probably wonder why people ask these things. But, we do see things differently. We see socio-economic management differently. To get an idea of how the diffusion of SEAM might progress in America, we took a look at how it progressed in Mexico, which is currently the best case outside of France, outside of Europe, in which SEAM has actually taken root. We used the classic diffusion model of Everett Rogers and, for the Organization Development (OD) students in the room, this is a great example of how one researcher's ideas inform the next

Decoding the Socio-Economic Approach to Management, pages 47–64
Copyright © 2016 by Information Age Publishing

generation, how ideas spread, and how knowledge transfuses or progresses through a social system.

THE PURPOSE OF THIS STUDY

One research question often leads to another. In a previous study of management consulting in China, we wondered whether socio-economic management might offer a cultural bridge between American and Chinese management theory and practice. While we found that there was potential for such a cultural bridge, we also learned that economic conditions and management practices were not yet favorable for the introduction of socio-economic management in China. Cultural adaptations in the delivery of socio-economic management would also be necessary to fit the context. The cultural questions considered in the Chinese study raised similar questions in our minds about the diffusion and adoption of socio-economic management consulting in America.

Lafayette was once a liminal (Turner, 1969) guiding figure between France and America because he embodied the human ideals that he hoped would release the benefits of intellectual and creative liberty in a civil society. He was a mediator of American cultural identity at a crucial period in our history, so it is fitting that the dialectical struggles to define his own identity in France (Kramer, 1996) are the same battles waged for the souls of modern organizations. We view ISEOR and its efforts to share the benefits of socio-economic management in the role of a present-day Lafayette. In this study, we employ elements of Rogers' (1995) diffusion of innovation model and Granovetter's (1973, 1983) social network theory to analyze the campaign for adoption of socio-economic management in America. We also look to ISEOR's experience in Mexico to anticipate the probable timeline and challenges in developing a supportive network for the sustainable diffusion of socio-economic management.

DIFFUSION OF INNOVATION IN SOCIAL NETWORKS

Innovations in management thinking have followed many paths into our collective consciousness. Rogers (1995, p. 207) investigated the diffusion of innovations and found that five variables explained most of the observed variance in adoption rate:

1. Perceived attributes of innovation
   a. Relative advantage
   b. Compatibility

  c. Complexity
  d. Trialability
  e. Observability

2. The type of innovation decision
  a. Optional
  b. Collective
  c. Authority

3. The nature of communication channels diffusing the innovation at various stages in the innovation-decision process

4. The nature of the social system in which the innovation is diffusing

5. The extent of change agents' promotion efforts in diffusing the innovation

The relative advantages of socio-economic management for organization performance have been well documented (e.g., Savall & Zardet, 2008) and ISEOR's publications offer forms of trialability and observability to potential adopters. From the perspective of a chief executive or organization director, the type of innovation decision is optional or voluntary. An intervention researcher can discuss the relative advantage of socio-economic management with decision makers, but cannot force an agreement. Out of the remaining variables, complexity, compatibility, and the nature of the social system are the most relevant to our culturally focused diffusion study.

COMPLEXITY

The complexity of socio-economic management favors diffusion through academically trained practitioners, with instructors who are well versed in the socio-psychological and technical-economic theory underlying the approach. In terms of Granovetter's (1973) social network theory, ISEOR expanded its strong tie network in France by doctorally training its own intervention-researchers in socio-economic management. For the purpose of this diffusion of innovation study, we apply the same logic and define a *strong tie* as one that carries sufficient knowledge to instruct others at the doctoral level in the theory and practice of socio-economic management. Note that this definition is somewhat more specific than Granovetter's (1973) strong tie that merely required direct and frequent communication between people, without regard for content. Once trained to this level, it may be more appropriate to shift our conceptualization slightly to an actor network model, especially if the intervention-researchers disperse. Outside of Europe, the greatest diffusion of socio-economic management has been in Mexico, where there are fourteen doctorally trained intervention-researchers (ISEOR, 2013) who serve as strong ties or actors in an emerging national network. This example provides convincing support for the effectiveness of strong tie creation in ISEOR's diffusion of innovation plan.

Table 3.1 depicts the timeline of SEAM diffusion in Mexico and offers insight into their experience of building a network of strong ties or actors. Notice that the second Mexican scholar to earn a doctorate at ISEOR figures prominently in later network development as a dissertation co-chair and faculty colleague. The shaded portions of Table 3.1 indicate the network of strong ties that was created following the doctoral training of Margarita Fernandez Rubalcaba. We can only speculate that the 11-year gap leading up to the planned introduction of SEAM into Mexico was necessary for ISEOR to develop sufficient personnel and resources to expand beyond Europe. From 1995 to 2009, concerted efforts to advance doctoral training, conduct interventions in Mexican businesses, and document research findings at conferences seems to have created a self-sustaining SEAM actor network.

Fernandez Rubalcaba (2007) gave us a preview of potentially relevant contextual factors in the Mexican SEAM diffusion experience that may apply to the American campaign. The most obvious common challenge is in the organizational culture of higher education. She noted that a SEAM intervention in a division of their university described an autocratic and compartmentalized organizational structure which prevented the very collaboration that was required for faculty to fulfill their work obligations. Teacher-researchers were separated from the committee charged with sharing their findings with potential users and

> professors lacked the experience to successfully connect with the organizations in their environment...Yet, the institutional structures that would authorize full-time professors to establish contact with real-world organizational problems had not been created, the only exception being a professor's private initiative. (Fernandez Rubalcaba, 2007, pp. 259–260)

There is no evidence to suggest that ISEOR will not encounter the same challenge in American university culture. The Universidad Autónoma Metropolitana, Unidad Xochimilco has a cluster of six intervention-researchers doctorally trained by ISEOR that is a cornerstone for training future doctoral students in Mexico. Efforts are also apparently underway to develop additional clusters of intervention-researchers beyond UAM, thereby reducing the dampening effects of isolation on the diffusion of SEAM. Perhaps this lesson is the driving force behind the formal SEAM training programs to be offered at the University of St. Thomas in Minneapolis.

Three additional contextual factors stand out in the Mexican experience that will likely present similar challenges in America. First, Fernandez Rubalcaba (2007) found that it was necessary to train "a core group of professors

TABLE 3.1   SEAM Diffusion Timeline in Mexico

Dates	Doctorant & Dissertation Title or Event	Current Affiliation
Dec 1982	ENRIQUEZ GALVAN Oscar: Analyse socio-économique des conséquences sur les conditions de vie au travail des décisions stratégiques de transfert de technologie. Cas d'entreprises mexicaines	Instituto Tecnológico de Veracruz?
July 1984	FERNANDEZ RUBALCABA Margarita Fernández: Interactions entre conditions de vie au travail et conditions de vie hors du travail. Applications à des cas d'innovation socio-économique	Universidad Autónoma Metropolitana, Unidad Xochimilco; AGSEO
1995	Socio-Economic Management Engineering presented (25-hour seminar)	
1996	SEAM method presented at the Mexican Directors of Applied Research and Technology Development Centers Conference	
1996	LIMSE formed at UAM	
1998	4 UAM professors begin studies at ISEOR	
1998–2002	1,248 days of interaction between ISEOR and Mexican intervener-researchers	
Nov 2000	MARTINEZ Y RANGEL Armando Luis: Formes de contrôle, systèmes d'informations stimulants et PME en croissance. Cas d'entreprises mexicaines	Instituto Tecnológico de Mérida in Merida, Yucatan, Mexico
April 2004	GONZALEZ Gerardo: Los desafíos para el cambio en organizaciones públicas en México. Dos casos de innovación tecnológica en el Sistema de Transporte Colectivo de la ciudad de México (Co tutelle)	Consultant, Zapopan, Jalisco
April 2005	MARTINEZ VASQUEZ Griselda: La contribution du management socio-économique à l'aménagement des performances économiques et sociales. Cas d'expérimentation dans trois petites entreprises mexicaines	Universidad Autónoma Metropolitana, Unidad Xochimilco; AGSEO
July 2006	PENALVA Laura Patricia Rosales: Inducción al Aprendizaje organizacional en la Universidad Pública para el desarrollo de estrategias de vinculación con el sector productivo. (Co tutelle avec Martha FERNANDEZ FERNANDEZ RUBALCABA)	Universidad Autónoma Metropolitana, Unidad Xochimilco; AGSEO
July 2006	RAMIREZ ALCANTARA Hilda Teresa: Elementos estructurantes de la confianza y su relación con el desempeño en una universidad pública mexicana (co tutelle avec Martha FERNANDEZ-FERNANDEZ RUBALCABA)	Universidad Autónoma Metropolitana, Unidad Xochimilco; AGSEO

(continued)

TABLE 3.1 SEAM Diffusion Timeline in Mexico (continued)

Dates	Doctorant & Dissertation Title or Event	Current Affiliation
July 2006	SÁNCHEZ TREJO Victor: Construction d'un processus de prise de décision stratégique dans la PME pour améliorer sa performance globale : Recherche–Intervention dans une entreprise mexicaine	Universidad Autónoma del Estado de Hidalgo; Franchised Consultant
Sept 2006	GONZALEZ PEREZ Claudia Rocio: L'organisation créatrice de connaissances. L'organisation synaptique	Universidad Autónoma Metropolitana, Unidad Xochimilco; AGSEO
Oct 2006	BRIONES Brenda: Les enjeux de l'interaction entre les comportements et les compétences, et son impact sur la coopération entre les individus. Cas de trois PME méxicaines	Universidad Autónoma del Estado de Hidalgo
Jan 2007	BRINDIS ALMAZAN María de Lourdes: Estructuras de Organización para el Desarrollo Socioeconómico local : la comunidad artesanal.	Universidad Autónoma Metropolitana Unidad Guajimalpa
Jan 2007	POMAR FERNANDEZ Silvia: La naturaleza híbrida de las organizaciones y el proceso de transferencia de modelos. El caso de las guarderías subrogadas en México.	Universidad Autónoma Metropolitana, Unidad Xochimilco; AGSEO
Oct 2007	IBARRA CORTES Mario Eduardo: Stratégie et gestion financières. Le cas de la municipalité de San Luis Potosi au Mexique	Universidad Autónoma de San Luis Potosí
2007	AGSEO formed at UAM	
2009	AGSEO holds first international symposium	

Note: Compiled from Socio-Economic Approach to Management in Mexico (Fernandez Rubalcaba, 2007; Réseau international des docteurs formés à l'ISEOR (126) http://www.iseor.com/reseau_docteur.asp; Thèses de Doctorat de Sciences de Gestion soutenues à l'Université (117) http://www.iseor.com/publications_ouvrages.asp?type=theses; History of AGSEO: Área de análisis y gestión Socioeconómica de las organizaciones http://csh.xoc.uam.mx/produccioneconomica/agseo/pagina_agseo/template_10a.htm

in social science research methodologies, thus enabling them to acquire the competency necessary for supervising doctoral research" (p. 271). Few doctoral programs in America actually accomplish this task, as academic careers depend much more on choosing an established ideological belief system along a false dichotomy and learning to recite its dogma.

Second, SEAM was presented to a conference of the Mexican Association of Directors of Applied Research and Technological Development Centers in 1996, with follow-up visits to several cities (Fernandez Rubalcaba, 2007). Although it is unclear whether this diffusion channel has been actively pursued by ISEOR, similar channels in America would likely provide direct access for SEAM to transfer into business practice. Research directors and their centers have a clear role to transfer knowledge to the public, often via commercialization in private companies.

Third, one of the objectives of their university SEAM intervention was to "adapt the SEAM engineering method to the culture of state universities in Mexico" (Fernandez Rubalcaba, 2007, p. 262). The research question of cultural adaptation is what led us to explore the current path of SEAM diffusion in America. From our research for this paper and our years of experience in teaching and applying SEAM in America, we would restate this Mexican objective. The methods of SEAM are not in need of cultural adaptation. Rather, the manner in which SEAM is taught and transferred should be adapted, as needed, to align with relevant cultural and contextual factors. For instance, it would be quite sensible to help students learn SEAM in a manner that is culturally appropriate and consistent with their learning preferences.

The Weakness of Weak Ties

To replicate the French diffusion model, ISEOR has set about building a network of American academic partners and institutions. By contrast with Europe and Mexico, diffusion of socio-economic management in America has had to rely on weak ties. For the purpose of this diffusion of innovation study, we shall define a *weak tie* as one that does not carry sufficient knowledge to create instructors capable of training others in the theory and practice of socio-economic management. The ideal form of a strong tie, as demonstrated in Europe and Mexico, is a doctoral student trained in residence at ISEOR/Jean Moulin University. Although the SEAM consultant training offered in seminar format is a mentored introduction to conducting interventions, this type of program is insufficient for creating SEAM trainers.

Granovetter's (1983) review of other researchers' work on social network analysis generally supported his theory of the strength of weak ties.

However, one unexpected finding was in the interaction of strong and weak ties. While information spreads rapidly via weak ties among unrelated network subgroups, adoption of an innovation into practice depends upon an organization's strong tie decision-making process. An official agreement for academic cooperation between universities is a formalized weak tie, even though it may have resulted from the strong ties of professional or friendship bonds between specific individuals. Granovetter's (1983) review found that while weak ties tend to remain in place over time, they generally do not transform into the strong ties needed for system-wide adoption of innovation. The diffusion of socio-economic management in America may, therefore, be limited if the social network consists entirely of weak institutional ties. Reiterating Fernandez Rubalcaba's (2007) experience in Mexico, organizational structures in higher education exhibit dysfunctional characteristics of mature bureaucracies. Personal initiative of individual professors is required for adoption of new ideas and, barring large-scale systemic structural reform, diffusion of SEAM will be limited to the professor's scope of influence.

Granovetter's (1973) work on social networks and much of the attention since has not been concerned with longitudinal changes in the networks themselves. This inattention is understandable, given that studies of events and similar transient phenomena must assume that the network parameters are largely fixed over short durations. Haythornthwaite (2002) recognized that latent, weak, and strong ties remain in flux over time as organization members, project teams, and communication media change in composition and emphasis. While latent ties can quickly become active or inactive as new project teams are formed and strong ties tend to seek out self-reinforcing communication media, weak ties remain most susceptible to disruption. Haythornthwaite (2002, p. 394) explained:

> From a tie perspective, we can also view the problem of group formation as the problem of individuals working against their normal tendencies toward weak ties. Time-limited groups who come together as weakly tied pairs need to expend effort normally reserved for strong ties, such as frequent communication, self-disclosure, and negotiation of communication norms. Moreover, there are more others to get to know. Faced with a whole set of weak ties, effort is greater because individuals must change their normal weak-tie behavior (such as waiting for opportunities to interact) into pro-active, strong-tie behavior. To convert these weak ties to strong ones—or even to sort out with whom to build a strong tie—does take more effort, partly because of the change in behavior, and partly because of the number of others with whom they must negotiate relations and media conventions.

The friendship and professional contacts within ISEOR's American academic and institutional partners have many other responsibilities in addition to their interests in socio-economic management. Thus, time and other resources intended for diffusion may be consumed in maintaining relationships, activating latent ties, and repairing disruptions.

Compatibility and the Social System

While the complexity of socio-economic management poses distinct challenges for developing sufficiently strong network ties to aid diffusion, a different set of issues arises when we turn our attention to compatibility with the existing purposes, beliefs, and practices of the social system. Broadly speaking, the social system in question is that of American business education, for it is through this diffusion pathway that academic partners will train intervention researchers, who will in turn spread socio-economic management to industry.

Bennis and O'Toole (2005) claimed that management is a practical profession that requires support from multiple academic disciplines. Indeed, prior to the ascendance of business schools, the atheoretical practice of management had a natural home in a liberal tradition and was much like crafts and trades that were learned through apprenticeship and on-the-job training (Perriton & Hodgson, 2013). Khurana (2010) explored the history of management education and found that a public call for the professionalization of management emerged after each economic calamity and ethical crisis of confidence in the institutions of capitalism. Emery (1993) observed that hierarchical organizations have great difficulty in setting objectives that are timely and relevant to the character of the global environment. Therefore, it is understandable that the leading business schools of the day decided to create a positivist academic discipline in isolation from the actual practice of management (Bennis & O'Toole, 2005). While this historical note has created debate and many publishing opportunities, we mention it only because we must understand the nature of the social system in which socio-economic management is diffusing. Socio-economic management developed outside of this historical constraint and therefore, the innovation may face a challenge of compatibility as it navigates a pathway to adoption.

Academia is intentionally fragmented into disciplines and specialties, therefore it would be reasonable to expect to find some subsystems within the larger American business education social system that are cognizant of the liberal arts discipline-spanning nature of management and are engaged with the work of managers in practice. Perriton and Hodgson's (2013) work suggests that such scholars tend to utilize critical, dialogic, and reflexive perspectives in their research and pedagogy. The field of organization development may be over-represented in this target group, with particular emphasis on those who study management as an individual/actor-network practice using ethnographic and phenomenographic methods. With these characteristics in mind, we examined the current list of American academic partners (ISEOR, 2013) to determine whether scholars in compatible subsystems had expressed affinity for socio-economic management.

The academic partner descriptions and interests of the personal/professional contacts in Table 3.2 were gleaned from each institution's website. Four of the six academic institutions matched the liberal arts affinity characteristic, while five of the six professional contacts had research and teaching interests in organization development or change, consulting, or critical management. The lone exception of Central Michigan appeared not to have any of the expected affinity group characteristics. However, upon further reading, we learned that their partnership with ISEOR began because they needed a model for developing an integrated management consulting option in their MBA program. Essentially, the contacts were searching for a liberal arts-inspired management curriculum that, in all likelihood, would be incompatible with the host institution.

To understand the current status of SEAM instruction and curriculum in America, we contacted the three institutions listed in *Realizations* 1975–2013 (ISEOR, 2013) for teaching SEAM and the newest official partner, the University of St. Thomas. Table 3.3 summarizes the curricula offered by these partners.

Tony Buono of Bentley University said that he began including SEAM in a comparative intervention frameworks module of his *Managing Organizational Change* course just after the sabbatical that produced the 2007 book, *Socio-Economic Intervention in Organizations* (Buono & Savall, 2007). He is likely the only Bentley professor to have ever included SEAM in a course, but his real contribution to the diffusion of SEAM in America has been in his work as editor of the Research in Management Consulting series for Information Age Publishing (personal communication, March 3, 2014).

TABLE 3.2   ISEOR's Network of American Academic Partners

Academic Partner	Description	Contact Interests
Benedictine University	Private Catholic liberal arts tradition	OD scholars/practitioners
Bentley University	Private Business School with integrated liberal arts tradition	OC scholar/consultant
Central Michigan University	Public comprehensive/teaching	Accounting
New Mexico State University	Public land grant	Critical management
Pepperdine University	Private Christian liberal arts tradition	OD scholars
University of St. Thomas	Private Catholic liberal arts tradition	OD scholars/practitioners

TABLE 3.3   SEAM Teaching Among ISEOR's American Academic Partners

Academic Partner	SEAM Curriculum Description	Current Status
Bentley University	Included in a module comparing intervention frameworks in Tony Buono's Managing Organizational Change course	No longer active
Central Michigan University	12-credit graduate consulting option launched in Fall 2003	Program ended in after Spring 2012
New Mexico State University	David Boje revised his Small Business Consulting course in Fall 2000 to utilize a SEAM diagnosis	Active
University of St. Thomas	OD Doctoral electives; SEAM Certificate and Masters Programs	OD Doctoral courses began in 2011; Programs beginning in 2014

Randall Hayes of Central Michigan University confirmed that their 12-credit graduate consulting option ended after Spring 2012 (personal communication, March 27, 2014). Returning to our three diffusion variables of complexity, compatibility, and the nature of the social system, the lessons in hindsight from Central Michigan University indicate why SEAM did not survive there. Bahaee, Love, and McGilsky (2005) note that the graduate consulting concentration looked to ISEOR as a model and SEAM as a foundation on which to build a program inclusive of a wider variety of consulting methods and tools. However, instructor training seems to have resembled ISEOR consultant training instead of something more appropriate for the depth of knowledge required to teach SEAM. The advisory council for the program also had no training in and presumably quite limited knowledge of SEAM. Savall, Zardet, Bonnet, and Peron (2012) described the Central Michigan consulting program as:

> focusing on the comparison of approaches to total quality management, and comparing results obtained through TQM, Six Sigma, coaching, and socio-economic approach to management in medium-size companies. As opposed to what happens in consulting firms, the rule of the game is to devote time and energy to document the interventions, pinpoint those factors which cut across all cases, and compare the results with the extant literature. (p. 87)

The history of SEAM at Central Michigan University is well documented in faculty publications and their business college newsletter. After the initial idea for a SEAM-focused graduate management consulting concentration in 2000, the program had to compete with SAP, Six Sigma, and entrepreneurship, as well as multiple college leadership and personnel changes and restructured programs. Consulting at Central Michigan University was always an internal cost center in contrast to large external funding for SAP, Six Sigma, and their entrepreneurship institute. According to Randall Hayes, the consulting option never reached its intended business student target, as it was most popular among Industrial and Organizational Psychology (IO Psych) doctoral students (personal communication, March 27, 2014).

David Boje has been using a SEAM diagnosis in his *Small Business Consulting* course at New Mexico State University continuously since Fall 2000. His publications on the theatrical and critical management aspects of SEAM have perhaps overshadowed his personal initiative and practical contributions for the diffusion of SEAM in America. Boje's Root Cause Chart and Story Chart/Narrative innovations have helped students to better understand complex causal relationships in client interview data. His work with small businesses and community groups has extended the benefits of SEAM to underserved and very weakly tied university constituents (personal communication, February 23, 2014).

The new programs starting in 2014 at the University of St. Thomas appear to be an innovative hybrid approach to create strong ties. ISEOR intervention-researchers have co-developed the new programs with John Conbere and Alla Heorhiadi, and have supervised interventions (personal communication, March 28, 2014). It appears that ISEOR has applied lessons from Mexico and Central Michigan to its efforts at St. Thomas to create an academic center for training students in the practice of SEAM consulting. An annual North American SEAM conference hosted by St. Thomas is another hybrid innovation that should assist in strengthening ties among SEAM scholars. Our analysis of the Mexican experience indicates that the institutional, regional, and national networks grew organically in successive stages from one seed over the course of 25 years. Intentional network development targeting SEAM affinity groups could occur in parallel with the creation of academic programs to jointly advance the diffusion process in America.

Diffusion of Innovation Among Weak Ties

As of January 2014, AACSB (Association to Advance Collegiate Schools of Business) lists 505 accredited business schools in America out of its total of 687 in 45 countries and territories. The remainder of the American business education social system includes non-AACSB accredited business schools, liberal arts schools with business programs or minors, and organization studies departments attached to non-business colleges. While this remainder group may actually be larger than the AACSB list and may have equal or greater affinity for socio-economic management, the limiting factor for diffusion in America is still the lack of strong ties or actors created by ISEOR's doctoral program.

Socio-economic management ultimately changes an organization at the individual psychological level (Hillon, 2005/2006), with specific actions for progress negotiated between managers and workers. Granovetter (1973) identified these sorts of dyadic relationships as weak ties relative to an organization's direction, yet found them to be extremely influential social system pathways. Given that weak ties are the most probable paths for diffusion of socio-economic management in America, it may be prudent to deconstruct and re-situate the diffusion narrative with a reinterpreted hierarchy (Boje, 2001). By this we mean to give primacy to actors who are not strongly tied to ISEOR and imagine from their perspectives how diffusion might occur. An advantage of people connected by weak ties is that they have access to quite different segments of the social system (Granovetter, 1973). We have already noted the choice of futures that largely disconnected American business education from professional practice. Thus, by elevating and giving voice to the current narrative's weak ties, we can move beyond the compatibility duality in a sub-system and gain access to a much larger cast of actors working in the field of business development and management performance improvement. If we change our perspective on diffusion to that of businesses that need assistance to improve performance, new channels and adaptations in delivery of SEAM become evident. This lesson is directly supported by the Mexican experience, albeit apparently as a missed opportunity to diffuse the SEAM innovation through the Mexican Association of Directors of Applied Research and Technological Development Centers.

The U.S. Small Business Administration provides funding for 63 lead centers that manage more than 900 local offices that offer counseling to approximately 590,000 small businesses each year (www.sba.gov). While many of the local offices are administratively attached to higher education entities, the daily work of SBDC counselors generally does not actively engage their host with business clients in any meaningful way. However, non-academic entities attached to universities have a degree of academic-like freedom in defining the nature and content of their work. One SBDC counselor in Missouri chose to work with Yue Cai Hillon to connect MBA students with small business clients for limited socio-economic management consulting projects. Between June of 2010 and December of 2013, a total of 109 MBA students in seven classes read *Mastering Hidden Costs and Socio-Economic Performance* and conducted a diagnostic and mirror effect for local business clients.

All 109 students could see value in the approach and 27 expressed intent to apply some aspect of socio-economic management in their current jobs. Of those who did not intend to apply lessons learned to their current jobs, 5 students were oriented toward or involved in Lean Six Sigma and process efficiency and thought that socio-economic management was too cumbersome to be practical for their work. Additionally, 4 students followed up with an independent study after the project. Overall, the instructor's appraisal of interest and aptitude indicated that, if given the opportunity, 6 students out of the total of 109 would seek further training to become consultants. Travel to France for advanced training was not a viable option for any of the students. Thus, to summarize the impact of an introductory applied theory course in socio-economic management on these MBA students, 100% became aware of potential benefits, 25% expressed limited behavioral intent, and 5.5% would adopt the innovation if professional training and support were available closer to home.

In this example, the SBDC host institution's culture was eventually confirmed to be incompatible with the practice of socio-economic management. However, the curriculum experiment lasted for 3.5 years because of the professor's security in a tenure-track job, highly favorable student course evaluations, an SBDC counselor who saw student projects as a viable means to leverage limited resources, and local business clients who saw value in working with students on socio-economic management projects. The relevant lesson of weak ties is that individual actors, not institutions, are the critical pathways for diffusion of SEAM in America. This experience has produced a wealth of data that will enable us to re-situate and enact a more comprehensive diffusion of innovation narrative for the practice of socio-economic management in America.

ADAPTATIONS IN PRACTICE AND PRAGMATISM

Our analysis has led us to practical and philosophical conclusions that indicate a way forward. First, experience in practice has shown that we should work within existing strong tie social networks that are compatible to our purposes. Tony Buono and Information Age Publishing are essential for disseminating knowledge of the SEAM methodology and case examples. The formal SEAM training programs coming online at St. Thomas in 2014 are another necessary component of a hybrid strong tie/actor network. However, drawing on the Mexican SEAM experience, one quickly realizes that other essential parts will be required before a sustainable network emerges in America.

Our second conclusion is also practical, but cultural in nature. The overall approach of socio-economic management is theoretically grounded at a trans-cultural human level. However, experience in practice has shown that adoption of the methods and tools of the approach may benefit from cultural re-contextualization. For instance, America is a low context culture that tends to frame problems in black and white, isolated from the relevant contexts in which they occur (Hill, 1977). Beliefs about management practice tend to reflect the extremes of order versus chaos, authority versus anarchy, and theory versus practice. America is also an adolescent culture that revels in defying authority (Repaille, 2006). The impatience for learning and the non-reflexive nature of perpetual adolescence adds to our superficiality, which accompanies a low context worldview because a belief that events occur unto themselves severely limits the search for complex causal networks and the meaning of extended relationships. In discussing relative advantage, Rogers (1995) contrasted preventative and incremental innovations. The long-term inoculative nature of socio-economic management makes the overall approach a preventative innovation. However, some of the tools could be implemented to demonstrate benefits in the shorter-term, as characteristic of an incremental innovation. One should anticipate and plan for a longer time horizon for knowledge to transform into reflexive practice.

Our third and final conclusion is philosophical and gives us reason to hope that socio-economic management is fundamentally compatible with American thought. Pragmatism is our only homegrown philosophy and probably exerts a more basic influence on our collective behavior than the cultural characteristics just mentioned. There seems to be a strong connection between American pragmatism and the responsible humanism inherent in socio-economic management. Rorty (1980) highlights this philosophical bond:

> Our identification with our community—our society, our political tradition, our intellectual heritage—is heightened when we see this community as ours rather than nature's, shaped rather than found, one among many which men have made. In the end, the pragmatists tell us, what matters is our loyalty to other human beings clinging together against the dark, not our hope of getting things right.... our glory is in our participation in fallible and transitory human projects, not in our obedience to permanent non-human constraints. (p. 727)

At the beginning of this study, we assumed Lafayette and ISEOR to be cultural mediators. To discover such a fundamental similarity in philosophy suggests that we initially misplaced them between countries and cultures. In reality, the liminal guiding role shows us all that in striving to live by human ideals, we can release the potential locked away by our own socio-economic constraints.

APPENDIX:
Conference Dialogue

Conference Participant: Were the people in Mexico cognizant of the struggle? Was the network self-aware?

Mark Hillon: From reading through the experience of Mexico, it seems in the beginning they weren't aware of the nature of the system. When you see what it took to get SEAM established in Mexico, you have to look at our own situation here to see whether we'll encounter some of the same issues. The most obvious one that stands out in their experience is the culture of higher education. Fernandez Rubalcaba found an autocratic system with structures that actually blocked people from fulfilling their job obligations and the result in their case was waiting for something to happen to relieve that barrier. They also noted that one of the key competencies in short supply among the faculty was research methods, the ability to conduct this type of social science research. That is surprisingly what you see in a lot of programs here.

We took a look at the academic partners that ISEOR has made over the years in America and there's a common theme running through all of them. They're not business schools, except for two, but they're really not exceptions when you look at the details. Most of them tend to be private liberal arts schools that are built on the idea of how things are connected and that you need a broad body of knowledge to be able to solve problems to function as a real human being.

If I could just sum up this whole diffusion model, the paper goes into more details about the earlier work on strong ties, weak ties, and latent ties. It seems when a network or new idea is trying to get established, the strong ties are important because you have to have frequent and direct communication between the people who have the knowledge and the people who need it. But later on, once the people, as in the case of Mexico, are getting to the stage where there might be enough knowledge transferred, you can switch to an actor network model in which the actors have autonomy to go forth from there. So, from where we are now, hopefully, this paper will lead to some discussion about building a stronger network in America and all the pieces that are necessary. It does take a very supportive community to get something like this going.

REFERENCES

Bahaee, M., Love, K. G., & McGilsky, D. (2005). Developing a Management Consulting Concentration within an MBA Program using SEAM Approach. *International Journal of Quality & Productivity Management, 5*(1), pp. II–1 to II–12.

Bennis, W. G., & O'Toole, J. (2005). How business schools lost their way. *Harvard Business Review, 83* (5), 96–104.

Boje, D. M. (2001). *Narrative Methods for Organizational and Communication Research.* Thousand Oaks, CA: Sage.

Buono, A.F., & Savall, H. (Eds.), (2007). *Socio-economic interventions in organizations: The intervener-researcher and the SEAM approach to organizational analysis.* Information Age Publishing: Charlotte, NC.

Emery, F. (1993). Management by Objectives. In M. Emery (Ed.), *Participative Design for Participative Democracy* (pp. 162–166). Canberra, Australia: Australian National University.

Fernandez Rubalcaba, M. F. (2007). Socio-economic approach to management in Mexico. In A. F. Buono & H. Savall (Eds.), *Socio-economic interventions in organizations: The intervener-researcher and the SEAM approach to organizational analysis* (pp. 251–278). Charlotte, NC: Information Age Publishing.

Granovetter, M. (1983). The strength of weak ties: A network theory revisited. *Sociological Theory, 1,* 201–233.

Granovetter, M. (1973). The strength of weak ties. *American Journal of Sociology, 78*(6), 1360–1380.

Haythornthwaite, C. (2002). Strong, weak, and latent ties and the impact of new media. *The Information Society, 18,* 385–401.

Hill, E. T. (1977). *Beyond Culture.* Garden City, NY: Anchor Books.

Hillon, M. E. (2005/2006). A comparative analysis of socio-ecological and socio-economic strategic change methodologies. Co-sponsored doctoral thesis. University of Lyon 3, France and New Mexico State University, NM.

ISEOR (2013). Realizations 1975–2013. Available at:http://www.iseor.com/ISEOR_ANGLAIS/pdf/default/fascicule-ANG-mai2013.pdf

Kramer, L. S. (1996). *Lafayette in Two Worlds: Public Cultures and Personal Identities in an Age of Revolutions.* Chapel Hill: University of North Carolina Press.

Khurana, R. (2010). *From Higher Aims to Hired Hands: The Social Transformation of American Business Schools and the Unfulfilled Promise of Management as a Profession.* Princeton, NJ: Princeton University Press.

Perriton, L., & Hodgson, V. (2013). Positioning theory and practice question(s) within the field of management learning. *Management Learning, 44* (2), 144–160.

Rapaille, C. (2006). *The Culture Code.* New York, NY: Broadway Books.

Rogers, E. M. (1995). Diffusion of Innovations. New York, NY: The Free Press.

Rorty, R. (1980). Pragmatism, Relativism, and Irrationalism. *Proceedings and Addresses of the American Philosophical Association, 53(6),* 719–738.

Savall, H., Zardet, V., Bonnet, M., & Peron, M. (2012). Preparing and training better management consultants through the socioeconomic approach to management curricula. In S. M Adams & A. Zanzi, (Eds.), *Preparing better consultants: The role of academia* (pp. 75–91). Charlotte, NC: Information Age.

Savall H., & Zardet V. (2008). *Mastering hidden costs and socio-economic Performance.* Charlotte, NC: Information Age.

Turner, V. (1969). *The ritual process: Structure and anti-structure.* Chicago, IL: Aldine Publishing.

CHAPTER 4

CAN SEAM WORK
IN UKRAINE?

Sergiy Ivakhnenkov, John Conbere, and Alla Heorhiadi

CONFERENCE REMARKS:
Chapter Prologue

Alla Heorhiadi

Very often at conferences, people ask us whether SEAM will work in a different culture. And, while the SEAM people say that there is no cultural variance here, SEAM can work anywhere, we had some doubt. We started actually with a research question, can SEAM work in Ukraine? You probably followed the news in Ukraine, something awful is happening there and the biggest thing about Ukraine is it's very corrupt. We talked to companies in two different parts of Ukraine and came to a conclusion that actually surprised us. I realize that geography is not a strength of many Americans, so we just wanted to show the map of Ukraine (see Figure 4.1). You see here, the river of Dnieper and it divides Ukraine. One case study comes from Kyiv, the capital in the center, and one from Lviv, near the Polish border. In the east are Crimea and the eastern part of Ukraine, where the Russian army is invading, although Russia pretends this is not happening.

Decoding the Socio-Economic Approach to Management, pages 65–82
Copyright © 2016 by Information Age Publishing

Figure 4.1 Map of Ukraine.

This case study explores a typical organization in Ukraine and asks if Ukrainian organizations are ready for SEAM. First we provide the context for the study. Next is a description of a small Ukrainian software company, to which we have given the pseudonym of Ukrainian IT, Ltd. Anecdotal evidence suggests that we might consider this case as typical for many modern Ukrainian businesses. As we analyze the case we explore readiness for SEAM in Ukraine, with additional reflections about what this might mean in other parts of the world.

THE CONTEXT: UKRAINE IN 2014

In 1991 two remarkable events happened in Ukraine. First of all, the relatively peaceful dissolution of the Soviet Union allowed Ukraine to become independent. Second, people could officially privatize businesses and entrepreneurship (in Soviet times, entrepreneurship was officially criminal). Thus, the process of privatization of state industrial property and the creation of new businesses began.

In November, 2013 Ukraine attracted the attention of people around the globe. On November 21, people took to the streets to protest against the fact that the Ukrainian government officially announced it was suspending preparations for an EU-Ukraine Association agreement. The protests, organized on social media, were soon named "Euromaidan" (European

Square). They were located primarily in Kyiv, around Maidan Nezalezhnosti (the Square of Independence). After the forced police dispersal of all protesters from Maidan Nezalezhnosti on the night of November 30, protesters proclaimed other political demands as well.

What were the demands of the protesters? It was not just Euro-integration. The Democratic Initiatives Fund (2014) on December 7th and 8th conducted a survey of people on Maidan. Among the reasons that led people to the square, the four most common were: the severe beatings of protesters on Maidan on the night of November 30 and repression (70%), refusal of Viktor Yanukovych to sign an Association Agreement with the European Union (53.5%), the desire to change life in Ukraine (50%), the desire to change the governmental corruption (39%) (Kvit, 2014).

Since those days, the conflict between protesters and government had enlarged and the government started to kill people. February 18–20, 2014 became the bloodiest days of riots. More than a hundred people were killed by the police. President Yanukovych then escaped from Kyiv and later fled to Russia. The Ukrainian parliament appointed a new Cabinet of Ministers and assigned early presidential elections for May 2014. But people stayed in Maidan to make sure the new government did not simply repeat its former corrupt ways (see Figure 4.2). They planned to occupy Maidan at least until summer.

Figure 4.2 A sign in a window in Kyiv: "It is not for Europe, it is against bribes given to the tax service. Go to Maidan!"

UKRAINIAN IT, LTD.

The company, which we shall call by the pseudonym Ukrainian IT, Ltd. was founded in 1993, two years after Ukraine became independent. Ukrainian IT, Ltd. was founded by a former PhD student in mathematics, who worked for the Soviet Ministry of Defense at a huge plant which produced electronics for the army. Formally, Ukrainian IT, Ltd. is a limited liability company with several minor co-owners who are also key employees. In actual practice, the company is controlled by a single owner/director and dividends are never paid.

When Ukrainian IT, Ltd. began, its focus was on software development for technological processes on railways. Later the company expanded to include software development for financial and managerial accounting and financial reporting. The software products include also those intended for public utility billing.

In 2014 Ukrainian IT, Ltd. had more than 20 active employees in Kyiv, and around 20 employees in Odessa and in Kharkiv. The payroll also contained several "ghost" people, who get an official minimal salary but no one saw them. Those people were close relatives of the owner. They actually did not work—Their interest was obtaining state social benefits, such as a state guarantied pension, which is higher if one officially were employed for a longer period of time.

The workers were mostly older people. There were several young workers, in their thirties, but the average age of an employee was 55. Eighty percent of the workers had reached the official retirement age, which in Ukraine is 60 for males and 55 for females. These employees received pensions and worked at the same time.

Ukrainian IT, Ltd. had a rented office. The company was located not far away from downtown Kiev, 4 subway stops away from Maidan, the central square of Kiev.

Business Practices of Ukrainian IT, Ltd.

The business of Ukrainian IT, Ltd. is software development and support. As a software company Ukrainian IT, Ltd. had a corporate tax privilege. The regular corporate tax in Ukraine is 20% of income, but registered software companies pay only 5% of income.

The sales volume of Ukrainian IT, Ltd. varied from year to year, fluctuating between 1,000,000 to 3,500,000 hrivnas. In U.S. dollars this would be $125,000 to $437,500.

The product line was based on the Microsoft FoxPro software tool. Software specialists outside of Ukrainian IT, Ltd. considered the FoxPro derivatives to be obsolete because they did not contain many options embedded in modern business and industrial software, such as multi-tasking, control procedures, and SQL databases. However, the key software developer at Ukrainian IT, Ltd., the aged programmer, who has PhD in technology, opposed any efforts to change from the use of FoxPro.

Ukrainian IT, Ltd. had a small number of clients. More than 95% of sales were done with one huge client, the Ukrainian state railways. The railway was a state-owned corporation with half a million employees. The railway had a complicated structure, with several thousand large and small departments and subsidiaries around the country. Almost all of the subsidiaries and departments paid small amounts annually for the software support to the company.

The main marketing tool of the software company was bribing railway officials. It works in the following way. When each contract was signed, 25% to 75% of the contract was used to pay kickbacks in cash to railway officials.

Quality control was non-existent. From time to time persons who actually used the software at clients' companies complained about the low quality and numerous bugs and mistakes in the software, no improvements or repairs were made. The bribed officials just did not care.

Periodically the railway management noted the fact that it was not safe for a large company like the railway to rely on one small company for its software, and that the railway should replace the software product either by SAP products (SAP is a world-wide famous German developer of business software) or by developing in-house its own products. These attempts were partially successful. For instance, the basic accounting product was replaced by one created by the in-house railway programmers, but most attempts to improve the software failed. There were various reasons for the failure, but the main reason was that change would limit the potential for bribery.

Most of the company's costs were labor costs. Most of salary payments, however, were done illegally, by cash "in envelopes." The payments were actually made by cash in envelopes. In Ukraine, the expression "money in envelopes" also is used widely for any illegal form of salary payments. By paying in cash the company avoids any records, and does not pay the taxes to the state for the cash in envelopes. Tax savings are approximately 33% of salary for the IT company and 18% of salary for the employee, so the saving is significant.

To pay salaries and bribes, the company needed a large amount of illegal cash on hand. This was obtained by the process that is called in Ukraine *obnalichivaniye*, cashing in, in which legally obtained money in bank accounts was converted to illegal cash. This scheme calls for creating a fraudulent company, or several such companies, which had accounts open in "special" banks. After contracts are signed, money is legally paid for goods and/or services. Services are better because it is harder to prove whether they actually were provided. But, instead of goods or services the vendor supplies the company with bags of cash. The commission fees are about 10%. Moreover, such fraudulent payments officially are considered as costs, and thus, they decrease profits and, consequently, corporate income tax payments, as well as VAT (value added tax) payments. Of course, by the Ukrainian law this scheme is completely illegal, but it is commonly known and used. Many state officials supported this because: a) it is a pyramid of "black" cash that is present from the bottom to the top of national and local politics, and b) it creates many opportunities for corrupt politicians to put political pressure on businesses.

The way business is done obviously makes all the official financial and tax reports miserable. Each year Ukrainian IT, Ltd. showed small profits or small losses, depending on the situation. The tax authorities several years ago actually stopped auditing to see if the tax laws were broken or profits and losses were distorted, and required companies not to show losses in their statements. Instead the tax authorities required a tax which was a percentage of sales. But it was possible to avoid large payments if one pays bribes of $1,000–$2,000 semiannually. Sometimes the bribe is paid by paying for office supplies but, of course, without the actual delivery of anything.

Working Conditions

Most employees of Ukrainian IT, Ltd. were programmers. The company did not have a reward system. Official salaries were low, slightly larger than the state-approved minimum for a full-time worker, which was approximately $100 per month. The evaluation of work results was made subjectively by the director. No timetables or formal results evaluations were used to evaluate work. The workers never knew the exact sum they could expect for their monthly salary. Sometimes they received less than usual, not because of their performance but just because "we do not have money this month."

The director avoided any talks about salary. Usually the illegal salary was 2–4 times larger than the official salary. Employees expected the same amount of salary from month to month, except for those whose salary included commissions (percent of sales). Thus, the sales employees earned a constant salary and on top of this a commission. Sometimes the income for these employees was less than they expected, because when the commission rose, the constant part of the salary could be decreased, depending on the director's mood. The director's explanation for the difference was, "It was too much for you."

The company had no job descriptions or document flow guides. Such written documents were strictly opposed by the director so that he could tell employees to do anything that he wanted. When the director was offered the possibility of having consultants calculate the hidden costs in Ukrainian IT Ltd., he said, "I don't need any consulting. I know who is working well and who is not." Two key employees were usually rewarded more than others. One of them was rewarded for hard work, the other because he was a lifelong close friend of the director. Generally speaking, external consultants are considered as potentially dangerous, because external parties could learn about illegal activities and actions.

INSIGHTS FROM OTHER UKRAINIAN COMPANIES

Ukrainian Enterprises

From a smaller city in Ukraine the owner of Ukrainian Enterprises (a pseudonym) described two kinds of corrupt behavior. The first was from the government, in which people forced him to pay bribes and unjust fines. Twelve times in the past year his company had been audited. Audits may be financial, or may concern other aspects of business, such as safety. The purpose of audits are to discern how much he might be able to afford to pay, and to find trumped up excuses to levy fines. In addition to the twelve audits, his company had twice been subjected to searches by machine gun toting police. The owner estimated that half of his time was devoted to dealing with the demands for bribes and fines. He described one incident. An audit was made of a site in which furniture was made. The company was fined 2 million hrivna ($250,000) because there was sawdust, even though it is impossible to cut wood for furniture without making sawdust. The fine was negotiated down to 45,000 hrivna.

The second type of corrupt behavior was from criminals, who would demand what ever they wanted form a company, such as 50% of the stock in the company, or buildings or materials. If someone one refused there might be violence, or a friend in the government would make it impossible for the company to do business. This owner had had several buildings stolen in this way, and had to relocate some of his enterprise in substandard rental places. Yanukovich's son was famous for this type of criminal behavior, and of course it was impossible to resist. If one tried to fight the theft in court, one lost because the decision went to the person who paid the largest bribe.

The system in place that requires bribes was described in this way. A police chief or chief prosecutor for the city paid between $300,000 and $1,000,000 in bribes to gain office. The average term in office was one year. In this time the police chief or chief prosecutor had to collect enough to cover the bribes and make a profit.

Is there hope? The owner offered several hopeful signs, and said he believed that change would be slow. The revolution in Maidan in Kiev was supported by business people and the young Ukrainians, and they were not highly trustful promises. They needed to see changes, which is why the people continued to occupy Maidan even after Tanukovich fled and elections were set for May 25, 2014. Formerly it cost the owner a bribe of $% per square meter to obtain permission to start construction on a new building. After Maidan he has not had to pay this bribe. In the revolution people barricaded the offices of two particularly corrupt mayors in western Ukraine. Both eventually resigned.

He added that the youth of Ukraine were strongly behind the revolution. One young man, a bright student, was in a university class in which the professor let students know she expected a bribe to complete the course. This is not uncommon, since a full-time professor makes $3,600 a year in official salary, the same as a heart surgeon who also expect "gifts" from their patients. The student told the professor, in front of the class that he would not pay the bribe. This refusal to accept corruption gave the owner hope.

Ukrainian Web Services

A business owner from Kyiv, who owned an IT industry that we will call Ukrainian Web Services, specialized in Web design and other connected services. The company had over 50 employees. The owner said:

> If you work with state-owned entities in the Ukraine, the very idea of competition is meaningless. And the SEAM approach is useless. The only important thing is to get an access to a person (i.e., state official) who will provide you with a contract. What is interesting, is that you, as a businessman, have to be trustworthy enough. State officials have to be sure that you: a) will bring the cash back to them, and b) will not disclose the case to police. And state officials are not interested in the end result. There are many firms that do not do anything—they just find subcontractors ready to imitate some activity for a fraction of the contract. At some point, we had stopped dealing with state companies. However, after Maidan won, we agreed to organize online streaming for a state-owned TV channel. They offered an honest price without kickbacks. The TV channel's management is afraid now because the new government wants to close them up due to low efficiency. So, there is hope.

DISCUSSION

We wish to raise this question. Can SEAM be effective in a nation which is highly corrupt, and if so, what needs to be considered? To start the discussion, we offer these observations:

For any organization like Ukraine IT, Ltd., as long as profit is made by bribes and theft, there is little motivation to improve the workplace. Resistance comes from several directions. Owners like the director of Ukraine IT, Ltd. make large amounts of money in their current system. In the railway the people who were enriched by bribes did not want to change the system that enriched them. The mafia groups also did not want to lose their influence. As long as people were acting illegally, the mafia had a means of forcing compliance with their demands for bribes. And of course they always have the potential for using violence to get their way. In a corrupt system it is easier for the mafia groups to thrive.

Part of the problem is that when corruption is so systemic, it seems like most people get caught up in it. It is easy to complain about the large corrupt practices, but more difficult to renounce the small ones that people have learned to use to survive. If one does not make enough money to live a moderate life, corruption is a means of surviving. Employees avoid the 18% tax on income when their earnings are in cash envelopes, so employees have a stake in continuing the corrupt ways. Companies avoid the 18% tax on payroll, so they have a stake in continuing the corrupt ways.

At the time of the writing of this article, the Ukraine is in a state of flux. In the Orange Revolution of 2004, Victor Yanukovich was removed from office for stealing the presidential election. The hope of many was for a more effective government. The presidency of Victor Yushenko was ineffective, and corruption remained the norm. Victor Yanukovich was then elected, and he exceled in profiting from the corrupt system. In addition, Russia opposes the Ukraine becoming closer to the European Union, and was willing to use force to take Crimea. The threat of Russia taking part of eastern Ukraine is real.

But, the impetus for the uprising in Maidan in November, 2013 was the withdrawal from the agreement with the European Union. Joining the European Union is synonymous with reducing corruption in many people's minds. So there is a force, a body of people throughout Ukraine that would like to have a functional, law-abiding government. When and if corruption is significantly reduced, then the ability to compete on the grounds of organizational effectiveness and the quality of goods and services will become important.

We suggest that SEAM could be an effective process for Ukrainian organizations even now if (a) their profits are not derived primarily from bribes and theft, and/or (b) if companies want to improve their efficiency to get ready for the day when corruption is reduced. The owner of Ukrainian Enterprises survived the bribes and theft, but unlike Ukrainian IT, Ltd., profits came from real work. For any company like this, becoming more efficient will increase profits, unless corruption is so bad that new profits will be stolen. As was hinted in the quote from Ukrainian Web Services, once the corruption ends, organizations will have to compete on the basis of efficiency and quality. Leaders who see this, and want to prepare for this, might use SEAM to prepare their organizations to compete in a fair market.

As a final thought, is Ukraine any different that the United States, or France, or many other countries, in terms of acceptance of SEAM? Organizations in the west are usually shaped by the "Taylorism-Fayolism-Weberism (TFW)Virus." At this time most organizations do not choose SEAM. Some of the reasons for this are cost of the intervention, preoccupation with short term gain, commitment to existing practices, and resistance to having flaws revealed. Most western companies choose not to use SEAM in spite of SEAM's demonstrated success. It takes an enlightened leader, and/or desperation, before an organization will take the risk, energy, time, and funds that are required in a SEAM intervention. Our guess is that the Ukraine will be no different.

Corruption in the Ukraine certainly may slow the development of SEAM in the Ukraine. The interesting point for us is when we compare the potential development of SEAM with France, or the United States, we also see very slow growth of SEAM. We expect that the reasoning is similar in France, the United States, and the Ukraine. In each, the organizational leader may not believe there is a problem because the leader's needs are met. After all, what is the essential difference between making 200 to 2000 times the salary of a worker at the bottom of the pay scale, and participating in the economic corruption in the Ukraine? Both are condoned by the government. In each, the leader or leaders receive immense profits at the expense of the welfare of the organization and (if one thinks of examples like the practices on Wall Street that led to the banking crisis in 2008) to the national economy. In the United States and France current practices are upheld by the business mental model, which we characterize as infected by the TFW Virus. In the Ukraine, current practices have been upheld by people who do not want to lose their lucrative thefts. In each country, leaders want to maintain their advantage. In each, it will take an insightful and courageous leader to embrace SEAM. And in each, leaders who want to improve their effectiveness, SEAM will work.

To take this a step further, organizational culture is a response to the environment. At the heart of culture is the set of beliefs and values that allow one to survive and perhaps thrive in one's environment (Schein, 2004). Organizations do not give up cultural assumptions easily, because they have worked. SEAM is a process that changes the way people manage, changes beliefs about people and management, and ultimately changes culture. Most organization resist changing their culture. So for any company, in any nation, to embrace SEAM is not simply an Organization Development intervention to improve efficiency. Embracing SEAM means beginning a much more profound transformation.

CONCLUSION

When we began this case study we had awareness of corruption in the Ukraine, and we were curious about the potential for SEAM. Our conclusion is that organizations enmeshed in corrupt practices will not use SEAM, because they cannot afford to be open about their business practices, and their concern is profit through theft and bribes rather than efficiency and competitiveness. At the same time, not all business owners are corrupt. Some are forced to submit to extortion, but they make their profits through being competitive. For these organizations, SEAM can work.

What surprised us was the realization that in some ways business in the Ukraine is not too different for business in France or the United States. Each nation has a dominant mental model about how to survive in the current business milieu. In the Ukraine the model involves surviving in a corrupt nation, after which we suspect there are elements of the TFW virus lying dormant, waiting to emerge as corruption wanes. In France and the United States the mental model is shaped by the TFW Virus which resists the process and cultural change implicit in SEAM, and maintains a status quo in which many employees endure the depersonalization and disrespect that are normative in virus infected organizations. In any of these countries, we expect that only leaders with insight and courage, have the potential to embrace SEAM. In this way, Ukraine, France, and the United States are not all that different.

APPENDIX:
Conference Dialogue

Conference Participant: I was in Ukraine two years ago with you doing an intervention for a school of business and, even though I've heard about these bribes, people talking about it, in that institution we went to, it was too kind of ethical. I know in reality it exists, but we did not see it. So don't think all of Ukraine is the same or maybe the business sector is different than the academic.

Alla Heorhiadi: Definitely we showed here extremes. There are companies who will not take bribes, who do not give bribes. First of all, we work with a Catholic university in Lviv and they are a bribe-free environment and they have a very high moral ethical standard. I don't think criminals will even approach them.

John Conbere: But, keep in mind we work with two universities in Ukraine. Ukrainian Catholic University in Lviv and National Univesity Kyiv-Mohyla Academy in Kiev. We work with them because they are the only two universities we know that don't do bribes. I know somebody at another university who writes doctoral dissertations for students and the Dean of the college markets these and gets most of the money. So you were in an exceptional place.

Conference Participant: So are U.S. universities really the best places for SEAM to grow because there are two old institutions in the United States. One is the Catholic Church and one is universities. The key in France seems to be actually the practitioner seems to be what's critical, since from my understanding SEAM is not spreading that much among academics in France. So, based on what Dr. Savall said about education and change, are U.S. universities even a good place for SEAM to grow in the Unite States?

Conference Participant: I think it's a problem that [is] the nature of the system in Ukraine, you have corruption, you have bribery. You have to learn to navigate that.

Alla Heorhiadi: Corruption becomes an environment. It becomes an environment within which businesses operate.

Conference Participant: I like the suggestion that SEAM could help an organization navigate that environment better. Maybe [if] they get their top officials in line better and corruption brought down to more reasonable levels, it would be more efficient all around. You have to look at the social system that you're trying to work in and unfortunately there doesn't seem to be a substitute for doctorally trained faculty who can explain everything there is to know about SEAM. At the consultant level of that level training, you might get enough information to do an intervention with some guidance and gradually you might gain the confidence to do those effectively but you don't get the amount of knowledge that you need if you say why can't we cut this part out or why can't we take a shortcut or why don't we just do this? You don't get that depth of history that you would get at the doctoral level. Now, coming back to your question though, there are some institutions you probably should avoid. And as you can see, the American institutions that have resonated so far with SEAM in adopting it, or at least being open to hearing the SEAM message, aren't your traditional business colleges. They are more the liberal arts schools and there are a lot of schools out there like that that don't have the funds to actually start their own business schools that might be open to doing a program that is more comprehensive which would include that management is a part of everything else that you learn in your life. You have to pick your partners carefully.

John Conbere: For me, part of what happens in SEAM is a major transformation in thinking. To leave epistemology out of the educational process, which is typically what happens below the doctoral level, would miss the ability to discuss theoretically the changes that have to happen for the TFW virus to be overcome. Not to have that epistemological frame would be a huge weakness for anybody trying to pass on SEAM.

Conference Participant: So I was just curious about the companies you described. Did you ask them how they . . . what role do they play in keeping the corruption in the system, the context in which they're operating, alive. What is their role in it? It seems they call it a blame game. Government and criminal organizations, have they explored other possibilities of how they create that?

Sergiy Ivakhnenkov: Thank you for the question. Unfortunately, I asked some owners of companies about their moral reasoning. Why are you doing this? Why are you paying bribes? Why don't you want to resist these demands? And the answer was well, everyone does and me too. I just want to earn money so I act as everyone and it was very bad but for me it showed me much because okay, it's like a broken person. Okay, they know that it is bad and the way they act isn't right, but they do it anyway.

Conference Participant: And the second part is do you see change now in their behavior and attitude and see an impact on their actions on a whole society as a result of these current events?

Sergiy Ivakhnenkov: Yes, it was actually the main reason why the events that became Maidan happened. Because people in Ukraine, the Ukrainians, just wanted to change. They just wanted to become civilized. They didn't want to act in old ways with corruption. I can [tell] you that this particular company in case one now experiences problems, financial problems, because of payments decreased and railway officials now just are scared. They don't want to participate in illegal activity. I cannot say anything about the future but currently, the events have an effect on the situation.

Alla Heorhiadi: The other company was a private business so it was an owner, not the state, and his reason was because he is doing this for his employees. Because if the business doesn't exist, then what happens to all those hundreds of people that work for me and it's a good intention to protect them. He said, "When people with machine guns come here, you do what they ask because otherwise it will be a different outcome."

Conference Participant: Maybe if we consider Ukraine as a new market for a SEAM project, maybe a strategy should be to contact an affiliate of international groups working in Ukraine. Maybe there are some U.S. groups working in Ukraine, an affiliate in Ukraine, you know? It could be maybe a solution. Because I suppose there are less bribes during this time for companies in Ukraine than another company.

Conference Participant: I was wondering if there were any culturally unique features about Ukraine that would cause you to change how you introduced or delivered SEAM because from our look at America, we wouldn't change anything about the method but we'd change things about the delivery. How it's presented to people and how we help them learn it. From your prospective, would you introduce it or deliver it differently in Ukraine?

Alla Heorhiadi: I agree with you. If you ask me to change delivery a little bit, it's the same in Ukraine, but delivery always depends on the mental model of the culture, and you cannot take one out of one culture. You know that Hofstede said every concept has a nationality so if one concept grew out of one nation it has to somehow adapt to delivery needs. Not the concept, but it has to be adapted to the other nation.

Conference Participant: Going back to our discussion about what Dr. Huber said, opening up the presentation today. I think part of it goes back to core values and Mark, in your presentation, you showed that the universities that are teaching SEAM the most in the U.S. are private, liberal arts colleges that tend to have core values that match the core values of SEAM in terms of developing human potential. The same thing that you have in Ukraine with the University of Kiev and the Catholic university in Lviv. So I think if we were looking at those common core values of the firms and of the universities, that's where we find that synergy. So just an observation, not really a question, it seems like it's those core values where we're finding similarity.

Conference Participant: But my argument is that SEAM is the stated core values of any private Catholic university are vastly different and I would say than the actual practice. The difference between execution and practice is very broad. I've lived the environment enough to know that that is true. Wouldn't we be better off to spread SEAM in the U.S. with one really large company that adopted it. Isn't the practitioner education spreading faster than the university piece?

Mark Hillon: The problem with large companies is that they have a luxury of waste and they can afford to treat people as if they don't matter and throw them away when their value is used up. One of the angles we're pursuing is with small businesses because they can't afford to lose people and often then have a more family mentality that they do want to take care of their employees and they want to be in business for the long term. There might be some large companies that might be good role models to start with but as you look at our labor force, over half of the population work in small businesses. A number of businesses, in the high 90%, the total number of small business versus large.

Conference Participant: Small, especially family-owned businesses, are not as subject to analyst's calls next week.

Mark Hillon: That and they tend to be the ones that don't have the resources on their own. They show up at the small business development centers asking for help and, I mentioned this in the paper, but there's some . . . if we could get .02% of the number of businesses that come for help to these small business development centers in one year, that would be more interventions than ISEOR's done in its entire existence. There's just a phenomenal number of businesses that need help. It's probably the right environment, just like we're looking at smaller schools that actually practice the values they espouse. You can separate the ones that actually are good candidates and work with them. It's a long term process, just like SEAM is a long term process. You don't do it all at once and you probably reach many more people and effect a lot more people working outside of these public channels. You know, the company that you see on the news is having great profits one quarter and the next quarter they're in some kind of scandal. It's not a great role model. You've got this silent half of the population that works for companies you never hear about but that want to stay in business.

Conference Participant: I want to give you an example of a Mexican company where someone wrote his PhD with Henri, applied SEAM in a smaller Mexican company. One of the dysfunctions was fraud—not reporting taxes. The evaluation of the hidden costs of fraud had an impact, and the mindset of the CEO has changed with this damage and he accepted to change his practice. And I think it's an application of how can we change the mindset of the CEO in this kind of case.

Alanna Kennedy: Just a couple points. Historically, if you look at the industrial revolution, Taylor had just published his book when WWI hit and all of a sudden, everybody needed goods and services to support the war and it just so happened his book was out there. It had been translated, picked it up and we had industry on a global basis. So it's the idea of preparation and then the opportunity. You can repeat that example by looking at Lean. I mean, it wasn't until the economic downturn of 1973 when the nifty 50 took the dive that everybody said well, how's Toyota making it, how are they profitable. I mean, up until that point in time when Toyota people came to Tokyo, they used to laugh at them and call them a bunch of farmers from the countryside. I mean, they weren't even respected at that time in Japan. So how will it get out there. I think it's the idea of what you had said earlier. Making sure that we write the stuff. Making sure that we have the information. Making sure that we have the research. And eventually there will be a shift.

Conference Participant: But you actually make my point. It was actually Taylorism that got put into the Carnegie report which then got into higher education. It wasn't higher education. So I actually think we agree about a lot of things. I think your approach to small businesses is perfect but really is the core of the question...are U.S. universities the best place to start to SEAM in a revolutionary kind of way. If we want 40 or 60 or 80 years to pass, the answer, I think, is probably yes.

Alanna Kennedy: You're overlooking the incubation point. At each point in time, Taylor was working on Taylorism for 20, 30...all of his career, really. It wasn't until he was around 45 that it takes off. So it was 25 years before he even published the five articles that then became his book. When you look at what happened with Lean becoming a continuous improvement methodology, which SEAM falls into that category, you'll find that the Toyota people came to this country for the first time in 1950 and on the plane going back after WWII, they hadn't been here for about 15 years, and on the plane going back they said you know, we can catch the Americans in three years. We can be more productive in three years. So you have Lean, then, lumbering in this obscurity. For 25 years they worked on their manufacturing to develop it and it wasn't until 1973. So I'm not shocked to hear that you're talking about a 30 year period or Mexico or even, for that matter, here at St. Thomas. It will take time. Again, it's that preparation point.

Conference Participant: A little bit different question but, as you're talking, I'm kind of wondering do you go back 10 years later? What's the longevity factor with a SEAM intervention? Are there tune-ups? How do you know whether a company, 10 years later, is still realizing the potential?

Henri Savall: The first part of our history was to prove to industry that organizations, regardless of the country or size or industry, private, for profit, not for profit, had the same pathologies, and that SEAM could heal these. That was the first part 30 years ago. Eight or nine years ago, the second part of our strategy is how long the results can be sustained. Then we keep sustaining the same organizations for a long time now. Ten years, 12 years, 20 years, 30 years. And we have longitudinal research assessing improvement results. Our present program is about what are the requisites to make sustainable results regardless of size or country.

Conference Participant: To your presentation, Sergiy and Alla and John, on is SEAM possible in Ukraine, perhaps the question almost needs to be changed to is SEAM probable? The couple of things going on that occur is that there's chaos there right now and so all the rules have been sort of broken. SEAM is ideology as much as it is a practice that they're searching for that they've been grasping for the future to eliminate the issues that have sort of imprisoned the growth and imprisoned their thinking. And so when we work with communities in Ukraine to talk about how we do business, how we do governmental entities, local government in the U.S., it's like drying an alcoholic out, like John, you put it. And we put them back into the family of alcoholics and expect change and it's impossible. Now they've got the family drying out, if you will, and it seems that SEAM is a comprehensive and ideal model to build not only the business structure but the governmental structure. You talk about the whole system. The whole system needs to change. I don't know if we have that critical illness in the U.S. Some would argue with some of your comparisons that we do but it may not as obvious. That's my thinking, anyway.

REFERENCES

Democratic Initiatives Fund (2014). http://dif.org.ua/ua/polls/2013-year/mogjor jghoeoj.htm.

Kvit, S. (2014). The ideology of the EuroMaidan Revolution. *Kyiv Post,* March 24, Op Ed page. Online at http://www.kyivpost.com/opinion/op-ed/serhiy-kvit-the-ideology-of-the-euromaidan-revolution-340665.html.

Schein, E. H. (2004). *Organizational culture and leadership.* San Francisco, CA: Jossey-Bass.

CHAPTER 5

AN EXAMPLE OF A LABORATORY IN THE FIELD OF MANAGEMENT INTERVENTION-RESEARCH

The ISEOR Research Lab

Marc Bonnet and Michel Péron

CONFERENCE REMARKS:
Chapter Prologue

The Socio-Economic Institute of Companies and Organizations (ISEOR) research center was created in 1974 by Henri Savall in order to carry out a research scheme focused on the discovery of a hidden value creation factor: Human Potential as the only genuine active factor of sustainable value creation; as opposed to passive factors such as capital, knowledge, and work. In a way, it calls to mind the Geneva particle physics lab, which includes a high-energy accelerator aimed at demonstrating the existence of the Higgs boson. Indeed, a number of scientific approaches (sociology, organizational psychology, education sciences, ergonomics, etc.) posited that there was a link between social and economic performance, but without succeeding in

Decoding the Socio-Economic Approach to Management, pages 83–102
Copyright © 2016 by Information Age Publishing
83

the demonstration of this link. In particular, there was a need to articulate sociology and economics and to create a "socio-economic" approach (i.e., the hyphen between socio and economic). The challenge of the ISEOR center was to pick up the gauntlet and develop a methodology to succeed.

VALIDITY ISSUES AT STAKE FOR LABORATORIES RESORTING TO RESEARCH IN THE FIELD OF SCIENTIFIC OBSERVATION IN ORGANIZATIONAL MANAGEMENT

Chris Argyris (2000) had raised the issue of the lack of actionable knowledge used by the practitioners. As he put it, "21st century companies have to be managed differently than 20th century firms. But much of the advice is not actionable." But which epistemology would be most appropriate for the ISEOR lab to avoid the two commonly observed entrapments?

Action-Researchers create local actionable knowledge, but consider that this has nothing to do with generalization as usually defined in the field of Organization Theory, even if it provides academics with first hand data. They can be used in the form of examples and case studies in their courses.

Academics who are doing research on organizational issues, drawing on quantitative methods have the purpose of discovering regularities (Glaser & Straus, 1967). However, such research often results in the kind of knowledge that is not relevant enough to assist companies in change management, because an analysis of past regularities is not sufficient to create something new, and also because of the difficulties encountered in generalizing results (Shipman, 1982). The contingency approach to organizations therefore gives little credibility to research in management consulting based on different kinds of industries, companies, or regions of the world. However, this type of research practice has been criticized by authors like Gopinath and Hoffman (1995) who highlighted the gap between the needs and interests of the business community and the output of the academic community. Indeed many of the management concepts and ideas appearing in academic journals are considered to be of little relevance to most practitioners.

This dilemma has also been analysed by Van de Ven (2000, p. 394), who called for complementarity between actionable knowledge and theory: He set the "pendulum" swinging between the social system of management and academic science, as shown in Figure 5.1.

Criticizing Validity in Action-Research?

In the field of epistemology, many authors have expressed criticisms against validity in Action-Research. Some of the weak points which are mentioned

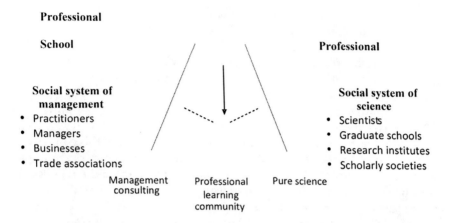

Figure 5.1   Pendulum swings to and from a professional learning community.

refer to bias stemming from subjectivity and ideology which influence both action-researchers and the company actors: Most characteristics of the epistemological positioning of action researchers cannot be defined independently from the interaction going on within the reality of the organization being studied. Action researchers and actors interact in the research project (Schwandt, 1994). Questions about the neutrality of the researcher and dialectical immersion and distancing with regard to the objects being studied can be discussed (Hatch, 1996). The subject who observes or experiments on himself or others may be, on the one hand, modified by the observed phenomena and, on the other, a source of modifications to the progress and even to the nature of these phenomena considered by Habermas (1973) who rejected the notion of action-research because participation in action will lock the researcher into the practical side of the equation in such a way that the ability to participate in theoretical discourse is lost: A process of liberation has to start with theory, not practice (Habermas, 1973). In the case of the ISEOR lab, there is a constant interaction between theory and practice, as opposed to some action-research labs which reject modeling.

A second kind of criticisms is that action-research projects don't enable generalization: They are context specific and produce partial pieces of knowledge, which are useful in the learning process of the company where action took place, but which can't be disseminated. What the action researcher observes has a fragmentary character, according to how the subjects observed perceive him (Devereux, 1980). Sanford (1970) argues that as a consequence of this fragmentation there is a fantastic proliferation of bitsy and disconnected and essentially unusable researches. Action research requires "highly contextualized individual judgments" (Van Maanen, 1998). This research is particularly difficult to describe because of its "flexibility and emergent character." Friedlander and Brown (1974) observed that action researchers suffer a tension between "action" (change implementation) and "science" (knowledge generation). Alderfer (1977) pointed out that the goal of most action research seems to be to change the system rather than to evaluate the intervention or to generate or test a general theory. Some argue that the purpose of action research is to generate specific knowledge to the situation so that the conditions can be improved. The status of the action researcher raises the question of analyzing the complexity of management science and the initial utilization of this complexity in the face of "real" situations, which can have multiple criteria, multiple actors, and multiple rationales and evolutions. In the case of the ISEOR lab, the objective is a kind of double-bind learning: On the one hand, company actors learn through the qualimetrics intervention-research process how to innovate when coping with tricky issues in a complex and blurred environment. On the other hand, the objective of the ISEOR research center is to discover the generic variables that cut across all case studies. For example, all companies suffer from six categories of dysfunctions, whatever the kind of industry, size, and cultural patterns: working conditions, work organization, communication-coordination-cooperation, time management, integrated training, and implementation of the strategy.

A third criticism is the excessive interpretative dimension of action research practices, while the dominant paradigm in the field of epistemology is the so-called hypothetico-deductive method, which is considered by some philosophers as the core of the scientific method (Kuhn, 1962). Authors comparing action research and scientific method have typically concluded that they are different and incompatible forms of inquiry. Action research is conceived of as inductive, interpretative, and qualitative (Van Maanen, 1998). Scientific method, in contrast, is a hypothetical-deductive and quantitative approach. Susman and Evered (1978) observe that action-research is not compatible with the criteria for scientific explanation as established by positivist science. Stone (1982) argued that scientific method is superior because it is more rigorous. Action-research studies phenomena in the environments in which they naturally occur and uses social actors' meanings to understand the phenomena (Denzin & Lincoln, 1994). On the contrary, quantitative, positivist research imposes scientific meanings on members to explain a singular, presumed-to-be-true reality that nonscientists may not appreciate. Is hypothetical-deductive model and positivist research more scientific than constructivist approach as action research? Interestingly, philosophers on science and knowledge production, such as Gibbons et al. (1994), have proposed models of research, which might be relevant to social sciences focused on action and change in the social system. Gibbons draws the reader's attention toward a new form of knowledge production (mode 2), which, although originally an outgrowth from its traditional counterpart (mode 1), is now becoming distinctive in its own right. This

TABLE 5.1   Models of Research

Mode 1	Mode 2
• Problems are set and solved in a context governed by the largely academic • Involves the community of researchers • Characterized by homogeneity • Hierarchical, tends to preserve its form • "Ivory tower" approach • Disciplinary • Focuses on 1 criterion	• Problems are carried out in the context of application • Involves the close interaction of many actors throughout the process of knowledge production • Characterized by heterogeneity • Hierarchical and transient • Socially accountable and reflexive • Transdisciplinary • Wide range of criteria

new mode is carried out in the context of application and involves the close interaction of many actors throughout the process of knowledge production. Table 5.1 shows how it differs from mode 1.

In some ways this mode 2 research method shifts away from positivist grounds, as mentioned by A. L. Cunliffe (2001): it leads to social constructionist forms of research, which intertwine knowing/being and see sensemaking arising with on-going practice.

Challenge of a Management Research Lab Creation Focused on Intervention-Research

So far, a few management research labs have tried to pick up the gantlet of implementing inductive research methods that resort to Gibbon's mode 2 of research, mainly drawing on action-research methodologies. Among them, feature the Tavistock Institute (London), Work Research Institute (Oslo), Society for Organizational Learning (MIT), University of Bath (UK), ITB Bremen (Germany), Centre for co-operative inquiry (Italy & New Zealand), Sigma program at Case Western University, OD program at Benedictine University, Waterford Institute of Technology (Ireland) , CGS-Mines and CRG-Polytechnique Paris, Action-research issues center (Australia), Society for Participatory Research (New Delhi, India), and ISEOR (France). This paper is aimed at presenting the case and specificities of the ISEOR research center creation (1974) and development (1974 onwards). The rationale behind the creation of this research center was to bring one step further the socio-technical approach of the Tavistock as well as Lewin's (1946, 1948) organizational development approach. The objective was to integrate the social and economic approaches to organizational issues into a coherent whole referred to as "Socio-economic Approach to Management" (SEAM).

Developing such a SEAM approach required designing the qualimetrics intervention-research methodology. Indeed, the ISEOR laboratory doesn't only consist of a headquarters, but also includes fieldwork, which goes by the name of "scientific observation field." As Henri Savall and Veronique Zardet (2004) put it:

> The enterprise is truly a crucible for forging, testing, and acclimatizing original concepts through an alternation of conceptualization and experimentation...The alternation between conceptualization and experimentation means that certain stages of fieldwork are devoted to testing, in the experimental sense of the word, concepts and tools in an observable situation of management. (p. 77)

This alternation results in an ongoing research creation process. The successive steps of the intervention-research method are continually put into question. The conceptualization of this step by step research process has resulted in replicable findings and in the creation of a socio-economic theory of management and the design of its key concepts: synchronization, periodical negotiation, steering, organizational cleaning-up, etc.

In depth and up-close observation of the object is required, the dynamic phenomena of organizational metamorphosis. There is a kind of trade-off between intervention-researchers and company actors. This is how cognitive interactivity developed. Company actors release information and give ideas to the intervener-researchers because it is a give-and-take process. Actors have a stake, and they provide intervener-researchers with valuable data because they are convinced that these data will help them succeed in reaching their objectives. This is achieved through interviews and training sessions focused on hidden costs calculation. In this case, company actors are not to be mistaken for lab rats: They are considered as pro-active collaborators of the research process. The research findings stem from a collaborative construct between company actors and intervener-researchers. The latter also have a specific objective while bringing their improvement project to a successful end—formalizing the underpinning principles of the outcomes of the intervention-research process. As for company actors, their specific objective is to reach consensus through the creation of value added for all, thanks to converting hidden costs into value added.

The quality of the scientific research scheme requires scientific independence. Two main conditions are to be met:

- The signing up of a research contract with each and every company willing to undertake the cooperation with the research center. It often requires a long negotiation process so as to ensure that the effective research requirements are met (e.g., all categories of actors have to be interviewed and involved in the mirror effect and in the focus groups).

- A variety of financing sources is necessary to enable the research center to be in a position to turn down proposals that don't fulfill the requirements. Refusing biased or shady proposals concerns both private or public organizations and institutions: The ISEOR proceeds to sorting out its clients in order to maximize the opportunity to get exemplary research sites and outcomes.

As time goes by, the ISEOR has set up a data bank progressively enriched by a number of intervention-researches. It enables to permanently test the relevance of the outcome of the body of information regarding the socio-economic approach to management, as a science applied to living and dynamic systems, as opposed to static ones. This is due to the two-fold nature of scientific research: On the one hand, knowledge considered as all but "acquired once and for all," and on the other hand, knowledge considered as a "never ended open-ended process." To give an example, an intervention-research carried out in Lebanese hospitals consists in applying the socio-economic methodology per se, resulting in an additional performance of the SEAM protocols. In addition, this intervention also provides an opportunity for furthering the research scheme: In this case, this experiment showed that instead of creating one jumbo size hospital, the best solution was to maintain three independent medium size hospitals whose staff would cooperate, thus enhancing synergy. This observation contributes to a research scheme consisting in putting into question the "economy of scales principle."

SNAPSHOT OF THE ISEOR LAB

When someone is asking to take a snapshot of the ISEOR lab, researchers just feel somewhat embarrassed. There are no stills, test tubes, nor crucibles to mix more or less mysterious ingredients. So should they be happy with a few pictures showing the lab: Should we take a picture of the archives, of the notes, of the books and articles, of the building, of the PCs and of the software, of the individual researchers and administrative staff, of the companies where intervention-research takes place, of the corpus?

It wouldn't be as nonsensical as all that, because it clearly points to collective working without any temptation for researchers to isolate themselves in an ivory tower. ISEOR lab is a locus of interplay and interaction where generic contingency knowledge is created and updated. This interaction is an intangible phenomenon that takes place when both intervener-researchers and company actors pick their respective brains to spark innovation.

All these statements don't mean that the output of the research lab is entirely intangible. Indeed, is there anything more concrete than a company experiencing sky-rocketing results and increased employee satisfaction.

Since 1976, ISEOR has conducted intervention-researches in over 1,300 companies and organizations in 34 countries. These interventions took place in a variety of industries and company sizes and patterns: 64 industrial sectors, non-profit making companies, family-owned companies, multinational companies, etc. The duration of these interventions ranges from 1 to 30 years. They are based on the same methodology that has been improved step by step. They are carried out in teams in order to enable the expression of different points of view on account of the complexity of the observed phenomena.

The intervener-researchers are trained through a long process and formalize their observations in papers, articles, and doctoral dissertations. It requires a specific set of skills: active listening, taking notes, making sense of the findings, using specific software to categorize the data (Segese software), running feed-back sessions, keeping track of the data and archiving them, interpreting the biases and taboos along with the expert-advice, etc.

Intervener-researchers also have to be trained in team working so as to exchange their findings with colleagues and thus resort to the contradictory intersubjectivity principle in order to strengthen the relevance and quality of their data. This is key when they need to compare their own findings with those of previous researches with a view to coming up to the generic contingency principle.

The stress was put on the accumulation of experiments over the decades, which required scientific independence. Common wisdom assumes that scientific independence requires only public funding, while private companies are considered to be only money oriented. ISEOR has put into question this biased belief for two main reasons:

- Public-sector decision makers are not "neutral": Experience shows that in any country under any kind or regime, they are influenced by their ideologies and their underlying specific goals.
- The research scheme was designed to be longitudinal over several decades, which required avoiding any dependence on stop and go or roller-coaster public policies.

The strategy was therefore to tap a wide range of financial resources, in order to only choose those projects and interventions in companies that comply with all the scientific requirements (i.e., the intervention-research contracting). It was necessary to demonstrate the feasibility of such a stance. The amount of $120,000,000 of ISEOR contracts over the first four decades speaks for themselves. Such amounts of investments in the field of research are only observed in other domains of science, as opposed to social science, where research schemes are often scattered and don't result in cumulative research.

Publications and Doctoral Dissertations

Publications play an essential role since they rely on the duration of the research implementation, which guarantees the quality of the longitudinal observation. We may consider the publication itself as a snapshot, as opposed to the movie of the ongoing development processes in the company taking into account that organizations are considered as a dynamic and evolving entity. In order to prepare their dissertation, junior-researchers have a 3-year contract. The first two years are devoted to learning the practice of intervention-research and capturing data in the field. The last six months of the three-year period are focused on making sense of the field materials as well as comparing the observations with other scientific analyses. As intervention researchers, doctoral students select a specific set of experiments and tally the results in order to distinguish between generic and contingent knowledge. An example of a doctoral dissertation is putting into question the theory of economy of scales: Through analyzing several experiments, it is possible to show that economy of scales can't but generate hidden costs, which in most cases negates the anticipated productivity increase.

In addition to doctoral dissertations, there are two main categories of publications: practitioners oriented books, and academic oriented books and articles.

Practitioners oriented books can be construed as on the job testimonies relying on the interplay between intervener-researchers, company directors, and other company actors. The impacts of the intervention-research process are assessed in terms of social and economic performance improvements. The report on the outcomes of the research draws on a contradictory intersubjectivity principle. This principle stresses the knowledge enrichment resulting from clashes in the opinions expressed and the attempt at reconciling them. This is key in a period when business schools and management research are more and more held accountable for the impact of their teaching and research. Like in the field of medicine research, scholars in management have to pay proper attention to the aftermath of the research work conducted in their institutions and the impacts on their stakeholders (and "patients")—company actors and society at large.

In academic oriented books and contributions, the objective is to enable debate and controversy between the ISEOR research lab and the other members of the academic community so as to compare the results and methods in order to enhance the overall research quality in the management science academia. However, the opportunities for that type of debate are scarce because there are very few publications outlets that focus on action and intervention research, which are not featured in the mainstream of management research as opposed to medical science. To provide some concrete support to this kind of approach, ISEOR has launched a tri-lingual journal called *Recherche en Sciences de Gestion-ManagementSsciences—Ciencias de Gestión,* having in mind to promote scientific debate in this domain and not to favor ISEOR members contribution.

However, the publications have a hard time getting accepted in top-ranking journals in the field of management. Indeed, the type of research resorting to Gibbon's mode 2 is not at all mainstream and can even be considered as outlier. This difficulty will certainly disappear in the long term, and one can already observe signals of evolution, such as the creation of the journal *Academy of Management Discoveries* by Andy Van de Ven and the supporters of evidence-based research.

Discussion of the Epistemological Positioning of the ISEOR Research Lab

The ISEOR research lab aims at reconciling positivism and constructionist epistemology because of bridging the gap between practice and conceptualization. In this perspective, ISEOR lab might be considered as very much in line with the genuine tradition of action-research, often times distorted by certain kinds of action-research practices. Indeed, Kurt Lewin, regarded as the father of action research in the field of management, declared in 1947, "There is no action without research and no research without action" (p. 81). Lewin (1951) defined the researcher's role in these terms, "He can investigate what ought to be done if certain social objectives are to be reached. He can secure data which will be important for analysing a given policy and its effect, and which will be relevant for any rational policy determination." (p. 168). He considered that theory and practice are linked methodologically and that such research is to a degree social action. The impact of research on action is taken into account, not as a bias, but as an actual principle of intervention and generation of scientific knowledge. As a legacy from Kurt Lewin, Argyris Putnam, and McLain Smith implemented some improvements and redefined "action research" in 1985. They believed that action science contributes simultaneously to basic knowledge in social science and to social action in everyday life. Action research covers a great variety of practices. Here we will simply mention the definition of "clinical inquiry," which seems to be close to a management consulting engagement as defined by Schein in 1987: The client initiates the project (as opposed to usual forms of action research, where the researcher initiates the project); and both researcher involvement and client involvement are high. Schein (2001) considered that clinical inquiry enables researchers to observe dynamic processes through the continuous testing of hypotheses. Replicability is fulfilled "when other observers see the same phenomenon that I do."

More recently David Boje has taken stock of large varieties of action research practices. He describes 16 important categories of large system change methods in his "Transorganizational Development Gameboard" (2001). He observed that forms of Action Research concerned with development are primarily trying to influence the particular situation in which the action takes place, and that this has led to schools for Transorganizational Development that generally do not compare their approaches to others.

When Henri Savall created the ISEOR research lab, based on his previous work on socio-economic approach to management, he explained in the book (Savall & Zardet, 2004), that the main issue was to determine how to combine the contextualization of knowledge (as provided by intervention research) and research into a generalized, formalized scientific framework for actionable knowledge (as opposed to cookie-cutting solutions): What are the procedures required to progressively enhance the reliability, validity, and credibility of interventions carried out by academics so that it might be considered scientific research. Any practice-oriented research method should obviously focus on fieldwork while avoiding the risk of being considered as unscientific in its observation. This paper is about a practice-oriented investigation method that reconciles scientific processes with pragmatic, on-the-job approach.

In depth observation necessitates numerous iterations to filter and improve the information's degree of significance in relation with practitioner's experience. Up-close observation points to the importance of the role played by the distance between the research and the object in obtaining quality information. The greater the distance, the more the information will be gross and confused and thus useless in practice-oriented researches.

Traditional management research instruments (questionnaires, interviews) are revisited in this new perspective. Those information-gathering instruments have to be combined with extraction techniques, in the metaphorical sense, due to the archeological characteristics of data buried in the organization as such or in its actors' minds. Archeological type research cannot be conducted in labs or libraries but on site.

Accessing the interior of an enterprise, being physically in contact with the persons, are indispensable conditions for up-close scientific observation as long as it pretends to be practice oriented. In that sense the approach to the material elements constituting part of the research object requires up-close observation but so do the intangible components in company operations. Up-close observation thus eliminates theoretical disquisition and subjective vision on the part of the researcher, which cannot but clash with a practice-oriented methodology. As Savall and Zardet (2004) put it:

Our direct confrontation strategy is instrumental in differentiating between wishful thinking and observable realization or attainable objectives. Our method leads to constructive interaction going beyond sheer instantaneous observation, though the creation of a dynamic field as a generator of signs, facts, and information giving pride of place to contextual data analysis. (p. 321)

Based on the ISEOR interventions carried out in the past 30 years in over 1,200 companies, Henri Savall (2003) claimed for a generic knowledge production system, which rests on three concepts:

- Cognitive interactivity: Taking into account the complexity of phenomena in the decision-making processes, no one can grasp all the data, and there is a need to build up a kind of collective cleverness.
- Contradictory intersubjectivity: Pure objectivity doesn't exist, but it is possible to come up to an agreement on a satisfactory knowledge when all actors involved agree for a period of time on the outcomes of the research process. This epistemological stance might be considered as close to Reason and Bradbury (2001) posture at the University of Bath, as they had recognized that objective knowledge is not entirely possible, either for action research or for positivist research "since the researcher is a part of the world he or she studies. Knowledge making cannot be neutral or disinterested. They add that all inquiry and all of life is necessarily framed by a worldview, therefore it is necessary to consider that the "reality" we experience is co-creation. In this sense, action research, management consulting in the field of change management, is close to institutionalism, as defined by Berger and Luckman (1966): Reality is the product of an absorption of socializations, assumptions; it is inter-subjective, situational, and is thus legitimized by successive steps. This approach to organization theory differs from what Harvey (1990) called the "positivist worldview" that sees science as separate from everyday life and the researcher as a subject within a world of separate objects, based on the metaphor of linear progress/absolute truth and rational planning.
- Generic contingency: The socio-economic concepts, methods, and tools share the distinctive feature of being quite easily adaptable to extremely different organizations, because they do not induce any standardized concrete solution, but only structuring principles for solutions worked out with and by the actors themselves, within the context of their organizations.

Commonalities With Other Types of Research Centers

In order to map out commonalities and differences with other research labs, we propose to compare the ISEOR lab with other research centers in the field of management, as well as research centers in another scientific field focused on improvement actions, i.e., research centers linked to university hospitals.

Other Research Centers in the Field of Management

The ISEOR research lab cannot be equated with other existing research centers because it doesn't satisfy itself with the usual scientific observation methods: There is an ontological and epistemological rift in the way the research object is apprehended. The title of Savall and Zardet's book, *Observing the Complex Object: A Qualimetrics Approach* (2004) testified to this specificity. In most management labs, the object is not as complex as it seems because the research bears on a limited set of variables, as opposed to the basic assumption of the ISEOR lab, which states that the object consists in a plethora of variables. Some management labs focus essentially on quantitative analysis of a limited number of variables and others are going for purely qualitative analysis on the ground that variables are too numerous to be taken into consideration. Conversely, the ISEOR lab has developed a research method referred to as qualimetrics with a view to reconciling qualitative, quantitative, and financial approaches.

In a way, companies are clients, and in another way, the phenomena concerning organizational development and metamorphosis are the objective of observation. To ensure its scientific independence, the laboratory has to self-finance with a variety of contributors. It thus enables it to turn down proposals when conditions of scientific independence are not met.

Metaphoric Comparison With Medicine Research Labs in University Hospitals

Professors of medicine who have also experienced the socio-economic approach (Thiébaut, 2009) could not but notice the similarities which exist between wording in both sciences: Pathologies and diagnoses are unavoidable references, so is the term "dysfunction." But, the most telling feature is the existence of numerous analogies between the socio-economic methodology and the therapeutic one. Like in medicine research and in university hospitals, the ISEOR lab develops and experiments innovative protocols to help organizations healing from their dysfunctions and "organizational viruses": Like human beings, organizations live and die and suffer from diseases and need medical assistance and physicians. In the field of management science, the research method practiced by ISEOR researchers is an evidence-based research, like in medicine.

The objective is to create innovative management methods and solutions with a view to converting dysfunctions and hidden costs into value added. One cannot but think of the principles put forward by Claude Bernard (Bernard, 1865), one of the founders of the scientific medicine based on experiments back in the 19th century, when he had to struggle with the proponents of the "experience in medicine" as opposed to "experimental scientific medicine" (p. 52). Bernard's experimental method encompasses both theory and practice. It includes four iterative steps: (a) stating facts or noticing unforeseen problems which don't match existing models, (b) surmising hypotheses, (c) setting up the conditions for experimentation, and (d) taking stock of phenomena stemming from experience. Throughout the experimentation process, researchers grope around and keep comprehensive track records of sometimes contradictory observations. As for ISEOR researchers, experimentation is a continuing process during which various hypotheses are constantly being altered. Similarly to university hospitals, ISEOR as an intervention-research center is at the same time a consulting firm and a fundamental research lab.

One of the most pivotal findings is the fundamental hypothesis of the Socio-Economic Approach to Management, which can be broken down as follows:

- A weak point of the financial and accounting systems is to fail in their attempt to account for overall company performance. In particular, those systems don't enable to elicit the link between social performance and economic performance.
- Demonstrating the fundamental hypothesis put forward in the book *Work and People* (2010): putting to light hidden costs which can be accounted for by poor management quality of the interaction between structures and behaviors in companies and organizations.
- Finalizing a qualimetric intervention-research method in order to study those phenomena interacting between intervener-researchers and company actors in the field. The scientific observation field can be defined as a constant shuttling between in vivo experiments and the data interpretation in vitro.
- Results of phenomena observation: Hidden costs and performance are high and hidden costs are convertible into value added creation through periodical negotiation of activity contracts, with a view to increase accountability of employees and at the same time to improve life in the workplace.

Impacts and Dissemination of the Research

The ethical legitimacy of intervention-research in the field of management rests on explicit values: those of researchers who believe that it is worthy to experiment innovative "organizational medicine" because so many people in and around organizations suffer from organizational dysfunctions and diseases. This stance differentiates from other kinds of mainstream management researches that rest on the Weberian non-intervention principle because of the risk of biased research. On the contrary, according to the intervention-research principle, abstaining from intervening is a biased attitude: This hands-off attitude would be somewhat cynical in management sciences and even a failure to render assistance to humankind who suffer and die from organizational diseases.

The knowledge acquired through 40 years of experiments in various industries and cultural settings throughout the world can't but benefit academics, practitioners, business schools, consultants, and politicians. Disseminating the scientific knowledge on socio-economic approach to management is necessary to give food for thought and subsequent action taking to all the stakeholders of companies and organizations.

CONCLUSION

As a conclusion, one can't but infer that designing such a type of lab in management science is not a pipe dream. This research has kept afloat during four decades so far and it is per se a feasibility evidence. However, the debate that could be opened bears on the following considerations, taking into account that there are not many followers up to now. In particular, we might raise questions such as:

- Is ISEOR research lab a model that can be easily followed in the future accounting for the economic and academic developments?
- Can the ISEOR experience inspire modifications in traditional mainstream management research labs?
- Could practitioners and management consultants undertake to build up such a type of management research center in a world where universities are no longer the only place of knowledge creation and dissemination?

APPENDIX:
Conference Dialogue

Conference participant: I was curious. In the companies that you sign up with, have you ever profiled the characteristics or industry or culture or style or whatever of companies that are more likely to want to enter into such an engagement than those that don't?

Marc Bonnet: Only one criterion, open-mindness about SEAM. Sometimes an introducer helps us convince the CEO but the key aspect is convincing the CEO and then step by step convincing or involving all the actors. But CEO's first as buy-in.

Conference participant: No drivers such as, you know, extreme profitability or extreme . . . ?

Marc Bonnet: No. In the database you have a variety ranging from large to very small profit or people who are in a very different position in developing country or developed country, etc. And we have worked with 64 kinds of industries up to now so far. So scientific independence. Well, one of the reasons why this kind of research has not been so much developed so far was common wisdom. In the academy or the field of business or management schools, common wisdom would assume that scientific independence requires only public funding. That is to say, the research is sponsored by the university, or you might have money, but there are conditions to go through the university system. And ISEOR has questioned this belief. The public sector decision makers are not neutral. In any kind of country, any kind of influence by their own indulges, their underlying specific values and goals. And second, we need scientific, in order to keep our own scientific independence, longitudinal research, that is to say the Dean might change, the president of the university might change, the provost might change and so on, but we have to stay our time for a long period of time in order to better observe and for long term observation.

In that observation, organizational metamorphosis is of interest to companies because, as we'll develop later on, organizational metamorphosis is what companies have a hard time implementing. They manage the company, the quality management, budgets, and so on, but succeeding in transforming is much harder and this is not so much told and even in OD programs this is a very tricky issue. So there's a kind of trade off and we need for that interactive connectivity. That is to say, we learn from each other. Researchers learn from practitioners and back and forth and vice versa. And company actors reveal information and give ideas, otherwise you send a questionnaire to the company and you ask or interview the CEO and some limited

REFERENCES

Alderfer, C. P. (1977). Organization development. *Annual Review of Psychology, 28,* 197–223.

Argyris, C. (2000). *Flawed Advice and the Management Trap.* Oxford, England: Oxford University Press.

Argyris, C., Putnam, R., & McLain Smith, D. (1985). *Action science.* San Francisco, CA: Jossey-Bass.

Berger, P. L., & Luckman, T. (1966). *The social construction of reality: A treatise in the sociology of knowledge.* New York, NY: Doubleday.

Bernard, C. (1865). *Introduction à l'étude de la médecine expérimentale* [Introduction to the Study of Experimental Medicine]. Paris: Baillière.

Boje, D. M. (2001). *Mapping the different kinds of action research practices onto a Transorganizational Development Gameboard,* http://web.nmsu.edu/~dboje/TDgameboard.html and EGOS colloquium, Lyon

Cunliffe, A. L (2001). Managers as practical authors: Reconstructing our understanding of management practice. *Journal of Management Studies, 38* (3), 351–371.

Denzin, N. K., & Lincoln, Y. S., (1994). The fifth moment. *Handbook of Qualitative Research, 1,* 575–586.

Devereux, G. (1980). *De l'angoisse à la méthode dans les sciences du comportement.* Paris, France: Flammarion.

Friedlander, F., & Brown, D. (1974). Organization development. *Annual Review of Psychology, 25,* 313–341.

Gibbons M., Limoges C., Nowotony, H., Schwarzman S., Scott P., & Trow M. (1994). *The new production of knowledge: The dynamics of science and research in contemporary societies.* London, England: Sage Publications.

Glaser, B. E., & Strauss, A. L. (1967). The discovery of grounded theory: Strategies for qualitative research. New York, NY: A. de Gruyter.

Gopinath, C., & Hoffman, R. C. (1995). The relevance of strategy research: Practitioner and academic viewpoints. *Journal of Management Studies, 32*(5), 575–594.

Habermas, J. (1973). *Theory and Practice.* London, England: Polity Press.

Hatch, M. J. (1996). The role of the researcher—An analysis of narrative position in organization theory. *Journal of Management Inquiry, 5*(4), 359–374.

Harvey, D. (1990). *The conditions of postmodernity.* Oxford, England: Blackwell.

Kuhn, T. S. (1962). *The structure of scientific revolutions.* Chicago, IL: University of Chicago Press.

Lewin, K. (1946). Action research and minority problems. *Journal of Social Issues, 2,* 34–46.

Lewin, K. (1947). *Participative action research.* Albany: State University of New York Press.

Lewin, K. (1948). Action research and minority problems. *Journal of Social Issues, 2,* 34–46. doi: 10.1111/j.1540-4560.1946.tb02295.x

Lewin, K. (1951). *Field Theory in Social Science.* New York, NY: Harper and Row.

Reason, P., & Bradbury H. (2001). Introduction: Inquiry and participation in search of a world worthy of human aspiration. In P. Reason & H. Bradbury (Eds.),

Handbook of action research: Participative inquiry & practice (pp. 1–14). Thousand Oaks, CA: Sage Publications.

Sanford, N. (1970). Whatever happened to action research? *Journal of Social Issues, 26*(4), 3–23.

Savall, H. (2003). International dissemination of the socio-economic method. In Special issue of the *Journal of Organizational Change Management, 16* (1), 1–128.

Savall, H. (2010). *Work and people: An economic evaluation of job enrichment, 2nd edition.* Charlotte, NC: Information Age.

Savall, H., & Zardet, V. (2004). Recherche en sciences de gestion: Approche qualimétrique—Observer l'objet complexe (préface de David Boje). Paris, France: Economica. [Translated into English (2011): *The Qualimterics Approach.* Charlotte, NC: Information Age]

Schein, E. H. (1987). *The clinical perspective in field work.* London, England: Sage Publications.

Schein, E. H. (2001) *Clinical Inquiry/Research.* In P. Reason & H. Bradbury (Eds.), *Handbook of Action Research: Participative Inquiry and Practice* (pp. 228–237). London, England: Sage Publications.

Schwandt, T. A. 1994. Constructivist, interpretivist approaches to human inquiry. In N. K. Denzin & Y. S. Lincoln (Eds.), *Handbook of qualitative research* (pp. 118–137). Thousand Oaks, CA: Sage.

Shipman, M. (1982). *The limitations of social research,* London, England: Longman.

Stone, E. F. (1982). In defense of rigorous research. *Contemporary Psychology, 26,* 629–630.

Susman, G. I., & Evered, R. D. (1978). An assessment of the scientific merits of action research. *Administrative Science Quarterly, 23,* 582–603.

Thiébaut, A. (2009). Intervenants-chercheurs d'universités et de grandes écoles en Europe [Intervener-researchers in universities and business schools in Europe]. In H. Savall, V. Zardet, & M. Bonnet (Eds.), *Management Socio-Economique: Une approche innovante* (pp. 369–422). Paris, France: Economica.

Van de Ven, A. H. (2000). Professional science for a professional school. In M. Beer & N. Nohria (Eds.), *Breaking the codes of change* (pp. 393–394) Cambridge, MA: Harvard Business School Press.

Van Maanen, J. (1998). Different strokes: Qualitative research in the Administrative Science Quarterly from 1956 to 1996. In J. Van Maanen (Ed.), *Qualitative studies of organizations* (pp. ix–xxxii)). Thousand Oaks, CA: Sage.

CHAPTER 6

RETHINKING LEAN

Combining Lean and SEAM for Improved Profitability and Support of Cultures of Continuous Improvement in Organizations

Alanna G. Kennedy

CONFERENCE REMARKS
Chapter Prologue

Alanna Kennedy

I've been anticipating this conference for months. As I was writing my paper, I would practice what I would say when this day finally arrived. One of the topics that I'm interested in and one of the things about SEAM that attracted me when I first encountered it in one of the classes here at the University of St. Thomas, was it seemed like it was a missing piece. To me, when I read about value, value creation processes in organizations, creation of wealth, value-added activities, and the organization of work and dysfunction in organizations, I thought maybe SEAM holds some answers. One of

Decoding the Socio-Economic Approach to Management, pages 103–118

the things that I had noticed in my work, I'm in manufacturing so I actually work on a manufacturing floor, is the failure of Lean implementations.

Many people believe Lean is complete and that Lean would do this and that in terms of continuous improvement. But what I noticed, through time, was even if we rearranged the manufacturing floor several times and we did, what did not happen was the development of a culture of continuous improvement. When I asked questions about this, they would say well you don't get it. It's a philosophy. You've got to get the philosophy. Get deep into the philosophy and then you'll understand how you can develop cultures of continuous improvement. Then they'd question me, well are you sure you asked "why" enough times. Did you ask five times, or did you only ask "why" four times. I'd privately wonder if asking "why" five or four times really makes that much of a difference. For that matter how would things improve if I asked "why" six times rather than five? The point is that it was heresy to question Lean, but honestly the more I thought about it and the more exposure to Lean theory I had, the more it seemed to me that Lean theory was not complete. Oh sure the Seven Wastes worked and the elimination of waste and the concept of value added activities was sound but for the most part that was just rearranging the physical factory. The development of cultures of continuous improvement still did not thrive. Something seemed to be missing.

When I came to University of St. Thomas and when I started to write my dissertation, I decided that I would look into the development of Lean cultures and Lean implementations and why they fail. Much to my surprise, I wasn't alone in my concerns or questioning of Lean. I had company and lots of it. I found estimates of the global Lean failure rates as high as 50%, in terms of cultures of continuous improvement failing to develop. That's high and I was shocked at the number. Actually, nobody really knows the number. But then when you read the literature on Lean, what is said is, well, you know, we do incur an improvement. We rearrange the factory floor and things get faster and waste is eliminated and yeah, we make more money. But again, often you don't have the development of cultures of continuous improvement or to put it a different way you don't have the comprehensive development of the wealth creation process on a continuous bases.

One of the things that attracted me to SEAM was the wealth creation process because that was new and it was a new way to think about continuous improvement that made sense. In the continuous improvement programs of Lean and Six Sigma, the wealth creation process in organizations is often over looked. It is there but it is in pieces. One of the things through studying SEAM that I began to realize is that in all my training and experience, the wealth creation and wealth destruction process was something that was almost totally invisible. We live it so deeply every day in our organizations and it so deeply permeates our environments and it's so fundamental to what we do in organizations that more often than not, we overlook the wealth creation process. I've realized that for most of my working life, I've missed it and underestimated its importance. As I began to study the wealth creation process, I began to think of wealth creation in relationship to Lean practices as having several sub-processes. Wealth creation and value creation processes that result in changes to the value-added activities are the link or hook. I see value-added activities as part of the value creation process, which contributes to the wealth creation process, as the link between Lean and SEAM. Wealth creation and value creation process influenced by value added activities is the common activity between both models. The difference is that based upon the SEAM model is that dysfunction is always present in an organization and that dysfunction act as a drag on continuous improvement and has a price tag. SEAM has a broader comprehensive view of the wealth creation and destruction process and value creation process within organizations. Understanding these processes greatly assists in understanding the creation of cultures of continuous improvement.

LEAN AND SEAM

The concept and application of value and non-value added activities and elimination of waste are important fundamental Lean concepts. In a Lean organization, there is constant organizing and re-organizing around the identification of activities that are perceived to have or not have value. Once identified waste is then eliminated from the system. The identification and elimination of non-value activities and subsequent waste ultimately influences profitability and the development and facilitation of cultures of continuous improvement within a Lean organization.

Identification of value and non-value added activities and eliminating waste are regularly carried out at the operational level of an organization. However, based on SEAM research, there is now evidence to suggest that value and non-value added activities can support even greater profitability and the continual support of cultures of continuous improvement. This is true when value and non-value added activities are addressed in the broader context of value creation and wealth creation and the minimizing of the dysfunction that the SEAM model theorizes is present in all organizations (Savall & Zardet, 2013).

The Socio-economic Theory of Organizations, or the SEAM model, was developed in the mid 1970's at ISEOR in Lyon, France, and was designed to address issues surrounding profitability and the broader processes of wealth creation and destruction in an organization (Savall & Zardet, 2013). The broader perspective and design of the SEAM model is inclusive of value and non-value added activities and the elimination of waste as found in Lean tools and methods. In addition, the creation and destruction of value processes that occur in an organization are also included. For those interested in increased profitability and sustainable cultures of continuous improvement, a broader understanding about Lean tools and methods in relationship to the SEAM model and the creation and destruction of wealth processes in organizations, is beneficial as it gives insight and broader perspective to the development of cultures of continuous improvement.

Manufacturing literature will at times also suggest that the failure of Lean organizations to implement Lean programs and develop sustainable cultures of continuous improvement is global in scope and widespread (Schonberger, 2007). However, often, the root cause of the failure is portrayed as, and attributed to, a lack of true commitment and support by executive management for their Lean programs and initiatives (Dixon, 2007, Pepper & Spedding, 2010). Prevalent in this type of thinking is an underlying assumption that Lean methodology is complete.

It is assumed that the current state of the development of Lean tools and methods offers executive management a comprehensive conceptual framework that supports improved profitability and sustainable cultures of continuous improvement in organizations. Often, imitation and mimicry of the manufacturing policies, processes, and methods of more successful Lean organizations, is the most common advocated approach for attempting to implement and develop sustainable cultures of continuous improvement. It is believed that these methods if carefully copied will lead to success. However, it is becoming apparent by the large number of failures in spite of best efforts, that imitation and mimicry is not enough to actively manage and support the viability and sustainability of a culture of continuous improvement. Something more is needed and it must be an approach that develops and customizes the uniqueness of each organization.

SEAM research, conducted extensively in more than 1,350 firms and 72 branches of industry, suggests that Lean tools and methods when used alone may not be as effective as when used in combination with the SEAM model and theory to improve the profitability and economic health of an organization (Savall & Zardet, 2008). SEAM research suggests that the development and sustainability of cultures of continuous improvement in organizations is more fully supported and sustained by actively managing the broader wealth creation process to improve the economic health and profitability of an organization (Savall & Zardet, 2013).

It is when Lean methods are used in conjunction with SEAM that profitability can be greater and cultures of continuous improvement can be developed and effectively supported through time.

To conduct our analysis, I will review the SEAM model as it pertains to the creation and destruction of value processes within organizations. Secondly, I will complete a comparison of the SEAM model and the wealth

creation process to the concept and theory of value and non-value processes present in Lean methods. In conclusion, I will summarize our findings.

The SEAM Model: Economic Value Destruction Process

Historically, the origins of the SEAM model stem from attempts to understand the failure of many of the established major theories of economics, such as Neoclassical, Marxist, and Keynesian economics, to fully account
for the difference in the realized levels of economic growth as compared to
the amounts of labor and capital input utilized. Studies estimated that the
dominant theories of economics only explain and account for as little as
50% of the economic growth experienced in relationship to the amount of
inputs of capital and labor (Savall & Zardet, 2013).

The SEAM model theorizes that the "gap" in accounting for additional
inputs of capital and labor is generated because of a chronic non-creation
of value of resources occurring within the organization (Savall & Zardet,
2013). It is theorized only a portion of all additional resources added create value in an organization. For a portion of all added resources, a loss of
earnings and a loss of opportunity are experienced. Further, under severe
conditions, it is possible for additional resources input into an organization
to evaporate and that no creation of wealth is ever experienced (Savall &
Zardet, 2008). Instead, a loss of earnings and opportunity occur.

The SEAM model addresses the non-creation of value by incorporating
the fundamental view of the organization as a set of structures interacting
with a set of human behaviors (Savall & Zardet, 2008). The non-creation
of value is theorized to occur due to the existence of dysfunctions in the
organization, which occur based upon the interaction of human systems
and structures within the organization as they pertain to the value creation
process in the organization. All organizations are theorized to experience
a degree of dysfunction. Dysfunctions are theorized to always be present, in
varying degrees, based upon human behaviors.

Dysfunctions occur because each individual in the system has a degree
of informal power based upon their will to act and choice of behavior. Each
individual's choice of behavior is viewed in the SEAM model as being subjective and chosen based upon what the individual perceives to be in their
best self-interest (Savall & Zardet, 2008).

A fundamental premise of the SEAM model is that when employees in
an organization exercise their informal power and create a level of dysfunction, their actions result in hidden costs (Savall & Zardet, 2008). ISEOR
research indicates that hidden costs in organizations can be very high and
range from $10,000 to $40,000 per person/per year (Savall & Zardet, 2013).
It is each individual exercising their informal power and the creation of

levels of dysfunctions and the resulting hidden costs that ultimately influences the larger more encompassing process of the wealth creation within organizations (Savall & Zardet, 2008).

SEAM research has discovered that dysfunctional behavior is known to create hidden costs and manifest as poor performance in six categories: working conditions, work organization, integrated training, communication-coordination and cooperation, time management, and strategic implementation (Savall, Zardet, & Bonnet, 2008). The resulting hidden costs and poor performance in the six categories are theorized to account for the difference between the inputs of capital and labor and the resulting outputs of the creation of economic value process (Savall & Zardet, 2013).

The SEAM Model: Improving Economic Performance and the Value Creation Process

The approach to minimize the hidden costs and improve the value creation process and profitability of an organization is to intervene and decrease dysfunctional behaviors. Ultimately, through time, the goal of a SEAM intervention is to prepare the organization for permanent socio-economic management so that through the value creation process profitability is constantly improving and a culture of continuous improvement is developed, supported, and sustained. On average, based upon SEAM research, the initial intervention and process to prepare the organization for continuous socio-economic management requires 3 years (Savall & Zardet, 2008).

A SEAM socio-economic intervention is designed to create change and improve economic performance and value creation by engaging both the human systems and structures of an organization (Savall & Zardet, 2008). The intervention process is highly synchronized and there are three distinctive features to the process. First, a SEAM intervention is a highly coordinated and methodical process. Second, the entire organization is engaged and all members participate. Third, large numbers of people are involved in the intervention in a short period of time.

The Socio Economic approach has often been compared to a ripple-through process because an implementation always begins with two very formalized and simultaneous actions that engage and encompass the entire organization and its systems (Savall & Zardet, 2013). The first act of the intervention process is a horizontal action that takes place with the executive management team and the second is a vertical action that begins with one or possibly two units within the organization (Savall & Zardet, 2008). These two simultaneous and synchronized, vertical and horizontal actions together are called the Horivert procedure. Ultimately, through synchronizing the implementations of the vertical and horizontal actions, every member of the organization is quickly engaged and the entire organization is very quickly working to improve selected dysfunctions.

The SEAM approach to improved profitability and development of sustainable cultures of continuous improvement is very effective. Generally, overall, improved profitability is experienced. Based upon SEAM research, methods have been devised to calculate the savings realized from minimizing dysfunctions and reducing hidden costs. During an intervention, hidden costs can be reduced anywhere from $4,500 to $71,700 per employee/per year (Savall & Zardet, 2008).

Further, because of SEAM's synchronized and simultaneous use of horizontal and vertical tools, the Horivert approach, and SEAM's quick deployment and inclusion of all organizational members, there is noticeably less resistance and withdrawal than other continuous methods such as Lean (Savall & Zardet, 2008). By utilizing the SEAM model, profitability is improved and cultures of continuous improvement are systemically developed and supported.

The SEAM Model: Different Economic Assumptions

The SEAM model of socio-economic management links the interaction of human behavior and system structures to the wealth creation processes and economic performance of an enterprise (Savall & Zardet, 2008). Within that framework, the SEAM model assumes that each individual will act in a manner they perceive to be in their own best interest. It is these individual perceptions and beliefs that prompt the individual to act, which in turn influences the creation of organizational dysfunctions and hidden costs that impact the wealth creation processes of an organization.

The SEAM theory about the impact of individual behavior differs starkly from the underlying economic assumptions and inferences that are made about the labor process and organization of work in Lean methodology and philosophy. Lean philosophy and methodology subscribe to the classical economic approach of rational individualism (Kennedy, 2014). This simply means that inherent in the design of Lean methodology and philosophy is an underlying assumption that an employee must always act in the best interest of the company because to do so is also in the best economic interest of the employee (Taylor, 2006). Classical economic rational individualism assumes that the economic health and profitability of the company is a mutually shared and supported common interest of the employee and employer (Stiglitz, 2013). It is assumed that the organization of work and the labor process, as determined necessary by management, must be accepted by the employee (Braverman, 1998). Acceptance is viewed as necessary for the economic benefit of the employee, the company, and ultimately society.

By their very nature, assumptions about rational individualism act as limiting factors in the support of the organization of labor, the work process, change and innovation, and ultimately the value creation process and resulting improved wealth and profitability of organizations. Assumptions that employee–employer relationships are only based upon mutual economic interest ignores, and ultimately negates, consideration of the vast array of human behavior and creativity that organically occurs in all human systems.

The SEAM model more realistically addresses the dynamic of human behavior and the organic nature of change in human systems (Kennedy, 2014). The SEAM model is designed to integrate and allow for the versatility and integrative nature of human behavior and structures in organizations. The model is designed to more accurately and comprehensively facilitate the support of the interaction between human behavior and structures within the organization as they pertain to the value creation process in the organization structures (Savall & Zardet, 2008).

The Lean Model: Lean Methodology Value Added Activities and Elimination of Waste

Historically, the Lean methodology was developed under the watchful eye of the brilliant Toyota engineer named Taiichi Ohno. Ohno's (1988) ultimate goal in developing the Lean system was to focus on the creation and preservation of value for the customer by eliminating waste in the production system (Dennis, 2007). Further, Ohno believed the workers were his most valuable asset and was able to include the worker as part of the planning and the elimination of waste process (Ohno, 1988).

In a Lean system, value is often defined as any action or process that a customer who uses and consumes the product is willing to pay for. As a means of creating value, Lean methods focus on eliminating all waste from the production system. By focusing on the elimination of waste, all actions except the actions the customer is willing to pay for have the potential to be reviewed and eliminated. As a result of the continuous elimination of waste in Lean systems, production time and cost are reduced and overall profitability and quality is improved within the system.

Lean methods are interrelated and mutually supportive. Conceptually a Lean system is often represented as two pillars. Together, the two pillars encompass the flow of materials and machines and equipment in a Lean facility. The first pillar of Lean is referred to as JIT or *just-in-time* (Dennis, 2007). The fundamental concept of JIT is to have only the inventory required when it is time to produce the product. Excess inventory in a Lean system is considered waste. When inventories are minimized, quality often improves due to an increase in focus on the remaining product.

The second pillar of the Lean system is referred to as *Jidoka* (Dennis, 2007). *Jidoka* roughly translates into automation with a human mind. This fundamental concept of Lean methods states that machines should be designed to stop when there is a problem, such as when the product is manufactured out of specification. The advantage of designing stops into machines is that overall quality is improved and the cost of producing inferior parts has been avoided.

Within Lean systems, improvements in the form of elimination of waste are a matter of daily practice and are never ending; hence the term *continuous improvement* is used. Continuous improvements are often, but not always, small-step improvements rather than big-step improvements. Within Lean systems, stability and standardization are viewed as requirements for ease in the facilitation, management, control, and implementation of the improvements being made.

In Lean systems, the way in which continuous improvements and the elimination of waste and non-value-added activities is determined is based upon an analysis of work processes that applies a standard criteria called the Seven Wastes. Often, upon analysis, only 5% of the activities in manufacturing work processes are value-added activities. The other 95% of activity can generally be classified as waste or non-value added activities. The Seven Wastes as outlined by Dennis (2007) are:

1. Motion: This waste has a human and machine element. Poor ergonomic design affects productivity. Productivity diminishes with unnecessary walking, reaching, or twisting by the worker. Waste of machine motion also exists when machines are placed too far apart on the production line or placed individually away from production areas.
2. Delay: This waste refers to delays caused by waiting. If a worker must wait for material or for a machine to finish processing, this causes a delay. Waiting is wasteful because it increases the time it takes for a product to move through the factory.
3. Conveyance: This waste is most often created by an inefficient workplace layout, overly large equipment, or manufacturing in large quantities. The inefficiency is created by unnecessary movement—of machines or workers. The concept is to eliminate costly unnecessary steps or transport time.
4. Correction: This waste is related to having to fix defective product. It includes all time, material, and labor required to fix the defective part.
5. Over-processing: This waste refers to doing more than the customer requires. Doing more than is required is considered a costly and unnecessary activity.
6. Inventory: This waste refers to keeping unnecessary materials. In Lean systems, having more than the quantity of materials required

to produce the product when it is time to produce the product is deemed wasteful.

7. Overproduction: This waste addresses producing product that does not sell. Once an item is manufactured and is not sold, it must be stored, handled, and administratively tracked, all of which are considered unnecessary costs.

Lean and SEAM Compared

Many regard Lean systems as a philosophy for conducting business and as a means of effectively managing organizations on a daily bases. The Lean philosophy frames improvements in the production system and achieving greater profitability in terms of a scientific approach to improving production (Ohno, 1988). As part of that scientific focus, value added and non-value added activities are constantly emphasized in support of the value creation processes within the organization. There can be many value creation processes or streams within an organization that support the overall wealth creation process. Subsequently, a Lean enterprise must constantly analyze, change, or obsolete tasks which add little value to the end result. In a Lean system, management time and skills are focused on consistently shifting the organization from low value-added tasks to high value-added activities and creating new activities and new tasks to upgrade the organization's performance (Dennis, 2007). The ultimate intention is to improve efficiency to the point of producing zero waste and to bring the percentage of work or value-added activities to 100 percent (Ohno, 1988).

In contrast, SEAM is designed to quickly organize and address not just the structural aspects of the system but also the human behavior and dysfunction within an organization. The SEAM model is intentionally designed to focus on and address the individual and collective behavior of employees. The intention is to reduce the overall level of dysfunction and to make known and decrease costs that have been previously hidden. It is through the process of addressing the behavioral dysfunctions that hidden cost is reduced and the creation of value and ultimately the wealth creation process is improved. It is the simultaneous use of horizontal and vertical tools—the Horivert approach and SEAM's quick deployment and inclusion of all organizational members that provides the foundation to address both the structural and human behavioral aspects of the organizations.

Although Lean includes the philosophy of respect for people, very few actual tools have been created in Lean methodology to link the social and economic performance of an enterprise and to provide a standardize method and tools for addressing the hidden cost that are incurred as the result of dysfunction of collective human behaviors. The SEAM model goes beyond Lean philosophy and is designed to view and address human behavior, regardless of it variability, to provide a systemic approach for addressing dysfunctions as they occur in any organization (Savall & Zardet, 2008).

CONCLUSION: LEAN AND SEAM COMBINED

Individually both the SEAM model and Lean methodology have distinctive features and each can contribute to improving profitability. However, when viewed in terms of the value creation process and ultimately the wealth creation process within an organization, the most beneficial and sustainable approach is to use both the SEAM model and Lean methodology. There isn't conflict in using both SEAM and Lean.

Upon close examination, SEAM and Lean can be mutually supportive and reinforcing in improving value creation processes within organizations. Each emphasizes different value creation processes but yet each supports and contributes to the overall creation of wealth of the organization. When implemented jointly, they strengthen the wealth creation process and increase profitability more than if implemented and relied upon individually.

The SEAM model is robust and more foundational than Lean in that SEAM links the structure of an organization and human behavior using a synchronized and simultaneous approach (Savall & Zardet, 2008). Further, SEAM's design includes the Horivert approach and the quick deployment and inclusion of all organizational members. SEAM quickly can encompass the involvement of the entire organization. Once implemented, SEAM can serve as a foundation to quickly organize and implement Lean and to hold discussions about value and non-value-added activities and the elimination of waste.

Jointly each can contribute to increased profitability and the improvement of the creation of value process in the organization. Lean methodology will emphasize the elimination of waste and SEAM will emphasize the exposure and minimization of hidden costs. Working together both can contribute the improved profitability and a more robust value creation process in the organization.

APPENDIX:
Conference Dialogue

Conference Participant: In one of your slides, Alanna, you talk about internal and external strategic plans. Can you say more about what that looks like?

Alanna Kennedy: Well, because of the fact that SEAM is so comprehensive within the organization, the idea of getting the organization in alignment with what you're doing internally with the organization and externally, SEAM, I think has much more adapted that than just using Lean.

Conference Participant: So in your estimation, and this is for both of the last presenters, is it actually possible to do both? Do you think it's possible for them to live side by side?

Alanna Kennedy: Yes, because I think that the faulty part is that without SEAM, you're not getting the development of the culture of continuous improvement. This is what the earlier presenters were talking about as far as the longevity of SEAM. Going forward you can almost say it'll take more work but what crossed my mind this morning is how close those two really align.

Conference Participant: But because you both pointed out that they're ideological in nature, how can you have both those ideologies, which seem to be conflicting, in an organization, side by side?

Leslie McKnight: I've participated in Six Sigma projects and they teach you how to manage the process but they don't teach you how to manage the behavior as a result of the change. So now you have all the unintended consequences that are occurring and there's conflict that they don't give you the skill set on how to manage it and manage it from an OD perspective. And I think that's where the gap is.

Conference Participant: So, Marc or Dr. Savall, is it possible? Would you recommend in any way doing Six Sigma or Lean alongside SEAM?

Henri Savall: Do you need a politically correct answer?

Conference Participant: No, absolutely not.

Henri Savall: I think in Europe now there is a campaign against psycho-sociological risks and Lean is supposed to increase such psychosocial risks.

Conference Participant: Stress at work?

Henri Savall: Yes, then SEAM could be the therapy to make Lean acceptable.

Conference Participant: Alanna, in your presentation you talked about fake Lean and my understanding of Lean is there's a difference between Lean and Six Sigma where Six Sigma is all about improving the process but Lean also includes the respect for people. And I think if you do process improvement without including the respect for people, it's doomed to failure. Would you comment on that and then give your perspective.

Alanna Kennedy: Sure. One of the things, when you read the Lean literature is that there's always this assumption that Lean is complete. But when you go back and look at some of the seminal works like Taiiche Ohno (1988) he's using sports analogies to describe team work and dealing with people. So, it's been 30 years since Lean's been out, if you're not successful, what's missing? The philosophy piece is really saying since it's a philosophy you might not understand, when in actuality it may be that there's an absence of structure. The method may not be complete and that would result in fake Lean. When I use the term fake Lean, if I wasn't clear, that's in response to not developing the culture of continuous improvement. Yes, I can rearrange my factory and I can improve my flow. I can improve my inventory turns. I can implement Six Sigma and minimize the variation in my processes, but that's not going to give me the infrastructure or support I need to develop the culture of continuous improvement within my organization. I think that that's the value that SEAM brings. It becomes this infrastructure then. If you have your culture of continuous improvement, if you can develop that, then you can bring in the other continuous improvement methodologies as you need them or let them go. They don't become your mainstay. They don't need to be.

Leslie McKnight: I absolutely agree and I like SEAM's perspective on the participative management and a whole reset on how to do that where there's actually contracts, individual contracts, team contracts, so it's control, it's accountability, it's participation and that will, in my opinion, release that human potential that we're talking about and the continuous improvement will happen on its own because now it's institutionalized in the system and it's coming from those that are within the organization that are affected by it every day.

Veronique Zardet: In my opinion, it's a question of mindset. Lean appears to me as a way to optimize production work but what about human behavior at work? What about team work? and so on. And it's a way to reduce production costs and to develop and improve, that is to say it could be compatible but SEAM is applied in a whole organization in a way to develop the company and not only to reduce production costs. And this is very different in the mindset of ISEOR model.

Conference Participant: For the people who know Six Sigma and Lean much better than I do, does it make sense that Lean and Six Sigma start with a different purpose in mind and don't necessarily incorporate what we know about human behavior, dynamics, etc. as part of the process, or not.

Alanna Kennedy: I'm just fascinated by the fact that both Six Sigma and Lean were developed in manufacturing environments and not university environments. You can trace Six Sigma back to the Western Electric plant in Cicero, IL. When you look at it, they were developed out of need because of process variation. The need is the same for the Japanese. I think that they are not exclusive. Rather they just address different aspects of the production process.

Conference Participant: I think there's an engineering structural piece. I don't know if it's critical but it also misses the human dynamic.

Leslie McKnight: Yes, that's the gap.

Conference Participant: Leslie had an interesting phrase in one of her responses. Unintended consequences. And that's what you get when you ignore part of your social system or at least the entire social system. Maybe if you use SEAM for the full diagnosis and then apply Lean or Six Sigma judiciously, and not let it take over, it might be viable but I think you've got to remember where it came from, what it's purpose was and that there was a reason they excluded the human element.

Conference Participant: But I've got to jump in here and say that not every company excludes the human element. It is because we have the virus and we're choosing to exclude the human element because Japan did not exclude the human element. It is so ingrained in the Japanese culture that when they write books about Lean, they don't talk about the need to develop the behavior of observation, they talk about the tool of 5S. So we take their books, we read them and we go oh, it's about the tools, oh, okay. So we must do this and here we go. And they forget to tell the employees the real reason why we're doing 5S is to develop the behavior and skill of observation. So if we link the behavior to the tool, now we are acting like Toyota, but what we do in America is we just take the tools and away we go. So it's our interpretation.

Conference Participant: But even if you were to do that, you still have to have a methodology where you can develop your own authentic culture of continuous improvement. My culture in "A" company may not be the same as your company in "B," and I think that when you start talking about Lean as a philosophy, that sort of falls short. It might have been engrained in the overall Japanese culture.

Conference Participant: I agree. When I did Lean for Honeywell, our tagline was developing continuous improvement through employee engagement. And we adopted and created a philosophy of the employee is the center of the universe. Not the employer knows best but the employee knows best, so we had to make mindful shifts but that was the authenticity that we created.

John Conbere: The comment I heard from the CEO of a company in Lyon, that has used SEAM and Lean for many years, is that Lean doesn't teach you how to manage. And if you have SEAM and change the management approach, then Lean is workable.

REFERENCES

Braverman, H. (1998). *Labor and Monopoly Capital.* New York, NY: Month Review Press. (Original work published 1974).

Dennis, P. (2007). *Lean production simplified.* New York, NY: Productivity Press.

Dixon, D. (2007). Lean in the job shop. *Fabricating & Metalworking, 6*(4), 16–19.

Kennedy, A. (2014). *Facilitating the socio-economic approach to management: Results of the first SEAM conference in North America.* Charlotte, NC: Information Age Publishing.

Ohno, T. (1988). *The Toyota production system.* New York, NY: Productivity Press.

Pepper, M., & Spedding, T. (2010). The evolution of lean six sigma. *International Journal of Quality and Reliability Management, 27* (2), 138–155.

Savall, H., & Zardet, V. (2008) *Mastering Hidden Costs Socio-Economic Performance.* Charlotte, NC: Information Age Publishing.

Savall, H., & Zardet, V. (2013). *The Dynamics and Challenges of Tetranormalization.* Charlotte, NC: Information Age Publishing.

Savall, H., Zardet, V., & Bonnet, M. (2008). *Releasing the untapped potential of enterprises through socio-economic management.* Geneva, Switzerland: ILO.

Schonberger, R. (2007). *Best practices in lean six sigma process improvement.* Hoboken, NJ: Wiley.

Stiglitz, J., (2013). *The Price of Inequality.* New York, NY: W. W. Norton Company.

Taylor, F. W. (2006). *The principles of scientific management.* New York, NY: Cosimo (Original work published 1911).

CHAPTER 7

THE CONVERGENCE OF LEAN SIX SIGMA AND SEAM TO MAXIMIZE PERFORMANCE IN ORGANIZATIONS

Leslie L. McKnight

The roots of Six Sigma methodology date back to the early 1980's from total quality management (TQM) philosophies and the sigma statistical metric that originated out of the Motorola Corporation (Arnheiter & Maleyeff, 2005). The Six Sigma metric was developed in response to sub-standard products traced back in many cases to decisions made by engineers when designing component parts. At Motorola, as products became more complex, defective products were becoming more commonplace while at the same time customers were demanding higher quality. Six Sigma statistical variations were applied to the process to measure the variability in production. The higher the process sigma, the more process outputs, products, and service meets customer requirements or the fewer the defects. In this methodology, the highest quality results in the lowest costs (Pepper

Decoding the Socio-Economic Approach to Management, pages 119–127
Copyright © 2016 by Information Age Publishing
All rights of reproduction in any form reserved.

& Spedding, 2010). Wall Street and corporations as diverse as Sony, Ford, Nokia, Texas Instruments, Canon, Hitachi, Lockheed Martin, American Express, Toshiba, DuPont, and Polaroid have embarked on corporate-wide Six Sigma programs and have netted in billions of dollars of savings over time (Schroeder, 1999). Proponents of the Six Sigma methodology believe that its application should be of paramount importance to every forward-thinking corporation seeking competitive advantage (Linderman, Schroeder, Zaheer, & Choo, 2003). The Six-Sigma metric is applied in a broad fashion, striving for near perfect performance at the lowest level of activity. Six Sigma programs generally create a structure under which training of employees is formalized and supported to ensure its effectiveness. All employees involved in activities that impact customer satisfaction are trained in basic problem solving skills.

In the 1960s, Japanese firms earnestly researched ways to enter the automobile markets. Toyota utilized western production techniques, improved them, and created a Lean manufacturing system known as the Toyota Production System. The Toyota Production System was built on the belief that the organization will succeed when it respects the knowledge of its employees and utilizes their skills and expertise to improve the production process (Stephens, 2007). Toyota's success with Lean manufacturing encouraged all other automobile companies to implement their own Lean systems. Today, the Lean philosophy is spreading from big automobile manufacturers to different industry sectors, including small businesses, service providers, retailers, and governments. Lean is a philosophy that advocates continuous improvement and analyzes potential sources of waste and reduces waste. Lean simplifies and standardizes business processes. The phrase Lean and Six Sigma were integrated to design a common model and theoretical compatibility that considers total quality management through process improvement strategies. The goal of Lean Six Sigma is to deliver the best quality products and services at the lowest cost and in the fastest time (Stephens, 2007).

Waste can be caused by unnecessary production, materials, effort, transportation, movement, processing, work defects, rework, and excessive wait times. Personnel issues, such as injuries, workloads, and misapplication of skills, knowledge, and abilities can result in forms of waste. Lean Six Sigma examines products/services through the customer's eyes and determines how improvements can eliminate "waste." The basis of the Lean Six Sigma methodology is to recognize the seven causes of waste in most processes.

1. Excessive motion
2. Waiting time
3. Over-engineering
4. Unnecessary processing time

5. Errors
6. Excessive resources
7. Unnecessary handoffs

Lean Six Sigma involves a project charter with a process owner within the organization and employees are trained as black belts, green belts, and yellow belts (Linderman, et al., 2003). Employees are part of the change effort. From this philosophy a team is formed to conduct an "Action Work Out" to implement improvements that will eliminate the waste. Lean Six Sigma strives to create a culture of continuous improvement operating at all levels within the organization. Process improvement strategies include the creation of Kaizen charts to induce continuous movement in organizations, control charts, and new process systems. The foundation of the Lean vision is still a focus on the individual product and its value stream (identifying value-added and non-value added activities), and to eliminate all waste, or muda, in all areas and functions within the system—the main target of Lean thinking (Stephens, 2007). The first step in a Lean transition is to identify value-added and non-value adding processes. Value stream mapping (VSM) emerged for this role (2007), and continues to provide a reliable qualitative analysis tool (if implemented correctly). It also provides the scope of the project by defining the current state and desired future state of the system. This future state map is then used to develop Lean improvement strategies, for example parallel working and flexibility through multi-skilling employees (requiring minimal expenditure).

The sequential steps are called The Six Sigma Improvement Model, or the Define, Measure, Analyze, Improve, and Control Methodology (DMAIC). In the define step, the customers, their requirements, and expectations are identified, along with the core business process. The project boundaries and the starting and stopping points of the process are defined. The process flow is mapped and areas where improvements can be made are identified. Any gaps between the customer's requirements and the process's output are defined. In the measure step, the performance of the core business process is analyzed. The output of the process that affects any gaps is quantified. A data collection plan for the process is developed and data is collected from different sources to uncover defects and metrics. In the analyze step, the root causes of defects are analyzed by examining the data collected and the process map. Charts, diagrams, and statistical process control tools are used to detect any disparity between the current performance and the target performance of the process.

Opportunities for improvements are prioritized and sources of variations are identified. The focus may be on achieving incremental process improvements or on major process redesigns. In the improve step, a process is improved by implementing innovative solutions to correct and prevent problems. Methods are redesigned or modified and an implementation plan is developed and executed. In the last step, control, the new process is monitored and managed by once again using charts, diagrams, and statistical process control tools. Monitoring ensures high performance levels are maintained and relapses back to former methods are prevented.

THE SEAM APPROACH

The ISEOR research center (Socio-Economic Institute of Firms and Organizations) is a research center in the field of management in Lyon, France. It was created in 1975 by Henri Savall, a professor at the University of Lyon. The institute's vocation is to experiment new management methods allowing improvement in compatibility between economic and social objectives of companies (Savall, Zardet, & Bonnet, 2008). Interventions are carried out by the ISEOR research center in many companies around the world. The approach has been validated through over 1,350 organizations for close to 40 years. SEAM has strong organization development values and is based on the premise that all employees (actors) in an organization have the capacity to help the organization grow and succeed (Conbere, Heorhialdi, & Cristallini, 2012). SEAM aids in the creation of supportive environments where human potential can be released. The SEAM intervention requires a commitment from top management and extends to the rest of the organization. Employees are trained on the SEAM process based on their position, knowledge, and experience in the organization.

SEAM consultants gather data from participants, synthesize the data, and present the data in a "mirror effect" to the organization. Six areas of social performance are explored using qualitative assessment tools to discover the organization dysfunctions and hidden costs of sustaining current patterns of social performance (Savall, Zardet, & Bonnet, 2008). The diagnostic narratives generated in the fieldwork are recorded and then arranged into main themes and sub-theme categories. From extensive action research in organizations and data profiles, SEAM has identified six common functions in an organization. When they work poorly, they become dysfunctions that can result in five main categories of hidden costs.

The six areas where dysfunctions can occur (2008) include: working conditions, work organization, communication-coordination-cooperation, time management, integrated training, and strategic implementation. The five main categories of hidden costs include: absenteeism, occupational Injuries and diseases, stay turnover, non-quality, and direct productivity gaps.

Once dysfunctions are identified and the leadership has an opportunity to reflect on the effects of their current practices, SEAM consultants implement the Horivert Method to explore the extent of the six dysfunctions and hidden costs, and develop sustainable solutions involving the actors of the organization (Savall & Zardet, 2008). The Horivert Method consists of horizontal interventions engaging top management; and vertical interventions which engage both management and personnel. Horizontal action interventions consists of three actions performed by top management. In the first action, managers are trained by SEAM consultants on the use of socio-economic tools relating to time management, competencies, and priority action planning. The second direct action involves a horizontal diagnostic inventory of the dysfunctions identified by management. The third action includes the development of focus groups charged to implement solutions through horizontal projects.

Vertical action interventions involve at least two units in the organization to conduct an in-depth socio-economic diagnostic analysis. A qualitative diagnostic is performed to estimate the units hidden cost. From thence, socio-economic innovation projects are developed by personnel to reduce dysfunctions identified during the diagnostic phase. SEAM equips organizations with coordinated tools such as piloting logbooks and activity contracts to ensure that the SEAM intervention will be sustainable and effective. New management skills can be developed because of SEAM's emphasis on teaching the firm how to convert hidden costs into value added competencies and develop human potential (Savall, 2010). In summary, the SEAM approach extends beyond efficiencies of Lean management and includes the intentional creation of an environment of inclusion, creativity, and engagement with all the actors within the organization.

CONVERGING LEAN SIX SIGMA AND SEAM

Lean Six Sigma and SEAM change management approaches focus on the elimination of waste and emphasize value added tasks. Both have a process improvement strategy based on the identification of wastes or "dysfunctions" in the organization. I would postulate that the Lean Six Sigma deadly wastes have social dysfunction implications that if evaluated could uncover hidden costs that may not be exposed during the Lean Six Sigma DMAIC process. The process mapping involved in Lean Six Sigma identifies wastes, but the SEAM approach in concert with the Six Sigma methodology, would uncover not only financial but hidden costs that would not be reflected in traditional cost evaluation reports. Lean Six Sigma focuses more on variability to the perfection of production of products and services and customer demand. SEAM provides indicators of flaws in management, human resources development, and organization strategy. Table 7.1 identifies the Lean Six Sigma Deadly waste causes.

Table 7.2 is the Lean Six Sigma and SEAM convergence chart that incorporates for each deadly waste, the SEAM approach to identify the type

TABLE 7.1 Lean Six Sigma Seven Deadly Wastes

Excessive Motion	Chasing approvals Searching for information
Waiting time	Waiting for approvals Meetings and conference calls
Over-engineering product	Poorly defined or communicated customer requirements Excess resources lacking clear work activities
Unnecessary processing time	Corporate policies getting in the way of accomplishing tasks at hand Redundant or unnecessary paper work Transcribing information multiple times
Errors	Rework Failing to meet customer requirements
Excessive resources	Poor resource leveling to meet demand Minimal understanding of bottlenecks
Unnecessary handoffs	Unnecessary approvals Verification loops

TABLE 7.2 Lean Six Sigma 7 Deadly Wastes and SEAM Convergence

Lean Six Sigma 7 Deadly Wastes	SEAM Social Dysfunction	SEAM Hidden costs
1. Excessive motion	Working conditions	Low value added productivity
2. Waiting time	Time management Working conditions	Wasted man hours Apathy Productivity gaps
3. Overproduction	Communication-coordination-cooperation	Excess salary Opportunity costs (customer demands) Overconsumption of resources
4. Unnecessary processing time	Integrated training Time management	Injuries Redundancy Non-value tasks
5. Errors	Work conditions Communication-coordination-cooperation	Loss of customer loyalty Overconsumption of resources
6. Excessive resources	Integrated training Strategic implementation	Redundancies Customer demand
7. Unnecessary handoffs	Work conditions Work organization Time management	Inefficient resource allocation Customer convenience

of dysfunction, and provides hidden cost indicators as a result of the waste and dysfunction. For example, the first Lean Six Sigma Deadly Waste is excessive motion. Excessive motion is characterized as the spatial location of resources and the process to exchange information or products from one stage to the other. In SEAM, this could be a result of dysfunctions in the working conditions in the organization. Further examination could reveal a scenario in which the organization has recently expanded to include new products or services but may not have redesigned their offices or facilities to accommodate the new productions. This is just an example to demonstrate a cause of dysfunction. The hidden costs related to the waste of motion are low value added productivity. Employees could be spending more non-value added steps in motion that causes delays in actual production or service.

SEAM-EMPHASIS
ON ORGANIZATION DEVELOPMENT VALUES

Lean Six Sigma and SEAM involve employees (actors) in the process improvement strategies. Both strategies identify wastes or dysfunctions within the organization. Both emphasize lowering non-value added steps and focus on customer expectation and satisfaction. Research has indicated that Lean Six Sigma is used by most U.S. or multi-national firms as a cost cutting measure that result in downsizing the firm (Porter & Lingenfelter, 2006). Downsizing can result in a loss of valuable human capital or the sacrifice of customer satisfaction and demands. The view that Lean is pro-company, not pro-employee, has some validity, and cannot be dismissed. For example, it is said that employees feel a sense of insecurity, perceiving Lean as a redundancy threat (Porter & Lingenfelter, 2006). The authors also contend that management avoids accountability when problems arise, letting it filter downwards onto the lower levels of hierarchy (Porter & Lingenfelter, 2006). This is to miss the fundamental underpinning of empowerment and cultural change, resulting from a failure by management to approach Lean with the correct goals. Without the preservation of organization development values, which is the basis for SEAM, there could be an adverse effect on morale which results in an increase of worker unhappiness and withdrawal, ultimately leading to operational failures (Schroeder, 1999).

The field and practice of organization development is a field characterized by a strong value base, a set of values that are highly influenced by the classic Organization Development (OD) scholars and founders, Kurt Lewin, Douglas McGregor, and Frederick Taylor (Yaeger & Sorenson, 2008). OD values are embedded in the SEAM approach by viewing all participants as invaluable resources and contributors to the organization's effectiveness. Furthermore, SEAM consultants hold a core belief that organizations exists to serve society and the employees in particular (Conbere & Heorhialdi, 2011). SEAM interventions are designed to flow from the top down and bottom up through a highly participative manner led by management. In Lean Six Sigma, management can tend to concentrate on tools and practices, aiming to teach new improvement tools to employees, rather than immersing them in the practical side of solving opportunities for improvement with a Lean approach (1999).

Unlike Lean Six Sigma, which focuses primarily on process and reduction of errors and defects, SEAM is a process improvement strategy that is both micro and macro, which incorporates strategic planning, policy changes, and the interactions between organization departments, division, and customers and how they relate with one another (Savall et al., 2008). SEAM also includes specific management tools to help top management and executives switch from a centralized to a more participative management style. This includes the Priority Action Plan which consists of scheduling work in each department. The Competency Grid is another tool to increase training participation and reduces shifts in responsibilities. Time management tools assist in delegation and oversight. The Strategic Piloting book provides custom indicators to focus on the improvement of converting hidden costs to value added costs (Savall, 2010). The Periodically Negotiable Activity contract (PNAC) allows management and employees the ability to collectively define personnel objectives and can include rewards when objectives are achieved.

In conclusion, the SEAM approach involves all the actors on every level in a synchronized coordinated fashion to align process and performance and to institute its internal accountability standards. The advantage to this approach is to maximize customer requirements and satisfaction but also positions for competitive advantage, flexibility, and agility within the organization. Second, SEAM embeds large system change within an economic and strategic analysis of the firm. U.S. based manufacturing corporations and other product and service corporations can benefit from the convergence of incorporating SEAM to their process improvement strategies to obtain a competitive advantage and maximize capital and human potential within their organization.

REFERENCES

Arnheiter, E., & Maleyeff, J. (2005). The integration of lean management and Six Sigma. *The Total Quality Management (TQM) Magazine, 17,* 5–18.

Conbere, J. P., & Heorhiadi, A. (2011). Socio-Economic approach to management: A successful systemic approach to organizational change. *OD Practitioner, 43*(1), 6–10.

Conbere, J. P., Heorhiadi, A., & Cristallini, V. (2012, June). The key to SEAM's effectiveness. ISEOR Conference. Lyon, France.

Linderman, K., Schroeder, R., Zaheer, S., & Choo, A. (2003). Six Sigma: A goal-theoretic perspective. *Journal of Operations Management, 21,* 193–203.

Pepper, M. P. J., & Spedding, T. A. (2010). The evolution of Lean Six Sigma. *International Journal of Quality & Reliability Management, 27*(2), 138–155.

Porter, J., & Lingenfelter, A. (2006). Nuclear fuel: Addressing the future. *International Meeting on LWR Fuel Performance, 10,* 22–26.

Savall, H. (2010). *Work and people: An economic evaluation of job enrichment.* Charlotte, NC: Information Age Publishing.

Savall, H., & Zardet, V. (2008). *Mastering hidden costs and socio-economic performance.* Charlotte, NC: Information Age Publishing.

Savall, H., Zardet, V., & Bonnet, M. (2008). *Releasing the untapped potential of enterprises through socio-economic management.* Geneva, Switzerland: ILO.

Schroeder, H. (1999). *Six Sigma: The breakthrough management strategy revolutionizing the world's top corporations.* New York, NY: Doubleday, Random House.

Stephens, J. (2007). Lean Six Sigma, *Journal of Organizational Leadership and Business. 1*(1), 1–7.

Yaeger, T., & Sorensen, P. (2008). Recognizing the value and values of OD. *OD Practitioner, 40*(2), 47–49.

CHAPTER 8

THE TFW VIRUS

Why So Many Organizations Act in Ways That Hurt Their Interests

John Conbere, Alla Heorhiadi, and Vincent Cristallini

Have you ever wondered why some behaviors persist in the workplace even though common sense cries out that the behaviors are destructive, wasteful, cruel, or downright stupid? Perhaps you have seen the examples of the boss who does not listen to his subordinates, or the boss who flies into rages and humiliates people; the executive who makes hundreds of times the salary of the average employee; the disruptive employee who is never required to behave in a civilized manner; the manager who does not have the skills to do what the job requires; or the number of people who waste time and energy gossiping about problems that never seem to change. We could describe more situations like these, but this is not the point. The question we want to raise is why are these examples so common? What is it that prevents organizations from working in a manner that most people know would make more sense, and which would make them more effective?

Decoding the Socio-Economic Approach to Management, pages 129–144
Copyright © 2016 by Information Age Publishing
129

In this paper, we present an explanation for the irrational and wasteful continuance of many destructive workplace behaviors. This is not a new theory, it is part of the socio-economic theory that has been developed by Henri Savall and his colleagues since 1973 (Savall, 2010; Savall & Zardet, 2008). This socio economic theory has been confirmed in over 1300 case studies of organizations since 1973. What we like about the theory is that it explains why organizations consistently put up with self-destructive behavior. This self-destructive behavior is like a virus that reduces an organization's immunity. While the idea of a virus is a metaphor, we will use it to reveal the deep beliefs that drive much of the management in the western world.

When Savall created the Socio-Economic Approach to Management (SEAM) in 1973, his intention was to respond to the inadequate theories about work and business. Savall created the virus metaphor much later and developed it at the Socio-Economic Institute of Firms and Organizations Research (ISEOR). The metaphor of the virus was first used by Savall and Zardet in their lectures in 2006, and then presented in papers in France, Mexico, and Argentina in 2009 (2009, 2009a, 2009b), and in a book in 2010. Our paper is an elaboration of the description of the TFW virus.

THE DISCOVERY OF THE TFW VIRUS

In socio-economic organization theory, the virus is named TFW, in tribute to the promoters of the ideas that allowed the virus to crystalize and develop: Taylor, Fayol, and Weber. Frederick W. Taylor (1856–1915) was a well-known American engineer who developed the idea of scientific management, in which he stressed the separation between the design and execution of work, and the study of how to obtain the maximum efficiency in work (Schachter, 2010). Henri Fayol (1841–1925) was a French engineer who promoted the idea of specialization and separation of business functions, and is credited for establishing much of management theory (Pryor & Taneja, 2010). In his fourteen management principles, he stressed the importance of division of work, the authority and responsibility of the boss to expect obedience, a hierarchical chain of command, and the importance of order. Max Weber (1864–1920) was a German sociologist who posited that the ideal organizational model bureaucracy is based on the definition of rules, which are then respected by subjects. He observed that bureaucracy does have a negative side, in which individualism, autonomy, and freedom are weakened, but these are inevitable and worth the benefits that come from bureaucracy (Houghton, 2010).

Together Taylor, Fayol, and Weber had great influence on our modern beliefs about organizations; beliefs that are taught in business schools and which have become common through all kinds of organizations, including business, ecclesiastical, educational, and government (Houghton, 2010; Pryor & Taneja, 2010; Schachter, 2010). There are some debates about whether the modern view of the theories of these men are accurate (see for example, Weisbord, 2011), but that is not the point. The point is that modern business is shaped by a mode of management that has emerged from the theories of Taylor, Fayol, and Weber, and this mode is destructive to the human soul. Let us note, though, that our concern is not with their theories, but how the theories are applied in the modern organization.

THE NATURE OF THE TFW VIRUS

Beliefs about people and work combined lead to beliefs about the workplace. These all lead to a series of symptoms and consequences which can be found in the workplace.

The core belief about people is that the economic human being is rational. This means that when faced with decisions that will affect the person's economic state, the person will respond with reason. The place of emotions is minimized. This allows managers to form plans based on the assumption that people will follow the places because this is the reasonable course of action. When stated this boldly, the belief is seen to be naïve, but nonetheless, it is a common deep belief.

There are two core beliefs about work. One is that when people are hired they must be obedient to the demands of the workplace. In other words, they sell their souls for the privilege of being paid. The other is that life at work is different than life at home. At home one attends to one's needs, at work one attends to the organization's needs. The rules are different in each setting. As a comment on how prevalent this belief is, think of the term *work/life balance*. The implication is there are two realms of human existence—work and life, and they are different. Does it not make more sense to think of work as part of life? One can argue that this is what is meant by work–life balance, but we suggest that this is a Freudian slip that reveals the belief of many in our culture.

As summarized in Figure 8.1, our beliefs about the workplace flow from the beliefs about human beings and work.

1. Hyper-specialization is most efficient, is the outgrowth of Taylor's Scientific Management. The more workers specialize the more efficient they can be at their tasks. The difficulty is the more workers specialize the more cut off they tend to be from others in the workplace. This is made worse by beliefs about separation.
2. Separation is the most effective way for organizations to be efficient. This comes from Weber's theories about bureaucracy. We separate

Beliefs about people	**Beliefs about work**
• The economic human being is rational	• When people are hired they must be obedient (i.e., they sell their soul for the privilege of being paid) • Life at work is different than life at home (the rules are different)

Beliefs about the workplace
- **Hyper-specialization** is most efficient
- **Separation is most effective** – separate: generating ideas from the execution of the work; "noble and menial" tasks;
- Business is about making a profit, so the work process is most important and **the value of the person is minimized**
- People can and should be **submissive** to the organization

Symptoms	**Consequences**
• The workplace is fractured – broken into many separate parts, divisions between people • Heartless processes – the needs of the organization are more important than the needs of the individual • Elitism – some people are superior to others • Depersonalization – people lose interest in their work, and lose hope that change is possible • Blindness – people come to believe that this is normal	**Social:** The 6 functional areas of the workplace have dysfunctions **Economic:** Many hidden costs are present (the French estimate is 20,000 € ($28,000) per person per year

Figure 8.1 The causes and consequences of the TFW virus.

    departments. We separate generating ideas from the execution of the work. We separate the "noble and menial" tasks, which is to say that those on the bottom of the hierarchy get the really menial tasks and as one rises one has increasingly noble tasks—tasks suited for the elite.

3. Business is about making a profit, so the work process is most important and the value of the person is minimized. Employees, in the end, do not matter much, so when it is convenient it is "ethical" to dispose of employees by firing them. The term for firing many employees, "rightsizing," illustrates this belief.

4. People can and should be submissive to the organization. This also comes from Weber. Since the organization is of primary importance, the needs of the individual are secondary, and employees are expected to submit to the needs of the organization. The needs of course are revealed by the managers, so the meaning is also that one has to be submissive to managers.

THE SYMPTOMS OF THE VIRUS IN THE WORKPLACE

The mystery is: Why do usually smart people, when put into organizations, engage in destructive and wasteful behaviors, without changing and without even believing there is a problem? What makes them so blind? The blindness happens because the beliefs and perceptions that constitute the virus are cleverly hidden in the minds of people. These deep beliefs are frequently unconscious, or at best semi-conscious, and they are only revealed by observing the expression and behaviors of people in the workplace. When Schein (2004) described organizational culture, he highlighted its three levels: artifacts, espoused beliefs, and deep beliefs and values. Organizational espoused values are wonderful. These values are about equality, justice, and fairness, and other similar things. However, when the behaviors are not in accord with the espoused values, it is time to look deeper in order to find the actual values and beliefs that drive behaviors. The virus resides in this inner, invisible place of unquestioned values and beliefs.

When in our consulting work we analyze the causes of organizational dysfunctions and hidden costs, we see that many of them are the result of lack of cooperation among actors within organization. In other words, team work is often lacking. What we find in workplace, more often than teamwork, is separateness, arrogance, and condescension. This observation may be surprising to many people. However, note that while at first this reasoning may seem unreasonable or too extreme, upon scrupulous analysis it can be found true for many organizations. And here is the first example of the virus, a story told us by a manager from a manufacturing company:

> In 2013, the top managers in a manufacturing plant in Minnesota decided that the line workers were not working as hard as they could. There were 18 people on the line, each at a work station. People worked 4 days, 10 hours a day. Most stations had a chair, so one could work standing or sitting. Every 2.5 hours people rotated to a new spot on the line, and we made sure that if they had a spot without a chair, next time they got one.

The engineers, trained in good Taylorist fashion, were redesigning the assembly line, and in their design they removed most chairs from the shop floor. Their thinking was if workers could not sit, they would work more. Management approved the plan. Two chairs were left. One was reserved for a woman who had recently had knee surgery. By medical necessity and company policy she had to have a chair. The workers said nothing, but inwardly fumed at the insult to them of removing the chairs. After three months, the woman who had knee surgery filed a harassment charge. A group of her co-workers constantly teased her about "being so special that she got to have a chair." Eventually the company bought new chairs for the shop floor.

The hidden costs were significant. The harassment suit ate up managers' time. Employees on the line had four months of discomfort, which they did not forget. They also knew that they had been insulted—judged as lazy. Thoughts of comfort, of the physical toll on the body of standing for 10 hours, was not in the engineers' vision. Nor was there any attempt to talk with the workers about the perceived problem.

We are claiming that unhealthy behaviors are actually the norm for organizations in the United States or France and most, if not all, other western nations. Here is the reasoning that leads us to make this claim.

Organizations tend to have espoused values that sound wonderful, but which are not aligned with the deep beliefs and values that shape behavior. We have become so inured to the cruel and selfish ways in which people are treated in organizations that the cruelty is taken for granted and is seen as inevitable. People either do not see the gap between what is espoused and what is actually done, or they dismiss the gap as irrelevant or an exception. For example, organizational theory espouses accountability for all employees. Yet when an organization is financially troubled, the usual recourse is to fire people lower in the hierarchy. The leaders, who made the decisions that led to the problems, are often not fired, or if they are fired they get the golden parachute. The gross unfairness of such behavior is obvious, but few seem to hope that such behavior will change.

Since 1973, intervenor-researchers at the ISEOR in Lyon, France have been observing and cataloging dysfunctional attitudes and behaviors that occur in organizations—these attitudes and behaviors reflect the symptoms of the virus.

- The workplace is fractured—broken into many separate parts, divisions between people
- Heartless processes—the needs of the organization are more important than the needs of the individual
- Elitism—some people are superior to others
- Depersonalization—people lose interest in their work, and lose hope that change is possible
- Blindness—people come to believe that this is normal

The Workplace is Fractured

At the heart of the virus is separation, so organizations with the virus cannot act holistically. The separation is obvious in numerous boundaries that separate units, divisions, or departments. Sometimes these separate parts of an organization are called silos. These silos are treated as separate elements rather than part of a larger system. This contradicts the systems theory, according to which all elements of the system are inter-related and interdependent, and the interaction, or relationship, between the elements are as important as the elements themselves. The impact on any element of the system impacts the whole system as well, which means all other parts of the system are also affected. However the virus works as if elements of the organizational system can be independent, which in turn reduces the ability for the organization to reach its potential efficiency. Examples of borders can be seen in divisions of business functions (production, sales, marketing, finances), workforce (men–women, old–young, superior–subordinates), business focus (long-term vs. short-term, local vs. global, customized vs. mass produced), etc.

The separation in organizations is cleverly disguised as specialization. The result, at its best, is that people, working in silos, see only a little goal of their silo without seeing a bigger picture of the whole organization. At the worst, people in the silos compete with other silos and often fight turf wars, which is detrimental to the organization. In our practice, we have seen examples when some departments in an organization would stifle the creativity of other units because that creativity was perceived as a threat to the department's survival, in spite of the positive effect for the whole organization.

Heartless Processes

Heartless processes are the ways organizations carry out their work without regard to the needs of employees. We know that this is not universal, there are people who care and a number of organizations who try to treat employees well. At the same time, there are many examples of people's needs not met because "there is a rule, and one cannot make exceptions." Here is an example from a manufacturing company.

> We are so busy that there is a lot of mandatory overtime. People work four 10-hour days, and by mandatory overtime rules, they can be forced to work another six hours a week. In addition, during periods of mandatory overtime, people cannot take vacations or family time. Mandatory overtime can go on for four or five weeks in a row. If you do not comply, once, you get written up, meaning no pay raise and no promotion is possible for over six months.

You have to follow the policies. A man's father was slowly dying of cancer, and finally he was put into hospice care. The man had used up all his sick leave for the year. He stayed out of work in the last few days of his father's life, caring for him in hospice. We had to write him up for his absence.

Elitism

The TFW virus is best represented by an elitist or aristocratic view of organizational life. The virus is rooted in the concept of "separateness" which is based on two premises.

The first premise is that some individuals are superior to others. This belief was described in *The Protestant Ethic and the Spirit of Capitalism* (Weber, 1930), in which Weber posited that Puritanism led to the belief that if one is successful, one must be favored by God, otherwise God would not allow the person to be successful. Thus the status reveals that the person has (or has not) been chosen by God. By this philosophy, to be successful means to have a status, or to be in a superior position. The person's faults or shortcomings are not very important.

The second premise stems from the first one. Because people believe they are superior, they have to be seen separately from those who are lower in rank, and thus they need to preserve and reinforce their place. To do this, those who feel superior create a series of laws, rules, and traditions that serve to protect their superior place.

These two premises can be illustrated by two images: the lottery and the royal court. In the image of the lottery, one's fate determines whether the person is "chosen," or in Weber's (1930) words, predestined to lead. So whether one is favored is a matter of chance. The image of the royal court, comes from old times, when having royal blood made a person automatically part of the royal court, which in turn led to having more perks than people of common blood. If one is in the "court," which means in-group, then the person is given prerogatives that are not available to out-groups. Often out-groups are perceived as those who are not smart, not responsible, do not deserve trust, have not evolved, and do not deserve freedom or creative expression.

The idea of separateness leads to a certain mindset that uses the following logic: (a) there are noble tasks and menial tasks; (b) status comes with certain attributes and symbols, which are deserved and important; (c) it is acceptable for leaders to be self-serving; and (d) the self-justification of differences helps to secure the status of those higher in the hierarchy.

Noble Tasks and Menial Tasks

The virus has institutionalized the separation of tasks into noble [pleasant] tasks, and menial [unpleasant] tasks. People who are higher in the organization hierarchy choose the pleasant tasks and delegate the unpleasant tasks to people who are lower in the hierarchy. In other words, the really crappy work is given to people at the bottom of the hierarchy, the "servant class." Why? Because people at the top can choose what they want to do. The espoused logic is that people who have a higher grade and can choose the pleasant tasks must, by rank, have more intelligence and/or more qualifications, so they should not be bothered with the unskilled work. Simple examples are requiring one's secretary to make coffee, or to shop for the boss.

Attributes and Symbols

The logic, affected by the virus, places much importance on the position one occupies in the organizational hierarchy. To demonstrate the higher status, one uses symbols or any other attributes of status. These symbols of higher position become paramount, and actors spend much energy to get them and then to protect these indicators of status. Examples of such symbols are the size and location of one's office, having an office with a door instead of a cubicle, access to the executive dining room, having an assigned parking spot or even a driver; flying business class or having a company jet available. People at the bottom do not get the perks. Why? The virus logic leads to the assumption that they either have not earned or do not deserve them. This is the heritage of Puritan Protestantism about which Weber wrote.

Self-Serving and Delusional Hierarchies

The virus that drives organizational hierarchy undermines the value of human capability and wisdom and endorses privileges for the top of the hierarchy as necessary. Privileges include better accommodations, perks, and salary. People at the top are given more not because they do more, nor because they are more skilled or more wise, but because they are at the top. The espoused reason is that one needs to reward people at the top to hire and retain their expertise.

The belief induced by the virus is that having a high position should bring privileges. Competence is not the criterion, in spite of the espoused claims that managers are always promoted for their skills. The SEAM approach, in contrast, argues that the only justification for managers' positions is their performance.

The Self-Justification of Differences

Of course having privileges is very pleasant and giving up on privileges is difficult. Therefore those in power want to keep their privileges, even if this calls for being arrogant, brutal, or exploitative of other people. The challenge for them is to justify why they have more than others, or why some must be dependent on them to enjoy the few benefits that they are allowed to have.

Here is a comment about training in a manufacturing company, from one of its managers:

> In the manufacturing environment, many supervisors and managers believe that a college degree makes you better. Those without a degree are failures, they are not smart enough. They have little awareness that people on the shop floor have been sifted by circumstances or learning style or language into their position. There is no acknowledgement of the blue collar workers as adult learners.
>
> There is an attitude among leaders that the blue collar workers do not need training. The implicit belief is that training is for white color employees. I have heard, "Oh they do not need to know that" and "It's inappropriate for them to know that." These beliefs are in keeping with the Tayloristic belief that blue collar workers do the menial work, and so do not need to learn anything.
>
> I suspect what happens is blue collar workers often have had a difficult time with education. It may be they are learning in their second language, or they are kinesthetic learners so do not do well with typical classroom training.

The manager also told about the attitude of supervisors.

> I am amazed at 20–30 year old supervisors. I have had eleven in the past year. They come in with a college degree, and maybe two years of experience, usually in retail, not manufacturing. In each one of them the TFW virus has done its work. They all think they are better than the people on the floor.

The Phenomenon of Depersonalization

One of the aspects of the TFW virus is to elevate the needs of the organization over the needs of the individual. The organization as an entity, the mass, is considered to be more important than anything else. Individuals and teams lose a lot of energy in friction, disputes, attending unnecessary events, and doing unnecessary activities. People are worn down and become resigned to their fate, believing that there is no hope of change. In this way, the virus weakens the creative power of the individual and eats away at the individual's vitality.

Fromm (1955) described depersonalization as:

a mode of experience in which the person experiences himself as an alien. He has become, one might say, estranged from himself. He does not experience himself as the center of his world, as the creator of his own acts. (p. 111)

Depersonalization then is the opposite of self-actualization, and results in the diminishing of the human person.

Today, many organizations focus on the organization as an entity without real concern for the individuals. The phenomenon of putting the organization above everything else is what Cristallini and Savall (2014) called *massification*, "the lack of an individualist approach—in which management views its employees as a herd of cattle for which 'you just need barking dogs'" (p. 14). The result is that individuals become depersonalized, they become cogs in the machine rather than individuals who deserve respect and care.

As depersonalization takes hold in organizations, people begin to believe that change is impossible, and freedom in the workplace is not possible. Once the belief spreads over the workplace, there becomes a sense of resignation and hopelessness. In our research, we have found that the resignation and hopelessness can be overcome by managers who listen well to their employees. At the same time, in large organizations, the sense of the organizational mass creates a tremendous pressure to comply with the organizational norms, rather than to treat each person as a valuable individual.

There are a variety of ways in which the importance of the organization or system is emphasized, with the result of devaluing the individual person.

- The job profiles and job descriptions can create rigid definitions of work, without taking into account the needs and abilities of the individual.
- Some systems of equal pay do not take individual effort into account
- The number of people under a single supervisor can be so large that there is no possible way for the supervisor to attend to the actual needs and abilities of each individual being supervised. The SEAM recommendation is 10 employees per supervisor.
- Procedures and standards are applied rigidly, without exception and without flexibility.
- Changes that are made in an organization that happen without consultation with employees, without explanation to employees, and without training for employees whose tasks will change.
- Inequities in the collection of resources lead to situations in which some parts of the organization are given different rules and expectations than others. This leads to inequities in the distribution of resources, either to individuals or to divisions of the organization.

All the points listed above have a trait in common, which is the lack of consideration of the people. The result of the resignation and hopelessness are huge amounts of hidden costs. ISEOR found that in 2014 the average hidden cost per employee per year ranged from €20,000 ($28,000) to €70,000 ($98,000).

Here is another example from a manager in a manufacturing company.

> In my company, funeral leaves are a matter of contention. If a parent dies, one gets a week off, without pay, to deal with all of the family affairs. If it is a relative overseas, one gets two days, without pay. If the family member is local, one gets two hours. A man came into my office, crying. His uncle had raised him. Their relationship was like son and father. The day before, the uncle had had a massive heart attack and died. The man said that he was the one who had to arrange the funeral and take care of the family. He asked for a week off. I knew that this would never be accepted, and gave him two days off. I knew HR would not like this, they would want two hours off, but the man was in deep grief. The workplace would be better off without him grieving in the midst of things, and besides it was wrong not to let him deal with the family needs. I was chewed out by HR. They said I did not have enough managerial courage. Their reasoning was if you let one person go, then you have to let them all go. In other words, what is important to the individual is not important to the company.

The hidden costs of episodes like this include lack of trust in or loyalty to the company, less productive work when one is grieving, when one works with someone who is grieving, or when one is angry because an employee's need to tend to family in a time of death is not honored by the company.

The TFW virus creates serious and destructive effects on people and organizations. This is an ethical problem, because lack of addressing the virus harms people and organizations. It is also an economic problem, because the virus reduces productivity and leads to hidden costs that hurt the organization's ability to reach its potential.

The Blindness That Results From the TFW Virus

One of the effects of the TFW virus is increasing blindness, which prevents people from the ability to critically look at the organizations and actors' modes of behaviors. Lack of a critical viewpoint leads to the assumptions (a) that it is impossible to have organizations that are flexible, cooperative, viable, and (b) more importantly, that organizations can have two foci in sight—achieving financial goals and also taking care of humans.

Chris Argyris (1990) described how, in many organizations, people become blind to what actually is happening and live in a semi-delusional world, in which they pretend to themselves and to others that life is better than it actually is. He called these phenomena "organizational defensive routines." One of the mechanisms that people use to maintain their delusion is *fancy footwork*, which Argyris (1990) described as including actions that permit individuals to be blind to inconsistencies in their actions, or to deny that these inconsistencies even exist, or, if they cannot do either, to place the blame on other people. An example of fancy footwork from our experience is a CEO who claimed he only wanted to help a manager and did not want to micromanage, and then micromanaged. When challenged about this behavior, he would deny that there had been any micromanaging. Here is another glaring example of fancy footwork. Some CEOs make tens of millions of dollars a year. Their earnings, which can be 500 to 2000 times the earnings of someone at the bottom of the hierarchy, are justified with reasons like the need to be competitive for the best leaders. Fancy footwork dances around reason, allowing greed to flourish.

A manager in a manufacturing company told a story about an engineer who was blind to the possibility that the people who did the work knew anything about improvements.

> We were designing a new packing station. Initially this had been done at a kaizen event, but the engineers refused to let any shippers attend. The decision was made that when an item arrived off the line, it would be weighed immediately. The computer would figure out the final weight, and bill accordingly. The shippers unanimously said this would not work. They have to do several things before the final packaging, such as arrange for boxes, packing material, more than one item in the box, and so on. There was too much variability to get an accurate assessment before the shippers did their work. The engineer heard all of this, and in the end refused to believe that his plan would not work.

SEAM as the Antidote to the TFW Virus

Socio-economic theory is based on a set of beliefs about people and work that are significantly different from the beliefs of the virus (see Figure 8.2).

CONCLUSION

The TFW virus is a metaphor. At the same time, the results of the virus are very real. In the end, an organization becomes the host for the virus. And as with every virus, the virus does not kill its host, it makes the host sick. The sickness becomes very apparent, and many either have worked for such sick organizations personally or heard stories about them. The patterns of the sickness are as follows. The dominance of an aristocratic

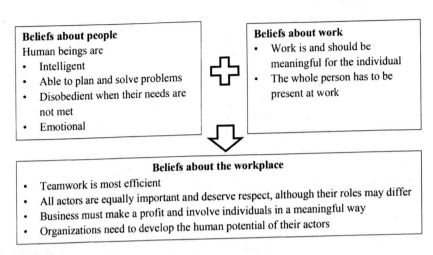

Figure 8.2 Beliefs about people, work, and the workplace on which socio-economic theory is based.

view of organizations is a common phenomenon. The blindness that results from the TFW virus is apparent to anyone who looks at the gap between espoused values and actual practice in the majority of organizations. Many organizations are divided internally, so they cannot work as a smooth system whose efforts aim at the same goals. The phenomenon of depersonalization is the norm and not the exception.

Our experience, as well as 39 years of the research by ISEOR, has shown that the TFW virus is alive and well in Europe and North America, and we suspect everywhere. The chapter on the TFW virus in the American workplace in this book, by Chato Hazelbaker, supports our claim. For some, the virus is transmitted through business school or managerial education. At this point, the mental model of management, shaped by the TFW virus, is part of the culture, so any manager, whether or not formally taught about managing, still has a strong likelihood of having some of the symptoms of the virus. Equally, workers expect the virus, and even if managers are genuinely attempting to manage in a manner that is respectful of each individual, many employees will project onto these managers their virus-induced hopelessness.

Is there a way to overcome the effects of the TFW Virus? Yes, such a way exists. The first step is naming the problem, and that was the purpose of this paper. Once the effect or presence of the virus are admitted, one can begin to counteract the virus. The next step is fixing the actual problems, which is the purpose of a SEAM intervention. In the process, the SEAM intervention beliefs are changed to be more in line with those in Figure 8.2.

We do have examples of organizations that work democratically and are very effective; they respect and value all actors by developing human potential and bringing a human soul back into a workplace. Let us make these rare examples a norm.

REFERENCES

Argyris, A. (1990). *Overcoming Organizational Defenses.* Needham Heights, MA: Allyn and Bacon.

Cristallini, V., & Savall, H. (2014). The Taylorism-Fayolism-Weberism virus. In H. Savall, J. P. Conbere, A. Heorhiadi, V. Cristallini, & A. F. Buono. (Eds.), *Facilitating the socio-economic approach to management: Results of the first SEAM conference in North America* (pp. 13–18). Charlotte, NC: Information Age.

Fromm, E. (1955). *The Sane Society.* Greenwich, CT: Fawcett Publications.

Houghton, J. D. (2010). Does Max Weber's notion of authority still hold in the twenty-first century? *Journal of Management History, 16* (4): 449–453.

Pryor, M. G., & Taneja, S. (2010). Henri Fayol, practitioner and theoretician—Revered and reviled. *Journal of Management History, 16* (4): 489–503.

Savall, H. (2010). *Work and people: An economic evaluation of job-enrichment.* Charlotte, NC: Information Age Publishing.

Savall, H., & Zardet, V. (2008). *Mastering hidden costs and socio-economic performance.* Charlotte, NC: Information Age Publishing.

Savall, H., & Zardet, V. (2009, June). *Mesure et pilotage de la responsabilité sociale et sociétale de l'entreprise : résultats de recherches longitudinales* [*Measuring and piloting the corporate social responsibility: results from longitudinal research*]. International conference proceedings and doctoral consortium, partnership between the Academy of Management (AOM) and Iseor, Lyon.

Savall, H., & Zardet, V. (2009a, July). *Responsabilidad social y societal de la empresa: Indicadores para dialogar con las partes interesadas* [*The corporate social responsibility: Indicators to converse with stakeholders*]. Paper presented at the ACACIA's Conference proceedings, UAM–México.

Savall, H., & Zardet, V. (2009b, September). *Los indicadores de pilotaje de la responsabilidad social y societal de la empresa resultados de experimentación* [*Piloting indicators of the corporate social responsibility—results of experiments*]. Paper presented at the 11th international conference of costs and management proceedings, Argentinian Conference of audit and cost academics, Trelew, Argentina.

Savall, H., & Zardet, V. (2010). Le non-dit dans la théorie socio-économique des organisations: Situations de management et pièces de théâtre [Unvoiced comment in the socio-economic theory of organizations: Management situations and theatrics]. In R. Ocler (Ed.), *Fantasmes, mythes, non-dits et quiproquo: Analyse de discours et organisation [Fantasy, myths, unvoiced and misunderstanding: Analysis of speech and organization].* Paris, France: L'Harmattan.

Schein, E. H. (2004). *Organization culture and leadership.* San Francisco, CA: Jossey-Bass.

Schachter, H. L. (2010). The role played by Frederick Taylor in the rise of the academic management fields. *Journal of Management History, 16* (4): 437–448.

Weber, Max (1930). *The Protestant Ethic and the Spirit of Capitalism.* London, England: Routledge.

Weisbord, M. (2011). *Productive Workplaces: Dignity, Meaning, and Community in the 21st Century 3rd Edition, 25 Year Anniversary.* Hoboken, NJ: Wiley, John, & Sons.

CHAPTER 9

LOOKING FOR EVIDENCE OF THE TFW VIRUS

A Case Study

Chato Hazelbaker

CONFERENCE REMARKS
Chapter Prologue

Chato Hazelbaker

I found evidence of the virus in every turn in a company that by every measure you and I would want to go to work for, in sort of the classic U.S. model. So why does this matter and I think this is where I'm going to throw out, very quickly, a couple of relatively radical ideas. The main thing that I think occurred to me is that ideology matters and we don't talk nearly enough about ideology. Ideology is what's driving our behaviors and it's what's driving behaviors in the workplace but is almost never talked about. I looked for and found one very good text on management and ideology written in 1980 that was specifically about management ideology and when I looked at accounting textbooks and I looked at other things, I found a common ideology but almost no discussion of that ideology. So the ideology that's moving forward is clearly the TFW Virus but nobody's talking TFW. They're just putting out this sort of virus as this is just an accepted fact; that is just the way that you do business in the United States.

So ideology is probably the most important thing I got out of this and I come back to it again and again. Really, ideology matters. We don't talk about it enough and we don't talk about it early enough. This requires, I think, a radical rethinking of management education and when I say radical, I was born in a very small town in Montana. I'm about as middle of the road, middle class as you can possibly get. I am a very, very reluctant and odd radical but I'm a very radical organizational thinker now because I absolutely think we need to burn it down. I absolutely think that the way we think about organizations is completely wrong and, when in my dissertation defense the other day Vincent said that he thought the implications of not recognizing the TFW Virus and doing something different was actually sort of the end to civilization, I didn't argue with him. I said "Amen."

Americans are not very excited about work. Disengagement is at epidemic levels. Gallup's (2013) "State of the American workplace report" classified 70% of the American workforce as disengaged with an annual cost of $450 to $550 billion. As I began my dissertation, I was interested in finding out more about why we are so disengaged, and why there seems to be so little conversation about what this disengagement really means and the effect on organizations. I also wanted to learn more about why Americans seem to expect so little of our workplaces.

One possible reason that Americans are disengaged at work was introduced to me by studying the Socio Economic Approach to Management (SEAM) as founded by Henri Savall at the Socio-Economic Institute of Firms and Organizations Research (ISEOR) in Lyon, France. SEAM is an approach to management that has been tremendously successful in helping organizations thrive, improve the lives of workers, and improve economic returns. Its success is partly rooted in the fact that it is one of the most closely studied change management programs in the world (Conbere & Heorhiadi, 2011). The body of knowledge is expanded through ISEOR, the institute teaching SEAM. ISEOR maintains an extensive database of outcomes from SEAM interventions, and contributes to an ongoing field of study through conferences, articles, and books.

Through ISEOR, Savall, Zardet, and their colleagues identified what they see as an underlying ideological flaw in the approach to management and used the analogy of a virus to help explain its impact (Cristallini, 2011). They named the virus TFW for Taylor, Fayol, and Weber, the three individuals they credit with promoting the management ideology that is at the heart of the virus. Taylor and Taylorism is well known to Americans with backgrounds in manufacturing. Taylor was one of the first to do time studies in factories near the turn of the previous century. He is credited with developing the idea of hyper-specialization, and separating the management of the task from the individual performing the task. American readers do not as commonly recognize Fayol and Weber. Fayol is French and Weber is German. Fayol was a proponent of the separation of business functions and specialization. A sociologist, Weber built an ideal model for organizations based on rules, a system which largely mirrors the modern idea in America of a legal bureaucracy.

THE TFW VIRUS

From the beginning, the work of Taylor, Fayol, and Weber has been a focus of research and discussion for ISEOR. Essentially, SEAM is the solution to the problem the researchers named the TFW Virus. Savall and Zardet first put forth the metaphor of the virus in 2006, and presented the concept to conferences in France, Mexico, and Argentina in 2009 (Savall & Zardet, 2009, 2009a, 2009b) and in the Academy of Management Conference in 2013 (Savall & Zardet, 2013). When thinking about the nature of the beliefs that damage the way people manage in organizations, the metaphor of a virus makes sense for three reasons:

- The virus is ideological in nature, contaminating decision making and analysis at a foundational level
- The virus causes changes in organizational structures and behavior
- The virus is continually transmitted within and to other organizations through training, practice, and management education

Cristallini (2011) described the virus as the root cause for the hidden costs and dysfunctions that ISEOR finds in organizations. He asserted that organizations are carrying this hidden virus. It is going undiagnosed, and current organizational change efforts are treating symptoms of the virus rather than the core problems of the organization which is the presence of the virus.

The TFW virus infects organizations with an ideological flaw at a foundational level. Since organizational behaviors are based on this flawed ideology the organization is less effective than it has the potential to be. This is evidenced by the work of ISEOR as interventions consistently find hidden costs that can be returned to the bottom line. These ideological underpinnings go unnoticed because few are looking there, and there are powers in place that discourage any one looking at the foundation.

The virus promotes a specific view of individuals that is core to the idea of SEAM, that is that for organizations to thrive they need to grow human potential. The key way that the virus inhibits this growth is by spreading a false view of individuals and their potential. Cristallini (2011) made the case that the proponents of the TFW virus view individuals as untrustworthy, and not intelligent or responsible. The individual is not free. In contrast to this, SEAM sees the individual as creative, and able to grow, change, and be trusted to do what is helpful to the organization given the chance.

The virus promotes the view of individuals as untrustworthy with the health of the organization and even the protection of their own interests. This baseline belief about the individual leads to the conclusion that individuals must be controlled in order to do what is in their best interest and the best interest of the organization. The effect of this view of individuals is manifested in the symptoms of the TFW virus.

LAUNCHING THE CASE STUDY

In order to look further into the TFW Virus and determine if it had an effect, I chose to engage in an interpretive case study as part of my dissertation research. The purpose of this interpretive case study was to discover if management practices in America revealed evidence of the TFW virus. By understanding the management practices that reveal the TFW virus, organizations would be able to look more closely at the virus and some of the strategies employed in SEAM to improve management practices. The research question was, "Do management practices of American organizations reveal and transmit the TFW Virus?"

Case study was the methodology that I chose because I wanted to get past the surface behaviors and see if I could find evidence for what was behind these behaviors.

Site of the Study

I chose a manufacturing site that appeared healthy, so there would be no obvious external factor, like mass layoffs or a recent transition in leadership. I refer to the site that was selected for the dissertation as Manufacturing Corp. to keep the confidentiality of the organization. Manufacturing Corp. is a manufacturing facility in the Pacific Northwest of the United States. The company owns similar manufacturing plants across the United States with a corporate headquarters in California. At the plant I studied they make high tech products that are used in manufacturing other products. The company as a whole is publically held with over a billion dollars in annual revenue.

During the course of the Case Study I interviewed 19 individuals, completed observations at the facility, and reviewed documents.

EVIDENCE OF THE TFW VIRUS

Two key resources helped define the four manifestations of the virus I used in the study. One was Cristallini's (2011) original work of which I had a translation from the French, and the second was a working paper by Conbere, Heorhiadi, & Cristallini (2014) that further refined the concepts of the TFW Virus and built on them. While there is some difference in terms, there is agreement that the virus can be observed in workers and in the organization in the exhibition of: depersonalization and submission, an aristocratic view of the organization, apathy, and separation.

FINDINGS

Themes

Themes are the key ideas having importance related to the case (Stake, 2013). Throughout my analysis, several of these ideas kept occurring across people and across shifts, though some variation is noted below. One of the challenges in developing the themes is that at the level of espoused values, individuals expressed a great deal of satisfaction with Manufacturing Corp. However, the more time I spent working with the data, listening to interviews, and reflecting on what I had heard, I began to see patterns of underlying assumptions and beliefs that drove what was happening inside Manufacturing Corp. and inside the lives of the people working there.

Five themes emerged. The first was that individuals expressed sentiment that Manufacturing Corp. was a good place to work. All of the individuals I interviewed spoke highly of the company in general terms when we started to talk, with some individuals sounding like they were actively recruiting for the company. Not one person expressed any desire to leave Manufacturing Corp. or that they were actively looking for other work. Pay and benefits, stability, positive relationships with managements, and a commitment to Lean Manufacturing were all noted as being reasons to work at Manufacturing Corp.

Despite the positive expressions about Manufacturing Corp. as a workplace, most employees expressed that they felt individually unimportant in the overall organization. This was most acute among the floor workers. Overall, employees at Manufacturing Corp. expressed low expectations for the role of work in life, which stemmed partly from feelings of a lack of control, little chance for advancement and boredom in the day to day tasks at work.

Individuals at Manufacturing Corp. expressed strong feelings that they as individuals were doing the right things and working hard, and in most cases felt that was true on their shifts or among the groups closest to them. However, once they began talking there often seemed to be a group of "others" who did not share those same values or perform to the same level. This most often manifested itself when talking about communication problems, interpersonal conflict, favoritism, and the subject of other's work ethic.

People reported isolation and separation from others at Manufacturing Corp. There are the walls, windows, clean room suits, and other factors that make up physical isolation. Part of it is also that it is a very large facility populated by few workers per square foot. Separation between shifts occurs and people do not often move from shift to shift meaning this separation is often long term. Discussed above the clean room environment requires a dress code that provides an additional level of isolation. At the floor worker level, observation and the interviews also indicate that individual jobs are very distinct. People do not move from one part of the process to another, and each job is made up of a set of tasks and then the product is moved on along the line to the next person who completes tasks. The majority of a floor worker's shift is engaged with the product, only interacting with other people in the plant when handing off the product to the next step or if something had gone wrong.

Throughout the organization there was a common view of management. One of the key ideas that came out was a shared organizational view of management categorized by command and control. Both the supervisors and floor workers indicated that the job of the manager was to control what happened. One man summed up the view of the supervisors overall by stating, "People want to be led, they want their problems solved." How people came to their ideas in management seemed to be consistently from what had come before them, and what they saw happening at Manufacturing Corp.

Below, the themes are expressed in overarching categories, evidenced by several comments and behaviors captured Table 9.1. I have added a key quote which sums up what a group of individuals reported.

Connecting Themes and Evidence of the TFW Virus

The TFW virus is ideological. As stated earlier, an ideology is a system of beliefs, values, and practices that reflect what is happening inside the organization. In the themes I could observe the practices and I heard about the beliefs and values. However, the real question for the study is where did this ideology come from and indicate the presence of the TFW virus?

The analogy of a virus works well to explain the next phase of the study because the themes show evidence or symptoms of the virus. I had to look at the themes and compare that to the evidence of the virus to see if a causal connection could be made.

TABLE 9.1   Themes and Key Quotes

Theme	Expressed by	Supporting Quote
Expressed sentiment that Manufacturing Corp is a good place to work	Positive expressions about pay and benefits Feelings of company stability Positive relationships with management Commitment to Lean Manufacturing	"Good benefits" "Layoffs are big in this industry and Manufacturing Corp. is better than most at holding onto people." "The best [supervisor] I have had in the past ten years." "Lean has taken hold,"
Individual feelings of unimportance	Low expectations for role of work in life No chance for advancement Lack of Control Boredom	"It pays the mortgage." "You are never going to make it out of production." "We worked so hard yesterday and then sometimes you come in and it's like—we're testing again." "I see a lot of bored people."
Suspicion and Lack of Trust	Communication problems Interpersonal Conflict Favoritism Complaints of others "Work Ethic"	"The biggest discouragement for me isn't projects it is the people issues." "Management turns a blind eye." "…watching people sit around while I'm busting my ass."
Isolation and separation	Separation by level in organization Separation by shift	"Management only talks to supervisors," "I don't feel like the other shifts are held accountable,"
A common view of management	Management as command and control A common path to management	"The main goal is productivity, making sure people are doing their jobs." "Learned under the people I worked under."
Expressed sentiment that Manufacturing Corp is a good place to work	Positive expressions about pay and benefits Feelings of company stability Positive relationships with management Commitment to Lean Manufacturing	

Going back to the research question, "Do management practices of American organizations reveal and transmit the TFW Virus?" the themes gave me an understanding of how people experience the work place. Because the virus is a metaphor for a set of beliefs and values underlying the behaviors, the next step of matching up the themes with the possible evidence of the virus was needed to answer the research question. It is the relationship between the themes and the evidence of the virus that is of primary importance to the research question. As I worked through this part of the analysis I asked myself, "In what people are saying, are they expressing things that could be explained by the presence of the TFW virus?" (See Table 9.2).

Depersonalization and Submission

Evidence of depersonalization and submission was not hard to find at Manufacturing Corp. because in many ways one of the unstated goals of the organization is to make processes as repeatable and as simple as possible, with each person doing the same thing the exact same way. Depersonalization and submission are also connected to the themes of individual feelings of unimportance and a common view of management. Though no one spoke about these in the interviews there are also several physical manifestations of depersonalization.

The nature of the shift work is depersonalizing. For instance, three workers spoke of a shift that they had previously worked over the weekend. They missed that shift. There did not seem to be discussion or options and even though the previous shift worked better for them because they felt they could better manage their personal lives, when the shift was moved over they were simply reassigned. Another small physical signal of depersonalization is in the dress code of workers in the "clean rooms." While clearly important for the manufacturing process, it is hard to tell one worker in a clean suit from another. Even little things like gender or age are hard to discern.

Many individuals expressed high levels of engagement during Lean events. However, what they talked about most was how engaging it was to be part of the process in which they changed something. One man expressed his joy, "We came up with the system." He explained that not only did his facility benefit, but a sister system benefitted as well as they adopted the same system. While the stated goal is to continuously improve in Lean management, another goal is also standardization, and that does not get the same level of support from workers.

Submission was also clearly present. One of the first things that happened in the training process is that one was introduced to the "job instruction

TABLE 9.2   Connecting Themes and the TFW Virus

Theme	Expressed By	Supporting Quote	As Evidence of the TFW Virus
Expressed sentiment that Manufacturing Corp is a good place to work	Positive expressions about pay and benefits	"Good benefits"	Apathy
	Feelings of company stability	"Layoffs are big in this industry and Manufacturing Corp. is better than most at holding onto people."	
	Positive Relationships With Management	"The best [supervisor] I have had in the past ten years."	
	Commitment to Lean Manufacturing	"Lean has taken hold."	
Individual feelings of unimportance	Low expectations for role of work in life	"It pays the mortgage."	Apathy
	No chance for advancement	"You are never going to make it out of production."	Depersonalization and Submission
	Lack of Control	"We worked so hard yesterday and then sometimes you come in and it's like—we're testing again."	
	Boredom	"I see a lot of bored people."	
Suspicion and Lack of Trust	Communication problems Interpersonal Conflict	"The biggest discouragement for me isn't projects it is the people issues."	Separations
	Favoritism	"Management turns a blind eye."	Apathy
	Complaints of others "Work Ethic"	"…watching people sit around while I'm busting my ass."	Aristocratic Approaches

(continued)

TABLE 9.2   Connecting Themes and the TFW Virus (continued)

Theme	Expressed By	Supporting Quote	As Evidence of the TFW Virus
Isolation and separation	Separation by level in organization	"Management only talks to supervisors."	Aristocratic Approaches
	Separation by shift	"I don't feel like the other shifts are held accountable."	Separations
A common view of management	Management as command and control	"The main goal is productivity, making sure people are doing their jobs."	Aristocratic Approaches and Depersonalization and Submission
	A common path to management	"Learned under the people I worked under."	Depersonalization and Submission
Expressed sentiment that Manufacturing Corp is a good place to work	Positive expressions about pay and benefits		
	Feelings of company stability		
	Positive relationships with management		
	Commitment to Lean Manufacturing		

sheets." A supervisor described training in a group of new hires on these sheets and his discouragement that they did not seem to follow the exact steps at the end of the training period. Again, there are business reasons at Manufacturing Corp., but there is also a depersonalizing element as well. The job a new person may learn during the training process may only change a few times over a ten or twenty year career.

When interviewing both floor supervisors and floor workers about their views about the role of management there was evidence of the cold technocratic approach of rule-making and enforcement that Cristallini (2011) indicated existed as an element of depersonalization. "Making sure people are doing their jobs," was the primary role of a supervisor according to one supervisor interviewed. Others echoed that, stating that they were largely concerned with the numbers and production.

An Aristocratic View of the Organization

The aristocratic view of the organization means that within the organization there is a chosen or privileged group within the organization and a class that is not part of the privileged class. According to Conbere et al. (2014) this is particularly seen when some individuals are superior over others, which results in those in power creating rules, regulations, and separating task in such a way to maintain the privilege of those perceived to be superior.

The aristocratic view of the organization was obvious when individuals talked about their view of management. There was a separation between management and floor workers and part of that separation was based on rank, both in the difficulty that people expressed moving into management, and the way that they talked about the role of management. Simply put, one position was higher than the other and was perceived to have special privileges. People also had an aristocratic view of shifts, noting that some shifts were favorable because those shifts overlapped with management, and that proximity to the top people led to more benefits. The privilege in this case is that the day shift workers received more recognition and had a chance to work on projects that would benefit their careers. The day shift was perceived as chosen, the night shift was not.

Apathy

Apathy is a lack of interest in work. Apathy seemed to come through most clearly under the theme of individual feelings of unimportance, but it was also found in the theme of suspicion and mistrust, and in individuals' expressed sentiments that Manufacturing Corp. is a good place to work. While this sentiment was positive, from the standpoint of the virus I got the sense that part of what is meant is that this is as good a workplace that particular workers think they could hope for.

Evidence of apathy and a lack of hope in the organization comes through in the low level of expectations that individuals have in the role of work in their lives. I was haunted by how well the statement, "It pays the mortgage," seems to sum up the expectations of work. Work was not seen as a source of energy, but rather as simply transactional with workers expecting only financial compensation for the time they spent in the manufacturing facility.

A lack of hope could clearly be found in the feeling that there is no room for advancement at the floor worker level. Workers at Manufacturing Corp. have on average been there a long time, and most clearly saw themselves in those same places for several years to come. In talking about interpersonal issues, people also expressed apathy in that they just did not have hope that they would get better. They simply felt that they were stuck with whatever interpersonal issues or conflicts they had.

The lack of hope was also seen in that workers reported both being bored and that they intentionally disengage or try not to pay attention because they find engaging frustrating. A participant stated, "You can't have a perfect job or a perfect company, but here is close." While this is indeed high praise, he also stated that he tried not to pay attention because it was discouraging to be too aware of what was happening.

Separations

Evidence of separations at work is found in the building of borders, walls and fences, and divisions where people interface either with other people or with technology. Separations are not hard to find in the themes and show up in the themes suspicion and lack of trust and isolation and separation. Separations can most acutely be seen between shifts, where individuals spoke of a competitiveness and communication challenges across shifts. Separations are also related to the aristocratic view, as people also expressed that there were separations based on rank in the company. Separations occur even within shifts as each part of the manufacturing process identifies with itself not in relation to the others.

CONCLUSION AND IMPLICATIONS

I found the more time I spent with the data, the more the major themes began to emerge and the more I found myself thinking about evidence that indicated the TFW Virus. In a way, it felt like a cycle of going from the data, to themes, to the virus, and then back to the data to ensure consistency. The reason this cycle emerged is because of the strong overlap between themes. Each of the themes were interconnected, suggesting a way of thinking in the organization that went beyond the experience of an isolated individual. At the end of the study I came to clearly believe that the TFW Virus was present in this organization.

There are three key implications I drew from the study and the previous work done on the TFW Virus. The first is that ideology matters, and that leads into the second implication that because of the existing ideology we may need to radically rethink management education and Organization Development (OD).

Ideology "...describes the system of beliefs, values, and practices that reflects and reproduces existing social structures, systems, and relations" (Brookfield, 2005, p. 68). An ideology is put forth as the true system of belief within the dominant group and is propagated as the one true way. Seeing the underlying ideology helped me to understand why the behaviors that I witnessed and heard about exist at Manufacturing Corp.

The main implication for me is that ideology matters. One of the criticisms that I can anticipate of this case study is that ideology is unimportant to individuals in the organization, and is unimportant to the goals of the organization. However, that argument in itself betrays an ideology. Edward Deming is credited with saying, "Every organization is perfectly designed to produce the results it's producing" (Clawson, 2012, p. 122). The ideology of the organization is the foundation of that design, and this case demonstrates that at Manufacturing Corp. there is an existing ideology that is consistent with the TFW Virus.

Manufacturing Corp. did not set out to have this ideology. In fact, it probably set out with positive motives, but in the themes I found the "virus ideology" inside the company. Behavior communicates the ideology of an organization, and in this case it was the themes gained from witnessing the behavior that brought me to identifying the ideological makeup of Manufacturing Corp. At the conclusion of this study, I saw that Manufacturing Corp. is a place where depersonalization, an aristocratic view, apathy, and separations were all apparent.

The founders of SEAM argue that over the past forty or fifty years the global marketplace has changed in such a way that the previous ways of management, with their basis in the work of Taylor, Fayol, and Weber are unable to meet what this new marketplace demands. They encourage a management style, "based on teamwork, involvement and empowerment, training, communication, and negotiation" (Savall, Zardet, & Bonnet, 2008, p. 11). Based on the discussions I had with supervisors and leaders at Manufacturing Corp., I believe they would agree that they see their current management style as being the best for their future, but I seem to have no shortage of evidence where they are doing things that inhibit those very things. It is the presence of the virus that explains why they are not able to make good on the promise to build this new style of management.

If the data indicates the clear presence of the TFW Virus in a specific U.S. manufacturing organization one of the questions I continually asked myself toward the end of the project was, "Does it matter?" This question kept coming up as I reflected on the fact that, as stated above, Manufacturing Corp. appears to be a very good place to work, and it turns a profit. In the end, I concluded that it matters because Manufacturing Corp. will never be able to sustain and grow its success if the current ideology is allowed to persist. If that happens, rather than growing the "human capital," they will burn it up. If you treat human beings like fuel in the industrial machine they eventually go the way of all fuel, they get costlier and costlier and then eventually used up. If you look at people as a resource, something that can be grown, the potential for ongoing production is limitless.

Depersonalization and submission matter because people do not do their best work when they do not engaged at a deeper level. With depersonalization and submission you can get people to change their behaviors, but not fully engage their hearts which is the true key to leadership and productivity.

The aristocratic view of the organization makes a difference because if people feel that they are born into their place or that they are not among the chosen then they are likely to strive to move beyond that. Additionally, in the modern, globalized workplace it has been proven that the best decisions are made by diverse teams. Organizations with and aristocratic view are inherently going to deny the contributions of some, leading to fewer ideas and again, less creation of human capital. In the aristocratic (or bureaucratic) organization, time is spent creating and enforcing rules that keep the aristocracy in place. A tremendous amount of organizational energy is wasted as individuals seek to control rather than to create.

Apathy keeps workers from contributing their best ideas and best selves to the workplace. At a place like Manufacturing Corp. this may show up in subtle ways like high absenteeism, but it is also dangerous and costly. In the manufacturing process there are times when not being fully engaged can lead to dangerous situations with machinery, chemicals, or other workplace hazards. Beyond that, as one person point out, in the organization there exists the possibility for million dollar mistakes. Each defect in the product is potentially damaging to the long-term bottom line for the company.

Separations may be the area that I have seen most commonly and are the most costly. When I think about the time and energy spent trying to get people to work together, or people and machines to interact, I see thousands of hours in lost productivity and energy sapping conflict. Because the conflict is negative and largely interpersonal, there is not the energy that comes from creative friction as people work together to solve problems. At Manufacturing Corp. many of these separations were reported as communication problems, and in my experience I see that time and time again. When people do not agree, they sometimes put the blame on the communication as a way of depersonalizing it and separating. However, this has the effect of making the separation wider.

One of the affects in an organization infected with the TFW Virus is chronic underperformance due to the loss of human potential. Organizations with the virus are not reaching their full potential, nor are individual employees reaching their full potential. In an organization like Manufacturing Corp. this may not be readily apparent as the current market forces do not require them to develop potential, but at some point it will.

Another effect of the TFW Virus is an ever increasing bureaucracy (Merkle, 1980). The divisions that take place require additional levels of management, and more and more separation is encouraged. This is a direct effect of Fayol's approach to managerial separation, and Weber wrote explicitly that bureaucracy had the effect of creating more bureaucracy. There are two areas of potential thinking about this. One is that organizations could be improved and made more profitable by effectively cutting down on bureaucracy and division. This is not a new idea. For instance in any company, workers immediately call for cuts in "management" when times come. However, like many of the implications of the TFW Virus, it caused me to ask, "What if they are right?" The TFW Virus expands the administration. The second related implication to this explosion of the administrative class is what the effect is on systemized thinking. This seems to be a key skill that successful businesses are employing, but the inertia created by the virus seems to reward ever widening division (Merkle, 1980) rather than encouraging the systematic thinking that so many organizations say they need today to be successful.

Implications for Management and Leadership

The presence of the TFW virus as a flawed ideology demands nothing less than a radical rethinking of management and leadership education. After framing the ideas of depersonalization and submission in the ways above, I needed to go further and ask if these are really a problem. Cristallini (2011) makes a compelling case that these concepts are indeed problematic. Additionally, in the words Einstein, "If you behave in the way you have always behaved you are going to get the results you have always gotten." Few would argue that the organization results we see in contemporary America are without room for improvement.

Implications for OD

In the world of OD there are implications at the micro and at the macro level. The entire idea of being an OD consultant owes itself somewhat to Taylor as he was one of the very first to work as a management consultant (Merkle, 1980). In his foundation book on OD, Marv Weisbord (2004) stated, "Indeed, he has stimulated all the social scientists whose lives I sketch in the next several chapters" (p. 27). If I have made the argument that Taylor, Fayol, and Weber at the heart of management ideology, it begs the question if the field of organization development has dealt fully with its own possible problems with the TFW Virus. However, in a more hopeful mode it might also explain why some OD interventions are less successful than others and call for us to continue to evolve.

Final Thoughts

There is arrogance in applying the elements of this case study to call for a fundamental rethinking of management education, OD practice, and the way that American organizations are managed on a day-to-day basis. Having that discussion allows us to talk at a core level about what we think and believe and those are likely to be hard discussions. It is also likely that in those discussions we will have to question some people and practices that have gone years without critical study.

As I was working on the final chapters of this study it was the work of Chris Argyris (2000) that I turned to for inspiration. In opening his book, *Flawed Advice and the Management Trap,* Argyris took on a few of the biggest names in leadership and pointed out gaps in their advice. He points out that it is the inconsistencies that are getting in the way of the good that each author is trying to encourage and states, "We need to better understand the costs—often the hidden costs—of this pattern, as well as the unintended consequences to which it so often leads" (p. 37). Imagining a better future for workers, organizations, and communities requires us to look at our ideology, and make sure that behaviors in our organizations are reflective of espoused organizational values.

REFERENCES

Argyris, C. (2000). *Flawed advice and the management trap: How managers can know when they're getting good advice and when they're not.* Oxford, United Kingdom: New York.

Brookfield, S. D. (2005) *The power of critical theory: Liberating adult learning and teaching.* San Francisco: CA: Jossey-Bass.

Clawson, J. G. (2012). *Level three leadership: Getting below the surface* (5th ed.). Boston, MA: Prentice Hall.

Conbere, J., & Heorhiadi, A. (2011). Socio-economic approach to management. *OD Practitioner, 43*(1), 6–10.

Conbere, J., Heorhiadi, A., & Cristallini, V. (2014). *The TFW virus: Why so many organizations act in ways that hurt their interests* (Working paper).

Cristallini, V. (2011, March). *The role of governance in the fight against the global pandemic of the techno-economic virus.* Working paper. Paris, France.

Gallup Inc., (2013). *The state of the American workplace: Employee engagement insights for U.S. business leaders.* Washington D.C.

Merkle, J. (1980). *Management and ideology: The legacy of the international scientific management movement.* Berkeley, CA: University of California Press.

Savall, H. & Zardet, V. (2009, June). *Mesure et pilotage de la responsabilité sociale et sociétale de l'entreprise: résultats de recherches longitudinales [Measuring and piloting the corporate social responsibility: results from longitudinal research].* International conference proceedings and doctoral consortium, partnership between the Academy of Management (AOM) and Iseor, Lyon.

Savall, H., & Zardet, V. (2009a, July). *Responsabilidad social y societal de la empresa: Indicadores para dialogar con las partes interesadas [The corporate social responsibility: Indicators to converse with stakeholders].* Paper presented at the ACACIA's Conference proceedings, UAM–México.

Savall, H., & Zardet, V. (2009b, September). *Los indicadores de pilotaje de la responsabilidad social y societal de la empresa resultados de experimentación [Piloting indicators of the corporate social responsibility—Results of experiments].* Paper presented at the 11th international conference of costs and management proceedings. Argentinian Conference of audit and cost academics, Trelew, Argentina.

Savall, H., & Zardet, V. (2010). Le non-dit dans la théorie socio-économique des organisations: situations de management et pièces de théâtre [Unvoiced comment in the socio-economic theory of organizations: Management situations and theatrics]. In R. Ocler (Ed.), *Fantasmes, mythes, non-dits et quiproquo: Analyse de discours et organisation [Fantasy, myths, unvoiced and misunderstanding: Analysis of speech and organization].* Paris, France: L'Harmattan.

Savall, H., & Zardet, V. (2013, August). *Linking Individual, Organizational, and Macro-economic Performance Levels: Hidden Costs Model.* International conference Academy of Management (AOM), Orlando, Florida.

Savall, H., & Zardet, V. (2008). *Mastering hidden costs and socio-economic performance.* Charlotte, NC: Information Age.

Savall H., Zardet V., & Bonnet M. (2008). *Releasing the Untapped Potential of Enterprises Through Socio-Economic Management.* Genève, Switzerland: ILO-BIT.

Stake, R. E. (1978). The case study method in social inquiry. *Educational Researcher, 7* (2), 5–8.

Weisbord, Marvin. (2004). *Productive workplaces revisited.* Hoboken, NJ: Pfeiffer.

CHAPTER 10

ENHANCING ORGANIZATIONAL AGILITY THROUGH SOCIO-ECONOMIC MANAGEMENT CONSULTING

A Case Study

Marc Bonnet and Véronique Zardet

The concept of agility has been developed by Williams, Worley, & Lawler (2013) through noticing that many companies had hard times in implementing the strategy. Tom Williams and Steve Wheeler (2009) observe that large companies are efficient in the process of designing strategies, but have a hard time in implementing strategies. Cummings & Worley (2008) (Center of Effective Organizations) have demonstrated that efficiency results from the ability to learn and change. Cummings et al. have carried out a research scheme on agility which shows that the ability to change is difficult to learn, as evidenced by the high failure rate of organization change processes. This paper is aimed at showing the contribution of the Socio-Economic Approach to Management (SEAM) to management consulting focused on agility enhancement.

Decoding the Socio-Economic Approach to Management, pages 163–183

SEAM CONTRIBUTION TO MANAGEMENT CONSULTING INTERVENTIONS AIMED AT ENHANCING AGILITY

A seminal book had been published by H. Savall in 1974 (Savall, 1981), followed by many other books (Savall & Zardet, 2008) based on over 1,350 experiments in 39 countries assuming that agility is enhanced by SEAM interventions because CEOs and company actors realize that lack of agility results in a huge amount of hidden costs. Socio-economic experiments also show that intangible investment needed to improve agility is paid back within one year, provided that companies implement a socio-economic management control, which enables the conversion of hidden costs into economic performance. This economic performance consists both in immediate results and creation of potential. One of the main findings is that the calculation of hidden costs stemming from poor agility unfreezes organizational defensive routines and speeds up the organizational learning processes and strategies required to get pro-activity. The conversion of hidden costs into performance through those processes results in improved agility through organizational metamorphosis processes. Organizational metamorphosis differentiates from other approaches to improve agility in that it taps endogenous resources and the hidden energy of the Human Potential of companies, as opposed to organizational restructuring.

Definitions of Organization Agility

Agile companies or organizations are those that out-perform for a long period of time the average performance of companies in the same industry. Their system of routines enables them to pro-actively react over time to the need of change. These agile companies orchestrate simultaneously four domains of managerial practice:

- *Strategizing* requires that top management teams shape a vision and design a strategic plan that is shared throughout the company. It is also necessary to implement a healthy social climate and to involve all employees in the implementation of the strategy.
- *Perceiving* means analyzing and interpreting change signals in the environment. It requires an ongoing, broad and in-depth analysis of the environment in order to monitor the changes. Changes perception have to be reported rapidly to decision makers in order to be interpreted so as to formulate appropriate responses.
- *Testing.* Agile companies experiment innovations, they implement those experiments and learn from them.

- *Implementing.* The most promising changes are implemented, they are both complex and incremental and their impacts on performance have to be assessed step by step.

SEAM Contribution to Agility

The HORIVERT principle. SEAM is a method that overarches all the company managerial processes. It involves both top management teams (Horizontal intervention) and all the departments and functions (Vertical intervention). The HORIVERT process enables the company to overcome obstacles to agility. Indeed, it helps articulate the projects designed at top management team level with those proposed by focus groups in various departments of the company. For example, an action plan aimed at streamlining delivery process and speeding up innovation processes may require both a horizontal project at top management team level to break the silos across departments and vertical projects in each and every department to improve productivity and efficiency.

Indeed, SEAM draws on a systemic approach to organization analysis: all the structures of the company interact with all actors' behaviors, resulting in both organizational agility and in hindrances to agility referred to as dysfunctions (e.g., it may prove difficult to change sales reps' habits who are accustomed to giving pitches on traditional product lines, and feeling ill-at-ease when trying to sell new company products). ISEOR database on company dysfunctions show the stiffness of company processes when trying to enhance agility. SEAM differentiates from other approaches to agility such as Lean-6 sigma, as it assumes that company actors are disobedient, even though they may not have any formal power: They can be absent, resign, refrain from giving their say and propose innovative ideas and refuse communicating with other colleagues to turn stiff processes into seamless functioning, etc. SEAM also draws on the *Human Potential* concept, which is opposed to the *Human Capital* concept because company actors decide whether they support the agility of the company or stay in a surface compliance behavior. The Human Potential approach consists in assuming that periodically negotiating the objectives and the means required to reach the goals spurs the actors' energy and pro-activity required to enhance company agility. The lack of periodically negotiable activity contract results in behaviors mostly focused on reluctantly improving company performance in a constrained strategic framework, as opposed to questioning their practices and move to more pro-active behaviors in order to increase company agility.

The Three Axes of the Intervention Process

The SEAM interventions consist in strengthening the three pillars of organization agility: processes aimed at enhancing strategizing, perceiving, testing and implementing (*Process of improvement axis*), the management tools aimed at sustaining agility overtime (Socio-economic *management tools axis*), and the design of strategic agility, its goals, values and rules of the game as regards to individual and team behaviors (*Policy and strategy axis*). This intervention process includes a listening process of all the company actors in order to make a comprehensive inventory of all the dysfunctions which are detrimental to company agility. The intervention is carried out through concerted training sessions and the facilitation of focus groups in order to accompany the company CEO and managers in an agility enhancement process. The three axes of the intervention are simultaneously implemented:

The Process of Improvement Axis

It starts with a diagnosis of the dysfunctions and hidden costs: SEAM interveners, along with internal consultants, conduct interviews with all the categories of staff to ask them what they observe on dysfunctions. Quotes are selected from note taking and they are categorized according to the six themes of dysfunctions which hinder organizational agility: working conditions, work organization, communication-coordination-cooperation, time management, integrated training, and implementation of the strategy. This list of field note quotes is broken down under key-ideas and sub-themes and presented as a mirror-effect, along with the calculation of the hidden costs stemming from the dysfunctions: absenteeism, work accident and occupational diseases, staff turnover, and non-quality and productivity gaps. Once presented, an expert's advice is also expressed by the interveners in order to give their interpretation of the root-causes of the lack of agility, such as: ill-designed synchronization, not enough elimination of low added value activities, lack of stimulating information systems, and phony negotiation processes concerning the development actions. Then, focus groups are set up in order to design innovative solutions and enable company agility. The innovative actions are proposed for decision making through the presentation of a socio-economic balance of visible and hidden costs and performance. Most of the time, the socio-economic balances demonstrate that payback of the development actions aimed at enhancing company agility is achieved within one year or less, which shows that what is costly is not the improvement of agility, but the lack of agility action plan.

The Socio-Economic Management Tools Axis

The rationale behind the SEAM intervention method is that usual management tools and management control methods are mostly focused on a bureaucratic design rather than on organizational agility. Therefore, the socio-economic intervention is aimed at upgrading the management tools so as to turn them into agility factors. Six main tools are set up through a concerted integrated training process.

The Internal and External Strategic Action Plan expands the scope of usual strategic designs through better taking into account the expectations and the projects, not only of external stakeholders of the company, but also the internal ones. Indeed, employees are part and parcel of the Human Potential of the company and they give their say and devote energy to improve company agility, as opposed to strategies mostly focused on core competences and external objectives, which prove to end up with resistance to change.

Priority Action Plans articulate strategy deployment actions and improvement actions related with the prevention of dysfunctions: Employees all the more accept to be involved in agility projects as they have also been involved in concrete improvement actions concerning their work-station, their team, or their department. The improvement actions particularly include the solutions to the six categories of dysfunctions that slow down the company agility enhancement processes: working conditions, work organization, time management, (communication-coordination-cooperation), integrated training, and implementation of the strategy.

The time management tool-kit is aimed at improving the quality of time devoted to agility (e.g., socio-economic time management methods reduce the number of disruptions, and concerted delegation enables the conversion of day-to-day management into time devoted to the implementation of Priority Action Plans).

The competency grid consists in mapping out all of the existing skills in each and every team, so as to set up an integrated training action plan in order to make up for competency weaknesses, or lack of multi-skills. It has been observed that when employees are encouraged to upgrade at least one skill per semester, it not only results in improved intellectual agility for themselves, but also in top-ranking company agility.

Strategic Socio-Economic Log-Book consists in a variety of indicators focused on both safety management and agility management. In particular, some indicators are referred to as strategic vigilance indicators and capture the weak signals which announce upheavals in the business environment. The indicators focused on the *creation of potential* enable the calculation of the payback of *intangible investments* aimed at improving company agility.

In the Periodically Negotiable Activity Contract, the objectives which contribute to organizational agility are negotiated every six months between each superior and his/her subordinates. This negotiation practice enables overcoming resistance to change and also includes bonuses that are more than self-financed through the improvement of company agility.

*The Third Axis of Socio-Economic Interventions is Focused
on Strategic and Political Decisions*

It particularly includes decisions regarding the coherence between the ambition of the strategy and the strategic consensus base required to permit high involvement of all actors in the implementation of the strategy required by agility goals. Decisions are also related to organizational choices that should be coherent with organizational agility: job enrichment, silo-breaking, innovative and comprehensive pay-reward systems, upgrading management skills, etc.

Shared Aspects of SEAM and Agility Concepts

- *Strategizing:* Working out an Internal and External Strategic Plan. Designing a Priority Action Plan by means of a socio-economic project. Rooting the strategy and up-dating it through the involvement of all teams and employees.
- *Perceiving:* Enhancing strategic vigilance to better detect untapped opportunities and foster innovation strategies in the fields of products, markets, technologies, and human potential.
- *Testing:* Socio-economic diagnoses and projects enable the experimentation of innovative solutions.
- *Implementing:* The socio-economic management control integrates the implementation of the strategy and the budgets because economic balances consist in calculating and monitoring the costs and performance of all the actions needed to implement the strategy.

THE SERLOU CASE STUDY

Serlou is a family business founded in 1974 in western France. Before it created and developed the brioche market, this specific industry did not exist in France, since those products were only sold in the city and countryside retail bakeries. Its original activity was therefore producing and marketing brioches in a single site in western France. After the 80s production and marketing plants were created throughout the country as well as in some European and American countries.

During its first 20 years, Serlou experienced a very strong 20% to 30% annual growth. To sustain its growth, the company decided in 1985 to build a second factory in Eastern France. At this point, Serlou first continued to expand by organic growth, then used a mixed approach combining internal and external growth through taking over small companies in its business area. This growth was achieved by the creation of new plants, since the company applied the organizational principle stating that an industrial and commercial site shall not exceed a 300 employee threshold, beyond which the company was considered losing its organizational, managerial, and strategic agility.

Since 1980, Serlou has become a leader on the French market. In the 1990s it has diversified into a second profession: pastry. In 2001, Serlou had a first international experience by acquiring a toasted-bread company in Spain, thus creating its third business domain.

Since 2000, Serlou stepped up its internationalization strategy, and now generates 16% of its turnover abroad, in particular in Belgium, England, Spain, United States, and Asia. In 1984, Serlou had 240 employees and integrated factory, sales force, logistics, and distribution, its current situation is summarized as follows. Nowadays, the company is structured into four main divisions: first, the brioche, business leader and driving force; second, the toasts; third, the pastry; and last a division was dedicated to international development. It has 17 sites, each one reporting to a division, 4,400 employees and revenue amounts to €594 million (750 millions USD).

Strategy

Serlou strategic development has been continuous, based on three strategic principles or values, referred to as *"fundamental"* by the company leaders (Pasquier & Pasquier, 2012), considering that the family business wished to keep financial independence at all costs.

The first basic principle is the *business organization into synchronized decentralized sites*, legally operating under limited liability companies or simplified joint stock companies status. The geographical location of the sites aims at better connecting the production and consumption places, in order to reduce the sales branches as well as the delivery delays, a key aspect to ensure the products freshness. Each site has both industrial and sales activity.

The second organizational principle is the *balance between operational and functional responsibilities*. It is applied to all sites, divisions, as well as to headquarters. A site flowchart illustrates the balance between operational and functional responsibilities (Figure 10.1). *Hierarchical proximity* is another key principle of the company: The hierarchical structure stretches to maximum of four hierarchical levels between top brass and rank and file.

The third principle is the *synchronized decentralization strategic vision,* so that sites fully contribute to the business development, construction, and strategy implementation. To support and enliven this strategic vision, Serlou has implemented since 1984 strategic management tools (see below). Then, in 1995, permanent focus groups strategic decentralized project called *"Strategic vigilance domains"* enabled checking out the lay of the land in each and every strategic domain as an input to the corporate executive

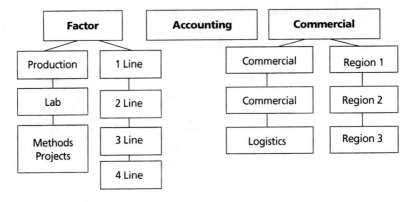

Figure 10.1 Serlou site flowchart.

committee in charge of overall strategic implementation. The originality of those strategic focus groups was that they were managed by a site manager, as opposed to traditional analysis proposed by experts at group headquarters or division levels. More details on the *"strategic vigilance domains"* operation and contribution to the business agility are presented later on.

In Serlou's strategic choices, we can notice that since the beginning of the company, specific attention was paid to the *human potential development* and to a balance between the *short and medium or long terms* economic objectives, which included equipment and intangible investments, specifically on potential creation.

Implementation of the Socio-Economic Intervention

SEAM was first implemented in Serlou in 1984. Indeed, the company leaders' motivation fit nicely with the key principles of SEAM: empowerment, high involvement on development objectives, trusting employees to enhance intrapreneurship, and appreciation of personal contribution to the collective company performance (Pasquier & Pasquier, 2012). Serlou leaders also chose this method due to its consistency and compatibility, as well as the enhancement of between economic and social performance. The SEAM had been considered as the best match to sustain over time a level of business agility whilst contributing to steady growth.

The first socio-economic innovative action took place on the Western France industrial site. It started with a socio-economic diagnosis of the company dysfunctions and hidden costs (see Table 10.1). Then, a participatory innovation project was carried out with the Serlou top managers and executives. A new organization of the factories was set up in 1985 in the first site, and was then adapted in each and every site, either created by the company, or taken over. This organizational pattern consisted in implementing *micro-companies* within the plants, each one corresponding to a production line, integrating kneading, cooking, and packaging. Each production line was led by a line manager in charge of the production, packaging and industrial equipment, maintenance, and employees. Each line had annual, semiannual, and monthly objectives regarding productivity, quality, and waste, as well as creation of potential objectives. To reach those objectives, all the employees were involved in a semestral priority action plan, as well as a team objective contract.

Two socio-economic innovation actions followed in 1987, on the second site in eastern France and in the sales teams, in order to detect dysfunctions and hidden costs and then convert them into value-added. Starting in 1990, the Serlou intervention team focused on the Serlou top management team, at the pace of one day strategic assistance per semester. Moreover, in 1995, an extensive additional intervention-research was conducted to help the company enhance its strategic pro-activity and innovation in terms of products and markets. This new stage of intervention-research gave birth to the concept of *"strategic vigilance domains,"* which has significantly contributed to the strategic business agility.

Figure 10.2 summarizes the dysfunctions and hidden costs identified in the 1984 initial socio-economic diagnosis (2a) and in the 1987 assessment of the SEAM impacts (2b). This assessment highlighted the high degree of conversion of hidden value added costs, reaching a 60% rate.

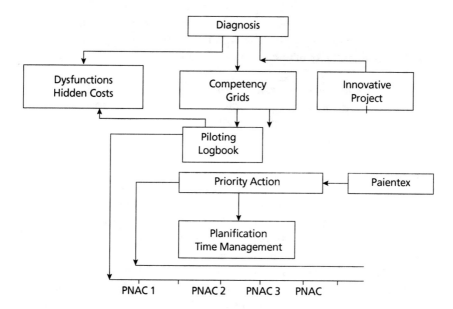

Figure 10.2 Hinging SEAM tools together.

TABLE 10.1 Synthesis of Hidden Costs per Person and per Year in the Initial Diagnosis—First Plant (1985, in 2014 USD)

Indicators	Qualitative Assessment	Quantitative Assessment	Financial Assessment
Absenteeism and occupational accidents	High level at packaging	5%	USD 5,400
Staff turnover		Not assessed	Not assessed
Non quality	• Twrown pulp	21 tons/year	USD 4,000
	• Unsold goods returns	1% of the products	USD 13,000
	• Ordering Errors	About 300h of annual overtime	USD 8,000
	• Loss of raw material	75 tons/year	USD 1,300
	• Products loss (waste)	4% per year	USD 19,000
Direct productivity gaps	• Frequent overweight of goods	50 tons/year	USD 2,600
	• Machines failures	20h/month	USD 13,000
Total of hidden costs/person/year: USD 68,000			

Enhancing Agility Through the Three Axes of Socio-Economic Intervention

As we have shown in the first part, the socio-economic dynamics unfolds in a company or an organization through the implementation of three simultaneous axes. We'll show in this part how the SERLOU group has developed its agility through the dynamic that it has created on each of the three axes.

Implementation of the Socio-Economic Management Tools

Since 1984, Serlou has implemented the main tools of the SEAM (Buono & Savall, 2007; Savall & Zardet, 2008; Savall, Zardet, & Bonnet, 2008) through an integrated training of all the managers that was then applied to the new managers, as internal and external growth of the company unfolded. Thus, the socio-economic management system of the company included the following main tools: An internal and external multi-year business plan, annually updated for the whole group, for each division and for each site. Table of skills allowed piloting the multi-skilling within their teams. Semi-annual priority actions plans were designed by each manager and were implemented by the line managers, sales team managers, and division managers in each site. Finally, periodically negotiable activity contracts were negotiated each semester, including production and sales objectives for the operational teams, individual goals for executives and managers, accompanied by bonuses paid each semester according to the objectives

TABLE 10.2 Assessment of Hidden Costs Conversion Into Value Added, per Person, and per Year (1987–in 2014 USD)

Indicators	Qualitative Assessment	Quantitative Assessment	Financial Assessment
Absenteeism and work accidents	• Increased motivation for presenteeism • Working time arrangements • Better training and accidents risks sensibilization	1% decrease in absenteeism rate in the packaging department of 1 point	USD 1,300
Staff turnover	Not assessed	Not assessed	Not assessed
Non quality	• Best regulation of quality defects • Less wasted goods	• 0.5% decrease in waste • Quality improvement: 50% decrease in returns of products	USD 2,700 USD 6,800
Direct productivity	• Implementation of socio-economic work organization on the production line	• 2% of productivity gain per day • Removal of an unprofitable line thanks to upgraded management tools • Streamlining the production process • Less maintenance and failures on equipment	USD 2,700 USD 23,100 USD 4,700 USD 4,700

Total of hidden costs converted per person and per year: USD 39,000

achievement level. We describe the day to day effective practices and operation of these management tools in Serlou as follows:

Each site operates with the same management system, built around a business plan, which summarizes each entity's three to five year project. This strategic action plan is then broken down into priority actions plans by each of the site managers (about fifteen, see Figure 10.1). The preparatory work of the priority action plans ends up with a semi-annual seminar of each site manager. It is aimed at arbitrating in case some priority action plans are overloaded, at synchronizing cross-departmental actions, and at communicating to the other departments of the sites the main forthcoming priorities. The seminar helps to significantly improve team cohesion in each site and to strengthen both the site and its departments operations improvements as well as the actors' professional skills and behavior improvements. Indeed, the priority actions plans are nurtured each semester by dysfunction *mini-diagnoses*, a bottom-up process conducted by each manager with his team.

Then, each division director runs a half yearly coordination seminar with the site managers and the key functional staff. They validate the division and its various sites priority action plans and start a coordination process on the objectives and priority actions.

Thereafter, the priority action plans are broken down into the managers' semi-annual calendars and, throughout the semester, are subject of an hour and half to three hour monthly piloting meeting between each manager and his/her superior. At the beginning of each semester, a periodically negotiable activity contract is also formalized between each manager and his/her superior in order to define the priority objectives and the appropriate means to achieve them. At the end of each semester, these periodically negotiable activity contracts are assessed and result in the payment of a bonus payment connected to the various objectives. Periodically negotiable activity contracts include objectives related to both the short-term performance of the company and to the creation of potential (development actions). This tool has replaced the job descriptions which existed in the company. Thus, the periodically negotiable activity contract, called CAP in the Serlou, encapsulates the contractual management system that is one of the fundamental principles of the management of the company.

The Socio-Economic Innovation Process Axis

Each semester, every team is used to meet during 2 to 3 hours to diagnose the dysfunctions, based on the expression of the employees and their manager. The latter plays a facilitator role during the meeting. Each employee expresses the difficulties, defects, and dysfunctions he/she encountered in his/her work. In these meetings local improvement and dysfunctions reduction or prevention proposals are proposed and included in the priority action plans, thereafter proposed by the team manager to his immediate supervisor. Then, during the semester, in each service, a monthly meeting of all the employees is organized to inform them on the progressive achievement of the team activity contract objectives, of the permanent productivity, quality, and losses objectives, and to coordinate those employees on the ongoing priority actions, considering their progress and their difficulties.

The Political and Strategic Decisions Axis

As it stems from the socio-economic management principles, Serlou is characterized by significant innovations on the political and strategic decisions axis, particularly when those are compared to the typical decisions of the companies in its business area or of its size. Moreover, it has been able to resort to such breakthroughs as sustainable strategic agility factors.

Since 1995, focus groups of strategic projects, called *Strategic vigilance domains,* have first been created to provide strategic intelligence, then to be a source of strategic proposals for the group executive committee, and last to pay particular attention to the harmonized implementation of those decisions. About twenty focus groups operate in the company, categorized per families of products, per markets (retailing, catering), and per core businesses (research & development, technology, human resources . . .). Each of these groups is led by a site manager, assisted by a group or division's functional expert, and associate executives from other sites or other divisions. These groups are cross-departmental and are particularly supported by operational managers, who supervise 100 to 300 person sites, whilst in similar size companies (4,400 people), the vigilance and strategic thinking function is commonly provided by a specialized headquarters team. This strategic and organizational choice is motivated by the desire of the top management team to develop an in-depth strategic analysis grounded into reality, and to enforce multi-skills plants. The headquarters mission is to organize the cohesion and consistency between the *"vigilance domains."* In each product family, key account and key function strategic intelligence is assigned to a site manager. For example the client "Auchan Distribution chain-store" is monitored by the Paris region site director, who negotiates each year for the whole company trading terms with this client.

The company also makes innovative industrial and commercial strategic choices, as compared with the competitors' strategic behavior and with the mainstream business models. For instance, the company is on a market with an extremely fierce price competition where the consumer constant euros prices steadily decrease. The company has nevertheless managed to keep up with its profitability rate through an efficient and effective periodic recycling of its hidden costs into value added. Unlike its competitors who outsource, Serlou has chosen to keep an integrated logistics function, considering that it allows more control guarantee and more reliability on the products freshness and fast delivery to the clients. The company also chose to decentralize its sales force across the different sites, as well as the key clients' accounts negotiation[1] to the sites sales managers.

Serlou has also taken the initiative to develop partnerships with some of its suppliers and customers about the new products, the information flows, the logistics flows, or on research and development. One of the challenges is to discuss beyond the prices and the discount matters with these partners. For example, the company partnered with a supplier to experiment internet orders placing so as to increase the data security and to gain speed and efficiency. Another example is a joint project group with a client on the marketing and merchandising of fresh pastry (Pasquier & Pasquier, 2012).

The organization into multi-skill sites also stemmed from an original choice of general strategic management, source of agility. The company's motto "power of sites, lightness of headquarters" is put into practice by major strategic and operational responsibilities carried by the sites and divisions directions and by a head office that employs less than 2% of group staff. Serlou also renounced to the economies of scale principle, considering a maximum site size of 300 employees threshold. Beyond such a size, the socio-economic approach suggests to create a new site. Serlou also renounced to the sites specialization on the production sole function (Zardet & Voyant, 2003) by providing each site with all the functions required to set up operational and strategic autonomy (see Figure 10.1). The company finally renounced to the cost minimization principle by series effect, by providing each factory—in the same product division—with all the necessary production lines to produce and sell all the products to its customer portfolio. This founding principle in the industrial and sales company organization, resulting from the socio-economic management concept, is still applied in the brioche and in the toasts divisions and, to a lesser extent, in the pastry division.

Serlou has developed a common operational and strategic piloting system used by the managers, concerning all managers ranging from top management to front line managers. It is a major explanatory factor of the 40 years in a row sustainable performance of the company (Savall, Zardet, & Bonnet, 2012).

Sustainable Performance

Since its inception, Serlou experienced a continuous economic performance (see Table 10.2). The company executives explain the company success by two main factors: on the one hand, an outstanding quality and popular product, which has kept over time its craft-trade characteristics—without food coloring or preservative—despite the sophisticated industrial facilities. On the other hand, a decentralized organization system has enabled the company to be connected with consumers and to work directly with the large retailers in order to short-cut all the production to consumption circuits. Serlou has set up ordering and manufacturing procedures that promote flexibility and allow customers to be delivered, within 24 hours, fresh products made on the same day, with orders that can be modified the day before into significant proportions. By comparison, in 1985, the average time delay between a product manufacture and purchase dates was about eight days whereas this delay is currently reduced to a single day in more than 80% of cases: The client buys in its hypermarket products on the shelves manufactured the day before.

The company has integrated for a long time the hidden costs and the risks in its decision making. For instance, some hidden costs were issued from the dissatisfaction of the mass-market retailing delay requests. A reflection and some major actions were realized at internal level to reduce these hidden costs by acting both on the orders forecasts, on sequencing, and on production. The company was the first in its market to show on all its products the manufacture dates whilst the only legal obligation was to mention the expiry date (Farré, Savall, & Pasquier, 2012).

Another example of hidden opportunity costs integration in the strategic decision making concerns logistics and supply chain of products. For the Serlou, the key point is not that the truck leaves the factory full of goods but that the client is delivered on time. Indeed, delivery consistency and punctuality result in sustainable economic performance, as opposed to the principle of additional cost of delivering a half empty truck.

We can assess the company sustainable economic performance steering from some highlights. From the inception of the company, the opportunity was provided to all employees to become shareholders through stock options. In 1985, when it needed cash to finance its growth, the company entered the stock exchange on the regional market in France. 22 years later, Serlou decided to leave the stock exchange to recover its lost independence, to facilitate the future acquisitions, and to have more cash for funding strategic projects (Farré, Savall, & Pasquier, 2012). Since their retrieval of the stock exchange in 2006, the purchase of stock options has been reserved to the executives, to the members of the company executive committee, and to the members of the divisions executive committees, which include site managers.

When the company was publicly listed on the stock exchange, a survey of the Boston Consulting Group showed that, amongst all European and international companies, Serlou ranked first among the companies which created value for the shareholder over the last 10 years (Le Journal des Finances, 1997).

Since the company creation, the evolution of the company main economic and financial parameters (Table 10.3) shows a continuous progression of the business volume, of the staff and sustained investments and profitability, even if the last ten years were less intense. Since the 80s, Serlou has acquired and maintained its leader position on the brioche

TABLE 10.3 Trends of the Economic and Financial Indicators of Serlou (1986–2012)

	Turnover (millions USD)	Net Result (millions USD)	Equity (millions USD)	Overall Staff
1986	36.93	1.24	7.47	350
1990	103.13	6.64	10.99	
1996	262.69	20.41	Not known	
2000	451.88	35.38	155.15	1,685
2007	683.10	11.56	179.64	3,000
Comp. 1986/2007	18.6	9.3	24	8.5
2012	808.49	18.91	308.94	3171
Comp. 2007/2012	1.18	1.63	1.72	1.05

TABLE 10.4   Benchmarks With the Main Serlou Competitor Within the Industry

Years	Serlou Turnover (millions USD)	Progression Rate	Barilla France Turnover (millions USD)	Progression Rate
2007	683		3.666	
2008	747	+9.37%	4.555	+24.24%
2009	721	−3.48%	1.292	−71.63%
2010	724	+0.41%	1.292	−71.63%
2011	748	+3.31%	662	−4.05%
2012	808	+8.02%	672	+1.51%
Comp 2012/2007		+18.30%		−81.67%

market. It has created many jobs, realized social innovation repeatedly hailed by the national press, whilst increasing human productivity.

A comparison of the company economic and financial performance with industry is unfortunately difficult over the long term, considering the major restructurings that most of the competitors experienced during this period (takeovers, mergers, acquisitions, etc.). Nevertheless, a comparison of the last five years with its main competitor shows that the Serlou has experienced a difficult situation in 2009, like all other companies in the same industry. However, it carries on a steady growth, as opposed to its competitors (Harris, Barilla Co.) which downsized and showed a dip in their revenue (Table 10.4). At present, Serlou holds a 30% of the French market share (even when not including the distributors' branding) while its main competitor, Harris Co., only owns a 13 % market share.

DISCUSSION

The synthetic case study of Serlou highlights the similarities between the theory of SEAM and the theory of agile organization, but also some specific agility aspects enhanced by the practice of socio-economic method implemented by the company.

Common Aspects on the Four Criteria of Agility

When analyzing Williams, Worley, and Lawler's (2013) four agility criteria, we easily observe that the implementation of the SEAM in Serlou has enabled to increase its agility on each of these four criteria.

Strategic Development

Serlou is characterized by its outstanding degree of strategic organizational and managerial innovation, but also by the company agility to break down a strategic idea into operational implementation in each site or department. Indeed, the company combines the use of strategic focus groups (*Strategic vigilance domains*), creators of both strategic and operational innovation with the decision-making power of the group executive committee, in charge of approving the proposals of these focus groups. Then, each semester, strategic and operational decisions taken by the group executive committee are integrated in an updated business plan. Those decisions are very concretely cascaded first in the different priority action plans of the divisions, then of the sites, thereafter of the departments, production lines, and sales teams. Eventually, the negotiation of activity contracts with all the managers at all levels of the hierarchy helps anchor and align the strategic objectives of the company at the finest level of individuals who will contribute, according to his/her position, service, and site, to the achievement of objectives. The whole articulation can be summarized in Figure 10.2.

Perceiving

Strategic vigilance is the shared function of actors who hold major operational responsibilities. Far from being a handicap, this organizational choice allows to spot with great anticipation the weak signals from the company environment, concerning competitors, current, or future clients and consumers as well as national and international legislation. The *Strategic vigilance domains* are particularly responsible for spotting new norms, standards, and regulations the company has to comply with, since thinking about their compatibility and implementation costs is required. Then, the focus group leaders present their proposals to the company executive committee (e.g., the 800 annually produced new norms and standards in the agrifood industry directly impacted the Serlou in the latest years).

Moreover, sales representatives are responsible for collecting and providing feedback on their customers, consumers, and competitors' behaviors. It is interesting to notice that it is one of their periodically negotiable activities contract objectives, in addition to the sales objectives.

Testing and Innovating

As previously highlighted, the company is featured by a high degree of innovation both at the external level, specifically in terms of products, markets, and services, and at the internal level, concerning technology, human resources, skills, organization, or management. Some of the most remarkable external innovations include partnerships with suppliers or customers, or the organization of regular tasting panels by consumers themselves, in order to keep direct relationship with them.

Among the internal innovations, a particular importance is given to the implementation of a decentralized strategic intelligence scheme, the integrated logistics, in spite of the fad consisting in outsourcing this function to specialized logistics companies, or the multi-skill sites and production lines.

Implementing

Figure 10.2 above elicits Serlou's agility both in the fields of strategic innovation and deployment. Indeed, the company's strategic deployment system is characterized by the articulation of three SEAM main tools: the multi-year internal and external strategic action plan, the semi-annual priority action plan, and the periodically negotiable activity contract that is individual for managers and collective for the administrative, industrial, and sales employees.

In addition, major decisions, for example the creation of a new site or a new production line necessarily follows the development of an *economic balance* that compares the amount to be invested to the expected earnings after the project implementation (see Table 10.5). Such a balance incorporates a hidden costs and performance analysis. Table 10.6 shows an example of economic balance designed before a decision to create two new production lines in a U3 plant (several million dollars). U2 and U3 are located in a near distance of 100 km and the company had first planned to specialize each of them. Then, an estimate was made of the hidden costs of the management of two specialized sites (Table 10.6) to €816,000 per year (1.11 million USD). By comparison, investment in two additional production lines and the creation of three director and executive posts was largely amortized by the new unit U3 forecasted commercial development: + €450,000 (612,000 USD) in the first year (Table 10.6). Furthermore, this scenario matched the group products freshness commercial policy as well as the plants multi-skilling policy.

Specific Aspects of SEAM Agility

We have insisted on the fact that the Serlou agility was greatly facilitated by a set of articulated management tools. We should also highlight the contribution of the extremely common company internal schemes of *coordination*, of *meetings*, and of other workshops in *project groups*.

Thus, *meetings on activities piloting* are planned every month between each manager and his immediate superior. It is a piloting tool of the profit centers, but also a strategy, concepts, and business fundamentals integration tool. Each manager, head of service, main line production manager, sales manager, site manager, and activity director is directly involved in these piloting meetings, which firstly consist in assessing the objectives achievement progress and the team security-management actions, the manager's

TABLE 10.5   Economic Balance of Scenario A: U2 and U3 Plants Specialization (in USD)

Additional Expenses		Additional Income
• Logistic, industrial, and commercial structures between U2 and U3 (trucks, fees…	78,000	0
• Additional litigation, assets, and exchanges costs (2% of USD 31 millions)	620,000	
• Travels and phone call costs between the two sites (time + fees)	87,000 8,000	
• Products flow waiting and storage costs between U2 and U3: 10% × USD 31 M × 2%	13,000	
• Overcosts on unsold goods return (1% de USD 31 M)	62,000	
Total additional expenses	+1,190,000	
Expenses Decrease		**Income Decrease**
Economie d'amortissements de 2 lignes de production à U3	–1,088,000	0
Expenses total variation	–102,000	Income total variation
Forecast Result of the Project: –102,000		

TABLE 10.6   Economic Balance of Scenario B: Multi-skilled U2 and U3 Plants (in USD)

Additional Expenses		Additional Income
• Investment on 2 production lines* 2 × 2,000,000 × 1/5° =	1,088,000	Additional turnover of U2 and U3
• Sites CEOs posts	68,000	31 millions × 10%
• 3 heads of servics at U3	108,000	× 60% (margin rate) = 1,878,000
Total Additional Expenses	+1,265,000	
Expenses Decrease		**Income Decrease**
0		0
Expenses Total Variation		**Income total Variation**
+1,265,000		+1,878,000
Forecast Result of the Project: +613,000 USD		

* Production lines are amortized in 5 years.

workload and results, and secondly to pilot improvement objectives through periodically negotiable activity contracts. Structural and strategic agility is accompanied by meetings, human interaction, and powerful support of all of the 400 managers who copilot the company development. These schemes promoting the activation of the human behavior are another key factor of the business agility (Savall & Zardet, 2013).

The SEAM includes tools for management control and financial analysis. The hidden costs assessment shows that every company has a sufficient potential to become more agile, because the hidden costs represent a pool of partially recoverable resources, provided that the company develops its energy and courage to tap them.

Thus, in the Serlou group, different division and sites directors have short term economic and financial objectives (EBITDA, turnover and yield on investments) and medium and long term ones. Annual negotiations on these economic objectives take place at two levels: divisions and sites. Then, the economic and financial objectives are translated into decisions and action by the division and sites directors.

A monthly reporting system is set up through the periodical meetings we previously described. Piloting strategic and operational logbooks include financial but also quantitative and qualitative indicators, such as market share, absenteeism, or the consumer panels' appreciation of the products tastes. In addition, once a quarter, a board of directors of the corporate company, including the division directors, examines various indicators and specific division strategic issues. The CEO, both family member and shareholder, ensures the link between the governance and the management of the company.

CONCLUSION

The example of Serlou shows how SEAM contributes to the enhancement of agility. It requires levering the four features of organizational agility: strategic development, perceiving, testing and innovating, implementing. In the field of management consulting interventions to help companies improve their agility, the specific contribution of SEAM is that it provides articulated tools which demonstrate how agility action plans are self-financed in a short period of time.

NOTE

1. A small number of clients provide most of the company turnover, particularly in the brioche activity.

REFERENCES

Buono, A. F., & Savall, H. (Eds.) (2007). *Socio-economic intervention in organizations: The intervener-researcher and the SEAM approach to organizational analysis.* Charlotte, NC: Information Age.

Cummings, T. G., & Worley, C. G. (2008). *Organizational development and change.* Boston, MA: Cengage.

Farré, D., Savall, H., & Pasquier, P. (2012). Entrevista a Pascal Pasquier. *Costos y Gestión (86),* 52–55.

Le Journal des Finances (1997), n°5742, 20th–26th December 1997.

Pasquier, S., & Pasquier, P. (2012). L'entreprise de généalogie: Réussir la transmission [The genealogy company: Successful transmission]. In H. Savall & V. Zardet (Eds.), *L'entreprise familiale: création, succession, gouvernance et management* (pp. 9–20). Paris, France: Economica.

Savall, H. (1981). Work and people: The economic evaluation of job enrichment. New York, NY: Oxford University Press.

Savall, H., & Zardet, V. (2008). *Mastering hidden costs and performance.* Charlotte, NC: Information Age.

Savall, H., & Zardet, V. (2013). *The dynamics and challenges of tetranormalization.* Charlotte, NC: Information Age.

Savall, H., Zardet, V., & Bonnet, M. (2000–2008). *Releasing the untapped potential of enterprises through socio-economic management.* Geneva: Éditions IOT-BIT.

Savall, H., Zardet, V., & Bonnet, M. (2012). Développer la croissance de l'entreprise par une démarche socio-économique endogène. In K. Richomme-Huet, G. Guieu, & G. Paché (Eds.), *La démarche stratégique. Entreprendre et croître.* (pp. 175–186). Aix-Marseille, France: Presses Universitaires de Provence.

Williams, M., & Wheeler, B. (2009). The Four Faces of Deploying Common Systems. *MIS Quarterly Executive, 8* (2), 59–72.

Williams, T., Worley, C. G., & Lawler III, E. E. (2013). The agility factor. *Strategy+Business,* 1–10.

Zardet, V., & Voyant, O. (2003). Organizational transformation through the socio-economic approach in an industrial context. *Journal of Organizational Change Management, 16*(1), 118–139.

PART II

ORGANIZATIONAL EXPERIENCES USING SEAM

CHAPTER 11

APPLYING SOCIO-ECONOMIC APPROACH TO MANAGEMENT IN LEBANON

Challenges, Design, and Results

Patrick Tabchoury

CONFERENCE REMARKS:
Chapter Prologue

Patrick Tabchoury

I will be talking about our experience of implementing socio-economic approach to management in Lebanon. It will be the case of three hospitals that belong to the same religious congregation of sisters. The first one is not far away from the capital of Beirut. It's about 30 minutes driving NE of the capital and has 180 beds. It is considered a mid-size hospital in Lebanon. It has 460 employees, 150 physicians, and a yearly turnover of $21 million. The second hospital is in Beirut, downtown. It has 300 employees and is considered also a mid-sized hospital with 150 beds. It has 150 physicians and its annual turnover is around $10 million. As for

Decoding the Socio-Economic Approach to Management, pages 187–193

**TABLE 11.1 Demographics for the Three Lebanese
Hospitals (H1, H2, H3)**

	Hospital 1	Hospital 2	Hospital 3	Total
Employees	460	300	240	1,000
Physicians	150	150	100	400
Turnover (Millions)	$21	$10	$9	$40
Beds	180	150	66	396
Accreditation Level	A	A	A	

the third hospital, it is 20 minutes driving north of Beirut. It is a small size hospital with 66 only beds and its annual turnover is around $9 million. It has 100 physicians and 240 employees. Table 11.1 summarizes the characteristics of the three hospitals:

EXTERNAL AND INTERNAL CHALLENGES IN LEBANON

So like other hospitals in Lebanon, these three hospitals were facing many external and internal challenges. First of all, the impact of the political instability in Lebanon and the region affected negatively the hospitals' development. Second, the economic situation affects especially the health care system in Lebanon. I'll give the example of the pricing system, which is imposed by the government—the last revision of the price list was in 1999. From other part, the majority of the receivables are related to the governmental institutions, and the average age of these receivables is more than 2 years, complicating a little bit more the work in Lebanese hospitals. We had to work with more than 100 insurance companies. Each one of them has its own regulations, its own system of telecommunication, its own system of control, of pricing, etc. so you can imagine how much the healthcare system is complicated in Lebanon.

We have a weak role for the syndicate of private hospitals. These hospitals are considered in the private sector, and the private sector counts 117 hospitals taking the lead over the 15 to 20 public hospitals. There are no updates for the regulations in the healthcare sector. There is a big competition on the national and regional level. And, as we all know, the demographic changes in the Middle East had a big impact on health services delivery. Patients are becoming more and more demanding; we have different cultures, etc.

As for internal challenges that are facing these hospitals, we can start by the difference in terms of culture, objectives, vision, mission, structure between the owners that are religious, and the other groups of work like physicians, nursing, etc. and team management. The second point is the scarcity of resources that exists in these hospitals. The repartition of these resources across the departments of these hospitals creates conflicts and tensions between the internal actors. So these challenges have led to many dysfunctions. Like an infrastructure that became less adaptable to scientific and medical development and progress. Many of our specialized physicians shifted away and went to other hospitals, and we started losing some key employees and know-how. These physicians were taking their patients to other hospitals in the region and the hospitals were also doing self-patient recruitment so that 50% or more of the admitted patients were admitted through the emergency room.

INTRODUCING SEAM

In order to overcome all these challenges, the management team of the three hospitals started searching for a new way of management that enables them to accelerate the pace of change; to enhance transparency; to increase the managerial competencies at all levels, especially for nurses and physicians; and to take into consideration both aspects of the economic and the social, both environment, external, and internal. The main problem was how to reduce costs without affecting the quality of the services provided at both levels: hospitality and medical.

The choice was made and the socio-economic approach to management (SEAM) was adopted. At the beginning, we were facing many problems: how to convince the owners to implement the socio-economic approach to management, especially when the notion of management doesn't exist for them; how to introduce new tools; the resistance of change generated from all the internal actors, employees, physicians, etc.; and the difference in language?

To overcome these hindrances, a decision was made to send some key persons to do the training and discover the socio-economic approach to management. This enabled them to discover the methodology of work, and the added value that may result from implementing such a method on both the individual and the organizational levels.

We started the implementation of the method in November 2010 and it was a team work between members from ISEOR and the already trained people from the hospitals. A steering committee was established, training groups and personalized assistance were done. Horizontal and vertical diagnostics were applied.

The design of the implementation method is summarized in Figure 11.1. Table 11.2 shows the yearly hidden costs resulting from the different dysfunctions at different levels. Like in medicine, if organizationally we are infected by a virus and we don't treat it, the situation will become worse from year

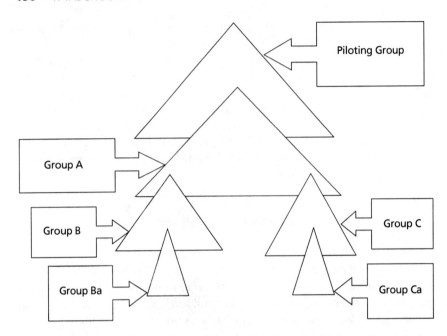

Figure 11.1 The implementation of the SEAM intervention began with a piloting group and then cascaded through the hospitals in several groups.

TABLE 11.2   Amount of Hidden Costs for 5 Departments in Which SEAM Was Carried Out, and the Average Hidden Cost per Person per Year in Each Group

Sector	Hospital	Number of Persons	Yearly Hidden Costs ($)	Wages Equivalent per Sector	Average Hidden Cost per Person
Operating room	H1	40	$484,300	100%	$12,100
Intensive care	H1	27	$389,100	120%	$14,400
Integral	H3	150	$848,300	42%	$5,600
Maternity	H2	20	$361,100	150%	$18,000
Emergency	H2	20	$794,600	330%	$39,700

to year. And if there is a hidden cost in 2010 in the operating room of St. George Hospital around $0.5 million USD, it will maybe increase in 2011 to $0.6 or $0.7 if we don't treat our virus. So, as we can see in Table 11.2, our human potential in our operating room was generating $500 million USD in hidden costs or the equivalent of $12,000 USD per person per year. In the intensive care department hidden costs were around $400 million USD for the same hospital or the equivalent of $14,000 USD per person per year. For the maternity department we found $400 million USD in hidden costs for the year 2010 which represents 150% of the department yearly wages and for the ER around $800 million USD or 330% of the department yearly wages, and so on.

In order to try to convert these hidden costs into performance, we started applying the socio-economic tools in conjunction with the socio-economic approach. The first tool we started with was the time management grid, followed by the competency grid that allowed us to develop internal and external strategic planning for the three hospitals with common strategic objectives for the three hospitals and dedicated objective for each one of the three hospitals. After elaborating the internal and external strategic plan, and in order to better implement it, we applied a departmental priority action plan for the departments concerned, and we linked it to the periodically negotiable activity contract to end up with economic balances and a log book with qualitative, quantitative, and financial indicators piloting indicators.

RESULTS

After one year of implementation of these tools, we made an audit especially on priority action plans and priority negotiable activity contracts. We audited 63 priority action plans and 164 priority negotiable activity contracts. The main reason for the audit was to train people to better perform when implementing such tools. Table 11.3 shows the repartition of the audited tools between the three hospitals.

A periodic evaluation of the results was conducted. Three categories of results were evaluated: Qualitative, quantitative, and financial.

On the qualitative level, a remarkable progress in terms of quality of patients' services and better accreditation results for the three hospitals were noted (Level A, 0 recommendations). A remarkable progress in managerial

TABLE 11.3 Number of Instances of the Use of the Priority Action Plan (PAP) and Periodically Negotiated Activity Contract (PNAC) per Hospital

	Total	Hospital 1	Hospital 2	Hospital 3
PAP	63	28	23	12
PNAC	164	58	53	53
Total	227	86	76	65

competencies at all levels especially for the heads of medical units and nurs-es was shown. Also managers noticed an improvement in employees behav-ior at all levels and an increase in the level of satisfaction for internal and external actors (from 76% to 91%).

On the quantitative level, we notice an increase in the number of pa-tients, internal and external, from $70,000 to $80,000 for the three hos-pitals, a decrease in the number of overtime hours by 70%, a decrease in the number of complaints by physicians, employees, patients, etc. and a decrease in nosocomial infection rate.

As for the impact on the economic level, Figure 11.2 shows the yearly evolution of the hourly contribution value added on variable costs. We no-ticed that the hourly contribution to value added on variable cost at H1 has increased from $16 to $23 USD. At H2 from 10 to 14 and at H3 13 to 17 and the consolidated for the group from $13.8 to $19 USD.

As for the global economic impact, Figure 11.3 shows the yearly evolu-tion in the three hospitals. After taking into consideration the two million working hours in the three hospitals, we can notice that we have an added value on variable costs of around $10 million in three years.

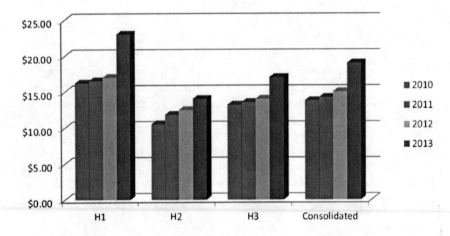

Figure 11.2 The hourly contribution to value added on variable costs (HCVAVC) for each.

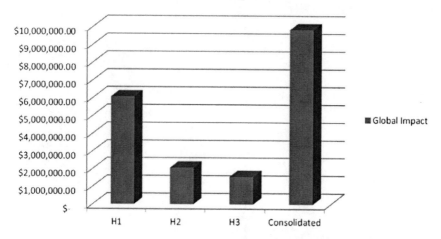

Figure 11.3   The increase in added value between 2010 and 2013.

CHAPTER 12

SEEKING ECONOMIC RESOURCES

SEAM Intervention-Research Case in a Belgian Subsidiary of a NYSE Listed American Group

Frantz Datry, Amandine Savall, and Philippe Lacroix

This paper reviews the outcomes of a change process implemented in a human resource service company. This company is the national Belgian subsidiary related to a New York Stock Exchange listed American group. We present the achievements we observed by applying a change management method that has been experimented by the French research center, the Socio-Economic Institute of Companies and Organizations (ISEOR) (Savall, 1979). In this paper, we referred to socio-economic intervention-research, which is a transformative longitudinal research carried out in a company that we call *M*, in an attempt at implementing a change process. Intervention-research is an exploratory and confirmation research technique that consists in actually getting into the company, to conduct the change process (Buono & Savall, 2007). Indeed, this research methodology is based on organizational immersion and cooperation between scholars

Decoding the Socio-Economic Approach to Management, pages 195–214

195

and company actors, in order to get reliable experimental materials and lead to organizational improvement.

We call M, the Belgian-Luxembourgish subsidiary of an 80 country based multinational group. This national branch had 330 million euros in annual revenue in 2012. It has 500 permanent staff on its payroll, 800 contractors (also called "ambassadors"), 37,000 temporary workers, and a 4,000 client portfolio. The subsidiary provides 5 kinds of human resource solutions to its clients: temporary work-recruitment, recruitment outsourcing and professional services, training, HR consulting & carrier management, and other outsourcing solutions, under 3 different brand names.

ISEOR has assisted M since January 2012 to carry out its change process. This assistance has been made up of 3 intervention research contracts. We will present them into deeper details throughout the paper. Before the first contract, an 8-month negotiation period defined the intervention research goals and specifications. In May 2011, the Belgian CEO attended a SEAM training seminar, organized by ISEOR. The CEO was also a Belgian SME administrator that has been collaborating with ISEOR for almost 20 years. This specific experience had allowed him to observe the SEAM method, concepts, and outcomes for a long period of time. Moreover, for almost 2 years, he was looking for a methodology to assist him in organizational development and change of M. These evolutions were necessary to support his proactive vision of the incoming market and environment changes. Between May and September 2011, the training seminar helped him make up his mind about the SEAM adequacy to support his organizational strategy. In September 2011, he asked for a meeting with ISEOR intervener-researchers to exchange views on how to implement SEAM in M. Since then, a 4-month negotiation process took place. It ended up in late 2011 with the 1st contract signature.

The main challenges of the 1st intervention research were based on the following internal and external analysis made by the CEO:

- The 2008 economic crisis consequences in a 12% collapsing market, a severe erosion in gross profit, and a high profitability demand from American shareholders.
- A lack of internal cohesion and professionalism among the Belgian staff, implying lack of rigor and bad quality of work in a poorly empowering and inefficient work organization.

Based on this analysis, the main objectives of the intervention research were co-established during 4 meetings between ISEOR intervener-researchers and the CEO:

- Reducing horizontal splits among the business units ("cross-collaboration") and lack of hierarchical vertical management.

- Increasing professionalism at each organizational level towards better quality of internal and external services.
- Improving efficiency of work organization with 20% productivity savings;
- Sustaining market shares and profitability to satisfy both shareholders' and local self-financing needs.
- Investing in human potential by training all managers and their teams in SEAM.

The 2012 intervention research program consisted in implementing the HORIVERT method (Savall & Zardet, 1987). "HORI" stands for a horizontal intervention involving top and middle management, while "VERT" stands for a vertical intervention in 3 different areas of the company. These 2 kinds of intervention need to be tightly aligned and synchronized. The main characteristics of HORIVERT method are aimed at improving the change effectiveness.

- It is a comprehensive and structured approach: The process involves all categories of actors (top management, middle management, and staff).
- The horizontal intervention goes after better cohesion among all managers and enhancing strategic decision making, such as business unit and position interface dysfunctions.
- The vertical intervention is focused on different areas of the organization (at least 2 of them). This enables detecting local dysfunctions and hidden cost potential that will self-finance the quality improvements of management, functioning, and client service production.
- The HORIVERT approach is intended to strengthen team leading and piloting roles of managers. Then, it goes to involving other staff throughout the change process in a participative way. This process focuses the attention on a good balance between necessary directivity and participation in the change process so to make sure that improvement actions are effectively implemented.

The 1st intervention research stage (2012) architecture is presented in Figure 12.1. At the end of 2012, the CEO asked for an extension of the intervention research area by carrying out diagnoses and project groups in both business units that were not entirely involved during the 1st year. He also asked for further advancements in SEAM method and concepts such as strengthening the internal intervention team, decentralizing management control function to better pilot economic performance, and implementing PNAC ("periodically negotiable activity contract"), considered as the cornerstone of the SEAM model. The PNAC is a "management tool that formally states the priority objectives and the means made available for attaining them, involving every employee in the company (including workers

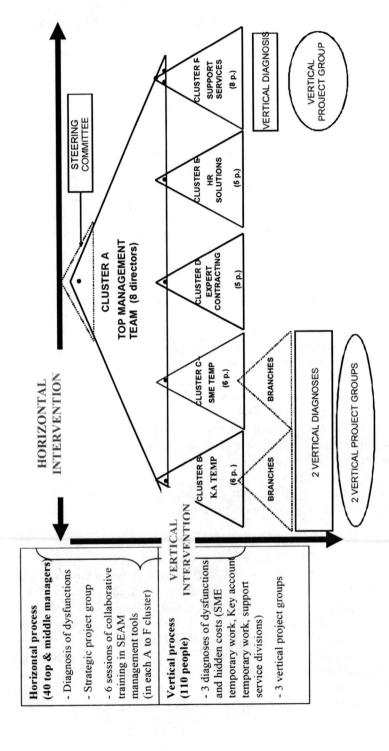

Figure 12.1 Architecture of 1st Intervention Research Stage (2012). *Source:* PJUC: Reproduction interdite et représentation réservée, document strictement confidentiel. ©ISEOR 2012.

TABLE 12.1   Composition of the Intervention Research Team and its Evolution Through Time

2012	%	2013	%	2014	%
1 expert intervener-researcher	60%	1 expert intervener-researcher	40%	1 expert intervener-researcher	30%
1 senior intervener-researcher		1 senior intervener-researcher		1 senior intervener-researcher	
2 junior intervener-researchers		2 advanced intervener-researchers		1 advanced intervener-researcher	
2 junior franchisees		2 junior franchisees		1 junior intervener-researcher	
4 internal interveners	40%	8 internal interveners (between 10 to 50% of their time)	60%	10 internal interveners (each one dedicated to a specific area)	70%
i.e., 10 people		i.e., 14 people		i.e., 14 people	

and office employees), based on a biannual personal dialogue with the employee's direct hierarchical superior" (Buono & Savall, 2007). The purpose is to link the company's strategy to individual objectives. This motivating and piloting tool is applied throughout the whole company: from CEO to workers. The intervention research has been carried out by a hybrid intervention team with both external (ISEOR) and internal interveners (see Table 12.1), trained by ISEOR.

OUTSTANDING ACHIEVEMENTS OF SOCIO-ECONOMIC PERFORMANCE

Figure 12.2 shows the 4 axes of M organizational change urged on by internal and external interveners.

- Axis 1: The socio-economic change management process suggested by ISEOR, includes 4 stages: socio-economic diagnoses, then socio-economic innovative plans, followed by their implementation, and the periodical assessment of achievements.
- Axis 2: SEAM management tools enable managers to better lead their teams and projects, and to support the "acting out" in the change dynamic.
- Axis 3: Important decisions are made throughout the change process, according to the company strategy. This axis is essential since these decisions can have great impacts on the change process ambition and success.
- The time dimension is a spiral expressing the essential time dimension of the change process. This process is progressive and falls into

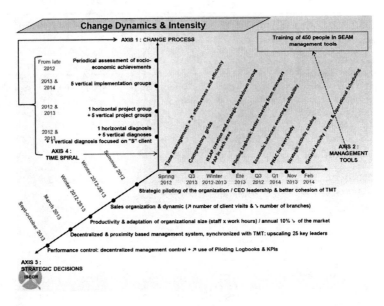

Figure 12.2 Change process on the 4 axis trihedral. Source: ©ISEOR 2014.

a 2-year period. The change dynamic is allowed through the alternation between synchronized and incremental inputs in the 3 previous axes. Each and every step on one of the axes generates new decisions and new steps on the other axes. In a heuristic manner, those steps eventually make up the organizational change.

Through 5 vertical diagnoses, we build the hidden cost assessment synthesis (Tables 12.2 & 12.3). Two components of hidden costs draw our attention: €8 million annual "overtime" (i.e., almost $11 million) represent 134,000 working hours, or 71 FTE. This potential was partially convertible into both productivity savings and self-financed creation of human potential, such as trainings, project groups, and more meetings with collaborators. €5 million annual "non-production" was a great promise for a potential increase of profitable sales. Those were very important regarding the current market; These 2 components weighed 50% and 35% in the €16 million overall amount of hidden costs.

These amounts of hidden costs were rather high-scale in the ISEOR 1,300 case database. We assume that the economic constraints of *M* combined with the actors' strong appetence for involving themselves in this economic assessment, were two main factors to explain these big amounts of money. This assessment was useful to detect economic resources (i.e., meeting the initial intervention research goals, and self-financing the incoming improvement actions to be implemented). These actions were elaborated

TABLE 12.2 Synthesis of 5 Hidden Cost Diagnoses (1/2)

	Overwages	Overtime	Over-Consumption	Non-Production	Non-Creation of Potential	Risks	Total
Absenteeism	€660,400	€4,300	N.A.	€121,800	N.A.	N.A.	€792,500
Work Accidents	N.A. (non assessed)	N.A.	N.A.	N.A.	N.A.	N.A.	N.A.
Staff Turnover	N.A.	€109,800	€97,300	€1,016,300	N.A.	N.A.	€1,223,400
Quality Defects	€206,400	€5,708,000	€659,400	€2,166,900	€73,600	€22,500	€8,836,800
Direct Productivity Gaps	€189,300	€2,534,000	€145,600	€2,110,300	€286,400	€45,800	€5,311,400
Total	€1,062,100	€8,356,100	€902,300	€5,415,300	€360,000	€68,300	€16,164,100
		328 people, i.e.: €49,300 per person & per year (average)					

TABLE 12.3 Synthesis of 5 Hidden Cost Diagnoses (2/2)

Date	Vertical Diagnosis	Amount of Hidden Costs	Hidden Costs/Person
June 2012	Key Account Temp	€2,121,000	€17,6000
June 2012	SME Temp	€3,950,000	€91,800
June 2012	Support Services	€3,937,000	€55,600
March 2013	HR Solutions	€3,126,000	€61,300
March 2013	Expert Contracting	€3,030,000	€70,400
Total		**€16,164,000**	**€49,300**

through 24 three-hour sessions of project groups (4 sessions after each diagnosis)—see Figure 12.3.

During the in-depth vertical project groups, the top management team (TMT) encouraged key strategic decisions into the different business units. This method led to the improvement of synchronization and coherence between the horizontal strategic axis and the vertical local one. The instigation intensity from top management depended on the capacity of each business unit director to carry out real changes. For instance, in the temporary work business unit, the improving actions were mainly supported by the local director and his managers, due to their large desire to implement

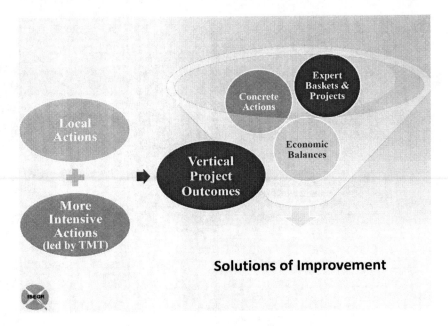

Figure 12.3 Socio-economic methodology to elaborate innovative projects.
Source: ©ISEOR 2014.

the decisions made; whereas the improving actions of the support service departments were mainly supported by the TMT due to the managers' inertia and resistance to change.

The "economic balance" tool has been systematically implemented throughout the project stage. This has allowed the managers to forecast and commit themselves into the economic impacts of the decisions they have been making since the beginning of the intervention. These economic impacts are mainly based on hidden cost conversion into value added. Their capacity to economic steering has led the managers to periodically re-examine budgets and forecasts and to better integrate these economic impact promise into their PNAC.

Table 12.4 shows what were the 5 main change levers on what M has worked on:

- Enhancing the strategic steering through stronger CEO leadership and TMT cohesion;
- Implementing a new sales organization for Temp business unit, and a higher number of customers visits;
- Seeking productivity savings by adapting staff number and implementing new organizational tree, working hour, administrative and accounting task decentralization decisions;

TABLE 12.4 Synthesis of Socio-Economic Innovative Projects

Horizontal Project (Spring 2012)	• TMT organizational tree reviewing • CEO leadership • TMT cohesion
"Temp" Vertical Projects (Fall-Winter 2012)	• From 100 to 700 customer visits/week • Geographic segmentation (not anymore by type of customers) • In-depth work on working conditions within local branches
"Support Service" Vertical Project (Fall-Winter 2012)	• Productivity & adaptation of support service staff (–15 people on 12/31/2012) • Support service organizational tree rewriting & temp-contracting payroll department decentralization
"HR Solutions" & "Expert Contracting" Vertical Projects (Fall 2013)	• Stronger involvement of these 2 BU into the change process • Successful conversion of ex-IT director into sales directors (from intervener-researchers) • Socio-economic management control "fall in love" from 1 sales director: strategic activity catalog, general activity forms, & controllers' decentralization • Slight cross-collaboration between the 3 BU • Awareness of contractors' potential: "take better care of them & they will increase sales & profit"

- Nurturing proximity management practices by building-up a strong 25 key leader team; and
- Launching new organizational change aspects—3rd intervention research contract with ISEOR in 2014—to improve the current economic steering practices: implementation of decentralized socio-economic management control, structured piloting logbooks, and the reviewing of failing financial processes such as monthly account closing and DSO management.

Table 12.5 shows how the 25 key leaders actually use the socio-economic management tools.

- Priority Action Plan (PAP) and PNAC implementation greatly orchestrate the strategic decision making—There is a big lack of effective use of competency grids and time management. Time management has always been touchy since the beginning of the change process: Some consolidation is currently being implemented, combined with new SEAM tools of management control, aimed at better piloting the working hour distribution and grant.
- Key performance indicators are widely spread within the IT system of the company. Managers have recently started their consolidation into individual and collective piloting logbooks. This will enable more accurate decision making and economic result follow-up.

TABLE 12.5   Effective Use of SEAM Management Tools (Intervener-Researchers' Assessment)

Tool BU	Time Management	Competency Grid	PAP	PLG	PNAC
TMT	▨	▨	■	▨	■
KA Temp	▨	▨	■	▨	■
SME Temp	▨	▨	■	▨	■
HR Solutions	▨	☐	■	▨	■
Expert Contracting	▨	☐	■	▨	■
Support Servcies	▨	▨	■	☐	■

Key: ■ Daily use mastery; ▨ Occasional use or incomplete mastery; ☐ Basic knowledge without practice

INTERVENER-RESEARCHER VIEWS

Change and Popular–Unpopular Decisions

The success of a change process tightly depends on the TMT capacity to make decisions. Some of them are considered "popular," others rather "unpopular." On one hand, the participative dimension of intervention research (diagnosis & project phases) is seen as a very popular investment by the actors: long and numerous collaborative trainings and new management tools to daily support them. Social performance is seen as an economic performance lever.

In contrast, managers have to make organizational choices and resource adaptation according to budgetary constraints and profitability objectives, set and required by American shareholders. This kind of decision is usually considered as "unpopular" in the first place. The managers' capacity to support this kind of decision is a key success factor to encourage social performance through new economic goals. These new goals are integrated within the Budgeted Action Plan and the PNAC, enhanced by intervener-researchers.

This popular–unpopular decision dialectic shows both "Push–Pull" orientations developed by alternating series during the intervention-research process:

- Perceived popular decisions aimed at improving working life conditions, drive economic performance; and
- Perceived unpopular decisions, mostly about money, drag social performance, by making people prioritize.

This dialectic was particularly fruitful in M, due to three factors:

- The proactive strategy of the CEO and his capacity to bear unpopular decisions: He started the change process way before economic results of the company would too much collapse. He escaped from drastic downsizing measures and human disaster, such as the competition had to.
- Setting new ambitious economic goals-constraints from 6 months after starting the intervention research: + €5,000,000 of additional value added, requiring at least 20% of productivity savings,
- €2,500,000 of cost savings by renegotiating with every supplier, and €1,500,000 additional sales gross profit.

Despite these economic constraints, the company reached on 12/31/2013: + €7,000,000 of valued added, +48% of net profit, on a 5% decreasing market, and many drastic downsizing measures of competitors.

Assessment of Intangible Investment Profitability in Human Potential Qualitative Development

The assessment of socio-economic change process achievements is based on the alternation between diagnoses and the measure of project impacts. According to Savall & Zardet (2008), this method aims to measure the intangible investment in human potential qualitative development (IIHPQD) and its profitability (i.e., the related creation of value added). The key concept called "hidden cost-performance" links social performance and economic performance. The capacity to convert these hidden costs into value added, through productivity savings and sales increase, is measured by the evolution of a global performance indicator called "hourly contribution to value added on variable costs" (HCVAVC).

The M intervention research team decided not to wait for the company to implement this method of assessing IIHPQD. From the very beginning of the intervention research, we started collecting any information that could help in building-up the assessment (HCVAVC values, productivity measures, economic results, sales increase). Figure 12.4 shows how M global performance has increased since 2012. The intangible investment in 2012 was fully self-financed (i.e., there was no damage of the company value

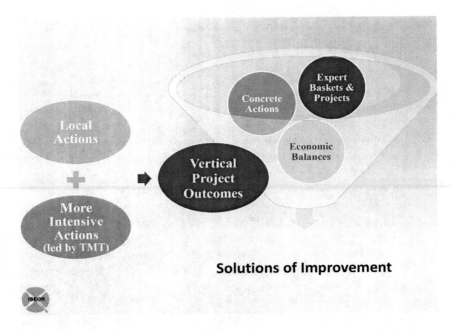

Figure 12.4 Periodical Assessment of HCVAVC by both intervener-researchers and company M: Global performance indicator. ©ISEOR 2014.

added). Since 2013, this investment has generated significant impacts such as 10% increase in HCVAVC, from €62 to €68.

The annual average amortization of intangible investment (see components in footnote n°4) related to the additional value added, reveals a 2000% global profitability ratio: 1 invested € (or $) generates 20 for the company. This ratio does not include some hidden performance (i.e., the creation of potential such as skill development, better work atmosphere, new organizational processes, given the increase in wages through PNAC implementation). Thus, performance earnings remain unappreciated.

Cyclical Energy of Change and Role of Internal Interveners

This intervention research experience has revealed the change energy cycles of internal actors. Their energy tends to deteriorate throughout the intervention process, according to the kind of changes being implemented (Savall & Zardet, 1995). For instance, decentralizing management controllers in the operational business units generated strong resistance to change from some finance managers. They considered this decision as a loss of power and a questioning of their traditional organizational pattern as they were used to. During this situation, internal interveners were useful in that they were representatives of external interveners for trainings and also to detect blocking specific people and aspects. However, their energy for change is more degradable than external interveners, since they are permanently exposed to resistance. Moreover, they develop new skills and employability with their in-depth SEAM training. They are promoted more easily than others, and have not time anymore to carry out the internal intervention. That is the reason why internal interveners should not be a permanent team: this team has to be cyclically and partially replaced so to sustain internal intervention potential within the company (Savall & Zardet, 2009).

CEO'S VOICE (BY PHILIPPE LACROIX)

The SEAM intervention process was named "iPower" within Manpower Group (see Figure 12.5). The four main aspects of this process were the impacts on strategy, the diagnoses, the management tools, and the change in mindset.

In terms of strategy, SEAM has been

- an opportunity to re-evaluate the developed strategy—everybody contributes;

Figure 12.5 Intervention process iPower.

- a change in mindset to question oneself keeps us alert for changes in the world of work;
- implementing the IESAP, a tool that keeps us focused on the strategy to realize and the future;
- implementing the PAP, a tool that help us to work very practically on the strategy and its planning;
- implementing the PNAC for each employee within the company;
- linking strategy & activities of each employee to give sense and make the work more rewarding because everybody has an impact; and
- improving alignment: It is a necessity.

The diagnoses highlighted four aspects to become a priority:

- Simplify the organization (work/structure)
- Improve/simplify processes
- Leadership & Alignment
- Technology

This led the company to understand the necessary awareness that we all have to change, to have a view on the gap that we need to close in order to be ready for the future, the need to simplify, the need for clear messages, clear focus and courage to make decisions, and the start of the dynamic of change.

The change mindset was very challenging for management. We realized managers had to get a new role, to become innovative managers, rigorous in their management practices that help their team win by integrating social and economic performance. The role of the management is key in order to implement and realize the methodology. The elaboration of a competence grid is meant for better "Leadership." And the key responsibility is to make sure to realize the strategy, "client first," and to be prepared for the future, developing the talents of the team. The managers within Manpower Group are now focused on three areas: we have to think, operate, and manage differently; it is our job to manage simplification; and we have to act concretely and now. Their major responsibilities of the management are to

- develop the strategy based on the vision and the market,
- implement the strategy,
- implement the vision,
- persevere,
- achieve results,
- develop human potential, and
- stimulate collaboration.

Despite this tremendous change mindset, we have encountered barriers to change, such as resistance to change (both personal & organizational), a lack of commitment from some people (both employees & leadership), and a lack of cross functional teams. We also realized that we set unrealistic expectations. One barrier is also not to be able to see the finality, getting stuck in tools and processes.

The main qualitative results we observed as practitioners are:

- Changes in the Senior Management Team
- Reduced number of managers (50 to 25)
- Detected/nominated Key Leaders within our organization
- Elaboration of a "Leadership" competence grid
- New structure Manpower
- New organization of our support services
- Regained "Client Focus"
- Improved collaboration between our different brands (common sales actions/visits—everybody sells all services to our clients/prospects)
- Introduction of first CAPN for each employee

This results in quantitative achievements such as:

- Increased productivity of our consultants: Gross Profit/Full Time Equivalent was €97,106 (2013) vs. €86,950 (2012) and Operational Unit Profit/Full Time Equivalent was €16,263 (2013) vs. €11,057 (2012)
- Increased sales thanks to cross-collaboration + €1,000,000
- Conversion of hidden costs into added value (2013): + €8,181,500
- HCVAVC in 2012 was €61.70, now €70.80
- The return on investment is €800,000/€8,000,000

The next steps to take on the SEAM process are:

- To develop and implement socials indicators
- To develop/create added value
- To let the methodology become our DNA—way of work within the company
- To lead by example, as managers
- To implement the "strategic list" in order to better manage our resources
- To implement SEAM management control including a new role for our financial controllers

To conclude, our collaboration with ISEOR and SEAM rely on the following principles:

- Has to be at all levels *an integral part* of our culture
- Has to be encouraged by *the management*
- Starts with the employees
- Is an investment of *time and money*
- Involves taking risks
- The development of *human potential* is a *shared responsibility* between the employer and the employee

Limits and Perspectives

This intervention research case is a great example of how a TMT put ardor and strength in piloting organizational change making and bearing the implementation of tough decisions about economic savings in the first place. Their energy was also supported by intervener-researchers, through SEAM tools and improvement process. However, we can imagine that in the second place, such decisions could have limited impacts: sustainable hidden cost conversion into value added must be combined with a real organizational development project (i.e., growth). This cannot remain about cost savings and downsizing the company forever. Therefore, we considered relevant to focus the 2nd and 3rd year of intervention research on sales team stimulation. The objectives of 2014 intervention research program are:

- Overcoming the 2nd crisis of TMT cohesion. According to our company knowledge, this new crisis lies in 2 factors: how earnings (€7,000,000) are distributed between each business unit, and the discrepancies of progress in the change process between business units & departments;
- Completing & increasing reliability of the current economic steering system by implementing a decentralized management control system towards a higher value added of working hours, new management control tools & KPI consolidation;
- Developing common sales practices among the 3 operational business units & preparing for the product portfolio evolution in the HR service market; and
- Taking up the challenge of internal support services more oriented towards salesmen and operational staff satisfaction, finding a balance between American shareholders' reporting priorities & reliable indicators for sales teams.

APPENDIX CONFERENCE DIALOGUE

Conference Participant: Could you talk a little bit more about the casualties? Who or how many didn't buy in, even though you tried to engage them? What was turnover like for people who just couldn't get it? And what was the impact of that? Also, when you talked about the number of top and middle managers, can you talk a little bit more to get a general sense of what the casualties were of people who just didn't get this, didn't want to be a part of it, couldn't make the adjustment, and what the impact of that was?

Amandine Savall: I don't know the exact number, but some of the managers quit, of course. But it was their own decisions because they didn't want to change; they didn't want to take care of their direct reports, so it was kind of a negotiation. I think some of them just changed their position or their department. Some of them were middle managers and since they didn't have the energy enough, now some of them are managers anymore, just experts with no direct reports. That's the kind of decision to make. But, only talking about firings, maybe five or six.

Conference Participant: So a lot quit on their own. How many in the organization?

Amandine Savall: Thirty people I guess.

Conference Participant: Was the effect of that overall positive? When they left, did the organization think that was probably good?

Amandine Savall: If the company was happy with their quit?

Conference Participant: Yes.

Amandine Savall: Yes, very happy.

Eric Sanders: It sort of goes to the combination of top down and bottom up change. You said that to get the change to work at Manpower, you needed to get closer to the people. I'm wondering if you could elaborate on that a little bit; how you did that and perhaps Patrick and John and Tom, you could talk a little bit about how you got SEAM closer to the people and got that front line buy-in and maybe how to help the top management team.

Amandine Savall: I think as external consultants, what we do best is to take care of the top and middle managers. But we realized after a while that we didn't know enough the bottom level, but the vertical diagnosis helped a lot in this way. It was going through all the hierarchy and that was the first time we put a foot in the local branches all over Belgium. We also invited some of the staff in the project groups. Also, thanks to the internal interveners, from the second year all the employees were trained by them through a lot of training sessions, as well as personalized assistance when they didn't get a tool or a concept in their collective training, they had the chance to get assistance. This team of internal interveners is kind of a sub-team in our intervention team. As external consultants, we see managers very often, but not enough the staff. Sometimes I feel like I want to see more of them, and the internal interveners are great partners to do that and keep us aware of what's going on at all levels.

REFERENCES

Buono, A., & Savall, H. (2007). *Socio-Economic Intervention in Organizations. The Intervener-Researcher and the Seam Approach to Organizational Analysis.* Charlotte, NC: Information Age.

Savall, H. (1979). *Reconstruire l'entreprise. Analyse socio-économique des conditions de travail* [Rebuild the enterprise. Socio-economic analysis of work conditions]. Préface de François Perroux. Paris, France: Dunod.

Savall, H., & Zardet, V. (1987). *Maîtriser les coûts et les performances cachés.* Economica. 5th edition (2010). Traduit en anglais (2008): *Mastering Hidden Costs and Performance.* Charlotte, NC: Information Age.

Savall, H., & Zardet, V. (1995). *Ingénierie stratégique du roseau, souple et enracinée* [Strategic engineering of the reed, flexible and rooted]. Paris, France: Economica. Traduit en espagnol en 2009: *Ingeniería estratégica: un enfoque socio económico,* Prólogo de Solis, P. México: UAM.

Savall, H., & Zardet, V. (2008). Le concept de coût-valeur des activités. Contribution de la théorie socio-économique des organisations [The concept of activitiy cost-value: Contribution of socio-economic theory of organizations]. *Revue Sciences de Gestion-Management Sciences- Ciencias de Gestión, 64,* 61–89.

Savall, H., & Zardet, V. (2009). Do internal consultants compete with or complement external consultants? Assessing experiences in companies? *Academy of Management* (AOM) conference paper, Chicago, IL.

CHAPTER 13

BLOOMINGTON TRANSPORTATION CENTER

Follow-Up Case Study

Tom Oestreich, John Conbere, and Alla Heorhiadi

CONFERENCE REMARKS:
Chapter Prologue

The Best Employee Quote of All:

> We need change. Most people don't like it, so we can't just say "Change—
> NOW!" SEAM says "What would help you work better, more efficiently, and
> happier?" That approach—the team approach—makes all the difference.
> Even those who put up the most resistance benefit. SEAM might just teach us
> all that change is, dare I say it, GOOD for us.

The Socio-Economic Approach to Management (SEAM) is designed to address human or social issues that have an impact on the financial outcomes of an organization. In September 2012 Conbere and Heorhiadi, with a small team of intervener-researchers, introduced SEAM into the Bloomington Minnesota Public Schools Transportation Center, of which

Decoding the Socio-Economic Approach to Management, pages 215–222
Copyright © 2016 by Information Age Publishing
All rights of reproduction in any form reserved.

Oestreich is the director. The start of the intervention was reported in an earlier case study (Conbere & Oestreich, 2014). This paper is a report of outcomes from the first year and a half of SEAM at the Transportation Center. We have divided the study into two parts, social and economic, although sometimes facts refused to be kept neatly into a designated category. The social is given by Oestreich, and the economic by Conbere and Heorhaidi.

The Transportation Center serves over 7,000 students daily, has a charter service for athletics and field trips, and a shop that maintains 110 buses as well as 125 trucks and mowers from around the school district. There are 125 employees, and we travel enough miles each year to cover the circumference of the earth 52 times.

In the 2012–2013 academic year a horizontal intervention was made, with the Mirror Effect in September, the Expert Opinion in October, and project teams starting in November. Vertical interventions with the office staff began in December 2012, then with the regular route bus drivers in January 2013. Projects began for the office staff and drivers in late spring. The vertical intervention with the shop mechanics began in August 2013, and for the Special Education drivers and aides and the trainers and stand-by drivers (who fill in on any route when the regular driver is not available) in September 2013.

We should affirm right away that the Transportation Center was very productive before the introduction of SEAM. The top priority is safety, and the Center had an excellent safety record. The next priority is getting students to and from school on time. With the usual exceptions that come from snow and ice in a Minnesota winter, the timeliness record was also excellent. The goal was to improve an already well-run operation.

Changes in the Office

I would like to begin with Claudia Carston, our Transportation Office Manager. As the SEAM process started, I knew that Claudia had reservations about SEAM. In her wisdom it did not take long for her to see the value and jump on board. After the Competency Grid was introduced, Claudia was asked to come up with a Competency Grid for her staff. She built a grid that immediately showed where there were deficiencies in current job duty practices and coverage. One of the problems was the lack of staff qualified to use the payroll system, and the reason for this was the system was difficult to use and learn. Using the payroll system also turned out to be a source of hidden costs. One of her first projects was replacing the payroll system, with group member coverage for backup. I believe the competency grid gave her a clear view of the office staff shortcomings, and/or how to better problem solve the ineffectiveness. It was not that she did not know the payroll system was poor. Rather the analysis provided the opportunity to realize how much time was wasted by the payroll system and thus inspiration for taking the time to find a new system.

We later used the Competency Grid to resolve a dysfunction in another project. Our Special Education Bus Assistant job duties and/or roles were unclear. In our small project group we developed a competency grid to clarify the needs and roles of the assistants, to better coordinate with the Special Education driver safety duties. It demonstrated a truth that, in Claudia's words, "if you believe in someone it becomes amazing the level they can rise up to."

I need to set the stage here a little about our morning bus dispatcher, who is a little German lady with a type A personality. She is one of the hardest working morning dispatchers we have ever seen. At the same time, as drivers come by in the morning to sign in she would yell out things like "You need to be here on time," or "We do not have anyone left to cover your route." Many people felt uncomfortable in response. That being said, I know Claudia and I have struggled with how to best work with her to improve her window-side manners. Through the SEAM process, I believe Claudia identified additional training needs based on the competency grid, and it has made a huge difference. Truly, she is responding like a gifted child who was not previously challenged enough.

A root cause of some office dysfunctions were unclear roles and/or expectations with many of the office staff. Claudia was able to start balancing some of the workloads to better handle the high traffic with staff interactions and radio emergencies. Resolutions included identification of roles, time management, and establishment of long range priority actions plans.

Time

One of the difficulties at the Transportation Center is there is always too much to do. The day starts at 5 a.m. and ends at 7 p.m., or later. We are driving buses that carry thousands of students every school day, and maintaining all the equipment to make sure each vehicle is safe. We have parents calling for a variety of reasons, plus calls from the schools we serve. We constantly have to adjust to situations, such as a snowstorm, or a sick child, or schedule changes. We never finish. So to take time for SEAM felt risky. We cannot afford to waste time. As one employee said, "There are many frustrations when trying to accomplish tasks when you already have too much work to do."

In spite of such frustrations, the overall response to SEAM has been positive. These are fairly typical comments: "The SEAM process has helped me to see things in a better light by clearing my thought process." "The SEAM process is one of fairness and understanding." "The employees work together to build a better business." "Work on the most difficult issues and the smaller issues will take care of themselves." "The result of SEAM is our drivers are more open, and the overall climate is better, although there is a small group of people who remain negative." "SEAM has helped us to have more communication with each other and to try to help what's broken, but I think we have a ways to go" (Office employee).

Changes we have seen: Through many projects and different interactions with groups, one of the largest successes we are seeing is with the new office staff assignments. Out of the competency grid and the feedback in the Expert Opinion, new tools were developed, such as protocols for radio and driver emergencies, and bus breakdowns. Improved communications were developed through discussions, and I see attitudes changing. Our radio clerk has more confidence in her role due to knowledge shared. Mr. Savall wrote about the Intrinsic and Extrinsic working conditions—the safety or framework of life at work. Through the SEAM process we have opened up to Horizontal and Vertical relationships which have changed the spirit within the workplace in a positive way—better working conditions and relationships.

Recent Wins With the Mechanics

Bloomington mechanics identified dysfunctions with present and future mechanical issues. Having identified this through the SEAM process, our shop team brought these concerns up with the world headquarters for the bus manufacturer. The hidden cost approach made at this meeting was very successful and saved many thousands of dollars to drive a resolution or fix for the problem. Bloomington benefitted from this, and we received valuable free equipment for being part of the solution. This was SEAM at work in a different dimension, by helping to correct dysfunction with the dealerships participation. I think what changed for us was the participation in naming and then fixing the problems in the shop. When the mechanics and I saw a problem that started with the bus manufacturer, we decided to fix that too. Before, we simply would not have thought of going to the manufacturer. So there were two changes. One is the mechanics began to own their expertise, and to speak up, even to a national manufacturer. The other is because they spoke up, we helped fix the manufacturer's problem and received $5,000 of free services in exchange.

After the SEAM Mirror Effect and Expert Opinion the mechanics were able to correct some long-standing problems. For instance, while working on these vehicles every day they saw where there were equipment break downs through poor driving habits, or problems drivers did not discover because they failed to make a thorough pre-trip inspection. The mechanics then created feedback loop trainers. Now, when mechanics see problems they share that information with the trainers. The trainers incorporate the new information into their training. As a result the mechanics are seeing far fewer problems on the buses of newly hired and trained drivers. The more difficult task is getting the previous drivers who have bad driving habits to change. At this time we do not have enough managers to address the problems, nor do the trainers have the authority in our unionized environment to take the initial corrective action to resolve the dysfunctions, even though these actions would be non-punitive, correctional support for our drivers and aides.

What is Not Working Well, Yet

While we have found great benefit in SEAM, we have some areas that remain difficult. We continually struggle with a constantly changing focus. Our Priority Action Plan is evolving quickly. Many additional projects have been added and assigned as high priority. Clearly, an additional dysfunction is created because we have not completed our original projects, thereby missing or leaving on the table hard cost of safety features that can still be captured. This appearance that nothing is being done, or things are not being done quickly enough, has created some dissatisfaction, which can be heard in some employee comments: "It is also frustrating when other departments have not been through this process and don't understand." "Some employees do not try to help the process."

One of the difficulties comes from the fact that the SEAM process was used for the Transportation Center, and not for the whole district. Where dysfunctions are within the control of the Transportation Center we are making good progress and are exceeding the goal of reducing hidden costs by 20% per year. However, many of our hidden costs involve other parts of the district. For instance, we have to work with schools to improve drop off and pick up efficiency. Currently we waste fuel, and the time of drivers and students. When we add it up, students sit on buses for more than 123,000 hours longer than is needed. At the same time, drivers waste time and fuel. To resolve these issues we need to create changes at each school. But school personnel are extremely busy, and working with the Transportation Center is not high on their priority list, so most individual schools have not made the time to work with us, and the district has not required schools to work with us to identify best practices or common practices to implement across the district. As a result our employees have said, "Support from upper management doesn't always exist."

One employee commented: "Tom—I have worked in the past with two organizations who implemented programs that mirror what the SEAM process is striving for . . . better communication and improved service. In both instances it worked because there was buy-in from the very top to the bottom of the organization. What I see here is a slow start with the drivers and an equally slow response from the top. Of the several meetings I have been involved in many of the conclusions point to the same changes and yet there is a hesitancy from the top to implement. The process will stall if there is no, or little, response to what the drivers, aides, and office staff see as necessary and obvious changes."

Another employee said, "There have been other issues where everyone seem to be in agreement and nothing seems to be moving forward. That is most frustrating. We are leaving an important group in limbo. We have repeated meetings about the same issues and the answers always come up the same. This group is at a standstill until something is resolved one way or the other. It is hard to get excited about the good things we have accomplished when some very urgent things are not being addressed."

TOM'S REFLECTIONS

My reflection: Learning about SEAM and working with Dr. Alla Heorhiadi and Dr. John Conbere on the process has been one of the coolest journeys I have had the opportunity to participate in. OK, obviously my wedding and my son being born come first.

SEAM has made a difference in the life force or spirit of the work place. I say this because of the attitudes that have changed through this process and how we all have opened up more. This is a slow process of change, and I have come to realize that changing slowly is the way to make this successful in a work environment. I have found new tools we can work with. Myself, starting out with the time studies and knowing there were job duties that I should not be doing, yet here I was doing them just to make things work; (a) tasks and duties that I could assign to our safety staff, (b) running the Priority Action Plan to keep me focused on the future and establish the goals set before us, and (c) utilization of the Competency Grid for project groups to develop positions within the organization. There are projects created from the competency grid that have helped us with dysfunctions from other departments, which are out of our control. Many ideas and suggestions that came out of the SEAM process are things I would not have thought of, such as "Staff members all need the ability to assist with certain functions in an emergency situation." I am seeing additional dysfunctions in so many places, and I know SEAM would be the right answer for companies to solve their issues. SEAM truly mirrors my life belief that we are all interrelated and we can work harmoniously given the right tools and process.

The hidden costs have been right on. I can share that our administration sees some of these as soft costs. I see many of them as hard cost, most in the safety area where the potential of hard costs becomes astronomical.

There have been many problems along the way. In particular, I had to take a lot of time to rewrite how the Transportation Center management would be structured. I believe that the largest hidden cost we have is lack of enough bodies to do the job correctly. Also, when we add technology we need the personnel who are able to operate the system to capture the dollars we were after in the first place, or correct the dysfunctions that are leading to additional hidden costs. At this point I have not gotten the help I need, and that has slowed us down, and frustrated many people.

Economic Analysis and Changes

We assessed hidden costs for the drivers, office, and mechanics (the shop) in the beginning of 2013, and again in the beginning of 2014. Table 13.1 shows the change. When we broke down the hidden costs for the shop, office, and drivers, we noticed that some of the actions to reduce dysfunctions came from the unit, some from the Transportation Center, and some from schools or the district as a whole. When we broke down savings, we saw a pattern. Where the dysfunctions were entirely within the realm of the Transportation Center, there was a much greater reduction in hidden costs than where other parts of the school district had to participate in resolving the dysfunctions (see Tables 13.2 and 13.3).

The lesson we take from this: We began the SEAM work at the Transportation Center. We included the superintendent, two district administrators and two union leaders on the advisory board, but the SEAM intervention did not include the administration nor the schools in the district. As a result, we believe that the rest of the district has not understood or bought

TABLE 13.1 Hidden Costs in 2013 and 2014			
	Hidden Costs March 2013	Hidden Costs March 2014	Savings
Shop	$284,352	$231,223	$ 53,129
Office	$134,875	$73,578	$ 61,121
Drivers	$276,780	$226,832	$ 49,948
Total	$696,007	$531,633	$161,198
Wasted student hours	123,729 hrs.	107,884 hrs.	15,845 hrs.

TABLE 13.2   Total Hidden Costs and Change in 1 Year

	March 2013	March 2014
Hidden Costs	$276,780	$ 226,832
Student hours	123,729 hrs.	107,884 hrs.
Savings in 1 Year		
Hidden Costs	$49,948 (18% reduction)	
Student hours	15,845 hours (13% reduction of wasted student hours)	

TABLE 13.2   Total Hidden Costs and Change in 1 Year

	March 2013	March 2014
	$55,390	$48,355
Savings in 1 year		
Hidden Costs	$37,726 (68% reduction)	

into the SEAM process, so reduction in dysfunctions leading to hidden costs is disproportionally low compared to what might have been. Working with the Transportation Center brought a reduction in hidden costs, but the potential was not reached. Similarly, the SEAM intervention transformed the morale and practices at the Transportation Center, but the lack of change in the rest of the district is a new irritation for the Transportation Center employees.

REFERENCE

Conbere, J. P., & Oestreich, T. (2014). SEAM Case study of Bloomington Transportation Center. The socio-economic approach to management within American companies. In H. Savall, J. P. Conbere, A. Heorhiadi, V. Cristallini, & A. F. Buono (Eds.), *Facilitating the socio-economic approach to management: Results of the first SEAM conference in North America* (pp. 49–59). Charlotte, NC: Information Age Publishing.

CHAPTER 14

IMPROVEMENTS FROM INTRAORGANIZATIONAL SYNCHRONIZATION TO INTERORGANIZATIONAL MONITORING OF STAKEHOLDERS

Intervention-Research in a Space Layout Consulting and Engineering Company

Thibault Ruat

CONFERENCE REMARKS
Chapter Prologue

This paper presents an ongoing case of socio-economic intervention-research conducted by an ISEOR interveners-researchers team in a space layout consulting and engineering company since October 2012. The first part presents the intervention and the diagnoses results. The second part

Decoding the Socio-Economic Approach to Management, pages 223–239
Copyright © 2016 by Information Age Publishing
All rights of reproduction in any form reserved.

covers the project intervention and the first ensuing results through the implementation of the improvement solutions and the appropriation of tools for SEAM. Finally, the third part explains the links between our team intervention-research and my doctoral research in management science addressing practical cooperation in the building industry.

OVERVIEW OF THE INTERVENTION AND THE SOCIO-ECONOMIC DIAGNOSES

The intervention-research was conducted in a space layout consulting and engineering company. The main activities of the company are to design and to manage the interiors set-up operations. The company designs and monitors layouts projects in three different areas:

- Prestigious places (e.g., Louvre Museum, luxury hotels)
- Brand networks and outlets, that is, shops, boutiques, and malls (e.g., Nespresso, McDonald's, Benetton)
- Service sector and public administrations (e.g., municipalities, banks, railway stations)

The building company seeks contracts as a prime contractor or as a coordinator, according to the project. Its missions are as follows:

- Analyze and size the global organization for the project implementation phase
- Define and analyze the technical specifications
- Schedule and control the setting-up and furnishing operations
- Ensure compliance with the price and delays in the contracts

The company was a French limited company with a Management Board and a Supervisory Board. Founded in 1987, its staff of 270 people included 35 fellow carpenters, 28 architects, and 24 building engineers. The company was located in eight geographical locations with seven sites in France and one in Italy. It also conducts projects in Spain, Portugal, and Belgium. In 2013, the company achieved 850 projects with more than 300 subcontractors, for a revenue of $78 million USD (€57 million EUR).

The Socio-Economic Intervention

The intervention-research began in October, 2012. The difficult context of the company was characterized by a decrease in sales and a net result operating loss of –\$6.7 million USD (–€4.9 million EUR). The intervention request came from the company's new CEO, in function since July 2012. The negotiation of the intervention-research lasted four months, from June to September 2012. This speed, unusual in the negotiation of such intervention-research, is explained by the specificity of the decision-maker. Indeed, the CEO is the former CEO of a security company in which ISEOR intervened for more than ten years. The client knew SEAM very well. The negotiations resulted in the intervention specifications agreement. The main objective defined between the company and ISEOR was: "Develop and mobilize human potential of the company and make everyone more committed to the strategy."

The main objective was broken down into seven intermediate objectives to define and formalize the methodology and benefits to perform (methods and products-products-services). These seven objectives were:

1. Improve service quality and delays through a better adjustment of supply and an effective coordination of subcontractors;
2. Create a true sales force in order to retain clients and win new ones, and to make everyone aware the vital sales function which prompts an "all vendors" individual position;
3. Adapt structures and working methods relying on shared management tools;
4. Develop cohesive management team to facilitate the decentralized monitoring of the strategic implementation and to reaffirm the unity of the group in Europe;
5. Strengthen local management to increase the business socio-economic performance, in particular the inclusion of human potential;
6. Set up reliable and relevant socio-economic performance indicators;
7. Set up an internal SEAM intervener team, able to keep up the effects of the process in time.

The intervention was conducted by an ISEOR interveners-researchers team, with the author's participation. The intervention began by a collaborative training assistance with all members of the management team. These actions were aimed at developing managerial skills by training persons, activities, and performances in innovative management tools. Thanks to the group time and the individual time alternation, collaborative training allowed for better monitoring and improved the implementation of socio-economic tools methods. These trainings also ensured the sustainability of the change action through the integration of tools in the current operation of the company.

In parallel to the SEAM training tools for managers, diagnoses were achieved. A Horizontal Diagnosis was conducted from October to December

2012. It involved all of the company managers. A second and more cross-departmental diagnosis focused on the Human Resource function during the second intervention phase, in October to December 2013. Two Vertical Diagnoses were achieved on two separate entities (Paris and Chambéry), corresponding to two clusters, the intervention in the first phase was characterized by 7 clusters following this architecture.

The Horizontal Diagnosis allowed for gathering the opinions of the 39 managers of the company about organizational dysfunctions. Thirty nine semi-structured interviews were conducted with five members of the top management team and 34 managers.

For the dysfunctions analysis of the two vertical groups, 81 people were interviewed (19 members of the management team, 52 persons without management responsibilities, and 10 representatives of representative bodies). The financial evaluation of the dysfunctions costs drew on 38 hidden costs interviews.

THE RESULTS OF THE SOCIO-ECONOMIC DIAGNOSES

The four diagnoses (2 horizontal and 2 vertical) achieved in this company highlighted 1,385 key ideas of dysfunctions. Two of the four diagnoses include a financial assessment of these problems by the hidden costs method (Savall & Zardet, 2008, 2011). These diagnoses required 212 interviews. Quantitatively, the diagnoses allowed us to identify $6.6 million USD (€4.85 million EUR) of hidden costs for both diagnosed sectors (see Table 14.1 and Table 14.2 for hidden cost assessment). More than half of the hidden costs came from overtime.

The difference between the two sites averages can be explained by the fact that site C integrated production activities while site P only undertook service activities. The amount of "non-creation potential" is underestimated due to the absence in the company of reliable indicators on this topic.

An example of non-creation of potential:

> Unsold but completed equipment services: "5 installers spend one hour per month to perform unsold and unbilled services." Calculation of the hidden cost: 5 persons × 10.5 months × 1 hour × €61 = €3,200.

The Synchronization Issue Within Project Groups

An in-depth analysis of the actors' interviews revealed that a significant proportion of failures were originated by monitoring and synchronization deficiencies between actors. We have gathered these problems into four foci and identified the amount of hidden costs that corresponded to

TABLE 14.1 Summary of the Hidden Costs of the Two Diagnoses Component

Sites	Full-Time Equivalent Staff	Excess Salaries	Overtime	Overconsumptions	Non-Production	Non-Creation of Potential	Risks	Total Site €/$	Total
Site P	31	€26,000 ($35,700)	€1,298,000 ($1,785,000)	€182,000 ($250,000)	€356,000 ($489,500)	€142,000 ($195,200)	N.E.	€2,004,000 ($2,755,000)	€4,850,000 ($6,668,000)
Site C	50	€107,000 ($147,000)	€1,580,000 ($2,172,000)	€438,000 ($602,000)	€721,000 ($991,000)	N.E.	N.E.	€2,846,000 ($3,913,000)	
Total %		2.70%	59.30%	12.80%	22.20%	3%	N.E.	100%	100%
Total %		Overload = 74.8%			Not produced = 25.2%		N.E.	100%	100%

TABLE 14.2 Amount of Hidden Costs by Key Ideas

Focus	Key Idea	Example of Elementary Dysfunction	Financial Assessment EUR 2,468,800 USD 3,400,000
Lack of monitoring of the stakeholders	Monitoring of the internal stakeholders deficiencies	"The staff short-cuts the workshop manager. They deal their applications directly with a business officer."	EUR 134,400 (USD 184,800)
	Wrong choice of the external stakeholders	"Subcontractors choice is badly treated because the choice is only based on price and not on quality. They make poor work and clients aren't happy."	EUR 109,200 (USD 150,100)
	Monitoring of the external stakeholders deficiencies	"The so-called flexibility of our subcontractors comes from the fact that we twist them. They are paid very late. Some are in liquidation or receivership and it is probably our fault."	EUR 244,400 (USD 336,000)
	Misallocation of the internal stakeholders	"The works foremen make the designers' work. Thus, designers are sidelined because they do not participate to the meetings and they take longer to draw."	EUR 56,500 (USD 77,600)
Lack of cooperation	Unsold and unbilled services	"The staff insufficiently takes into account the customer requests. It causes additional but unpaid work by the customer."	EUR 121,500 (USD 167,000)
	Poorly organized worksite	"For a two weeks project, we spent four to five weeks. This excess is due to the fact that he had to go back six times on the worksite because of organization deficiencies."	EUR 49,400 (USD 68,000)
	Compartmentaliza-tion between internal stakeholders	"There is neither connection nor rules of the game nor working strategy between the areas of work. It creates enormous economic conflicts between those areas. Decoration, business managers and manufacturing services are partitioned."	EUR 549,600 (USD 756,000)

(continued)

TABLE 14.2   Amount of Hidden Costs by Key Ideas (continued)

Focus	Key Idea	Example of Elementary Dysfunction	Financial Assessment EUR 2,468,800 USD 3,400,000
Lack of coordination and of teamwork	Deficient planning	"The sites are poorly anticipated and not programmed. Everything is done at the last minute and in emergency."	EUR 329,400 (USD 453,000)
	Lack of coordination consequences	"The plans always change during the construction because the designers constantly give elements without proper validation. We have to make changes, it increase time and costs."	EUR 76,400 (USD 105,000)
	Lack of coordination between stakeholders	*"Installers are never consulted in the furniture design phase, it would avoid many mistakes, both on the plans and in the choice of materials."*	EUR 31,500 (USD 48,000)
	No compliance to the process	"The decorators modify manufacturing without going through the engineering office. It causes problems at installation and impacts on time and costs."	EUR 126,800 (USD 175,000)
Bad communication and bad transmission of information	Lack of meetings	"There are no meetings held between business managers, works foremen and designers that would provide opportunities to share information. It generates a tremendous loss of time, because everyone has to run after the information."	EUR 128,800 (USD 177,100)
	Conception errors	"There are errors in the dimensions taken by the engineering department. Carpenters-installers must rework the furniture on site and sometimes return them for making the necessary changes.	EUR 308,200 (USD 423,700)
	Failures on files transfer	"There is no information transfer between the engineering office and the works foreman who was not there from the start and who is in total ignorance of the project. Works foremen never transmit descriptions that specify what there is to be done by installers. Then, installers make work they should not do."	EUR 202,700 (USD 278,700)

each of them in Table 14.3. Hidden costs related to monitoring and synchronization deficiencies represented \$3,400,000 (€2,468,800), which is more than half of the total hidden cost. In the project phase, the expert opinion of the four diagnoses confirmed this, because 9 out of 16 "baskets" of dysfunctions highlight stakeholders' synchronization and monitoring deficiencies. Freeman (1984) defined stakeholders as "any group or individual who can affect or can be affected by the company achievements." These problems led us to provide a specific collective training and to work on the managers and supervisors' monitoring role through communication–coordination–cooperation methods. In parallel, according to the process of the SEAM intervention, some focus groups were set up after each diagnosis.

One focus group aimed at proposing improvement and socio-economic innovation solutions in order to reduce the diagnosed dysfunctions while recycling the hidden costs into value added. For this purpose, each manager of the diagnosed sectors was responsible for looking for solutions for each focus. They involved staff without hierarchical responsibility into working groups. Thus, more than 120 people were included in making the improvement solutions suggestions.

Improvement Proposals and Economic Balances

During the project phase, four working groups were set to deal with each of the 44 key ideas, which meant there were 176 working groups over a twelve month period. On average, there were six improvement actions proposals for each key idea, which means 264 proposals in total. Table 14.4 shows a sample of improvement actions proposals for four baskets on site C.

More than 90% of the proposals submitted to management have been validated, even those requiring significant financial investment. The proposed renovation of the workplaces represented an investment of \$962,500 USD (€700,000 EUR). Other proposals, such as investing in a CNC machine, required an economic balance before being validated. Economic balance highlights the financial consequences of the company improvement actions proposals (see Table 14.5). The CEO just took a few minutes to validate a €200,000 EUR (\$375,000 USD) investment for a CNC machine thanks to the economic balance.

TABLE 14.3 Composition of 8 Dysfunctions Baskets of Two Vertical Diagnoses

Basket	Vertical Diagnosis Site C	Vertical Diagnosis Site P
1	• Develop internal and external cooperation and teamwork • Lack of inter-service cooperation • Ineffective means of communication and of information transmission • Poorly integrated teams	• Develop synergy and communication-coordination-cooperation between the various sites, services and subcontractors • Compartmentalization of the conception and the operational functions • Absence of external partnership relationship • Ineffective relationships with functional departments, teams and sites
2	• Improve the monitoring and build implementation performing tools • Procedures heaviness an non-compliance • Lack of efficient control tools • Ineffective time management policy	• Create reliable activities planning to improve the quality of service • Poor anticipation and distribution of the workload to the actors • Lack of efficient control tools Mismatch between service quality and clients requirements
3	• Improve the human potential management • Underdeveloped integrated training • Lack of professional dialogue	• Strengthen responsibility and autonomy of the management and personnel management functions. • Lack of responsibility and of robustness of the managers • Lack of professional dialogue • Lack of decentralization of the integrated training for managers • No buy in tools and of the monitoring indicators by management • Lack of team management
4	• Improve the material conditions of work • Ineffectiveness of the physical working conditions	• Encourage the decentralized implementation of the strategy and of the company policies • Lack of equipment and of storage space • Failures of the purchase and trade policies that affects the margin • Gap between the communicated and the implemented strategy

TABLE 14.4   Sample of Improvement Actions for Four "Baskets" at Site C

Basket	Root Causes	Root Solutions	Improvement Actions
1	Difficulties in the relationship with HRD and the general services	Centralize and track collaborators' requests	Create a requests indicator and raise and systematize resolutions chart
2	Workshop competitiveness deficiency	Invest in automated manufacturing machines	Make an economic balance to study the feasibility of investing in a CNC machine
3	Lack of consideration for other work people's	Inform people of the business constraints and specificities	Conduct an internal seminar to present the different business areas and perform a role-play
4	Poor insulation of the workshop	Insulation of the workshop	Achieve a thermal study and install sectional doors in the workshop

The Implementation of Improvement Action Proposals and the First Changes

Among the 264 improvement actions proposals, more than half have been implemented by spring 2014. Table 14.6 below shows an example of the outstanding implementation by basket three months after the end of the project phase.

Improving the socio-economic performance, although it still needs to be developed, has already strengthened the bargaining power of actors (Savall, 2010; Savall & Zardet, 1995). The many dysfunctions actors suffered placed them in a position of inferiority or of submission to clients-as-kings, and they could only answer "*yes*" to any request, even if those requests go beyond the scope of the contracted works. The internal reinforcement now allows them to say "*no*" to important clients while renegotiating the terms of their partnership.

ARTICULATION OF INTERVENTION-RESEARCH WITH THE PHD RESEARCH

This intervention-research, by providing results on synchronization practices in the building industry, enriched our doctoral research on practical cooperation in this business area. It prompted us to consider synchronization as a component of cooperation.

TABLE 14.5 Economic Balance of a CNC Machine

Expenses			Income		
Extra Expenses	Year 1	Year 2 to Year 4	Extra Income	Year 1	Year 2 to Year 4
Material investments			*Incomes development*		
• Equipment (tooling)	€5,000	€5,000	Gross margin on:		
• Designers loss of productivity	€38,529	€0	The company subcontracted markets	€9,404	€10,671
• Designers training	€27,632	€0	Markets that could be subcontracted to the group	€0	€4,706
• Workshop training	€4,132	€0	Workshop hours valorization (productivity gain)	€46,713	€76,380
• Computer engineer travels	€1,040	€0	*Self financed potential creation*		
• Workshop loss of productivity	€25,738	€0	Pre-conceived deneric furniture (designing time gain)	N.E.	N.E.
• CUGN Maintenance	€3,000	€3,000	Manufacturing and stocking the most sold furniture	N.E.	N.E.
• Network connection	€3,000	€0	New markets	N.E.	N.E.
			New type of materials	N.E.	N.E.
Project cost amortization					
Amortization or leasing (N=5) see Amort. Table	€35,000 PM	€35,000 PM			
Software TOPSOLID cost (€17 000 EUR)					
Permanent overcosts					
CUGN Control	€3,050	€3,050			

(continued)

TABLE 14.5 Economic Balance of a CNC Machine (continued)

Expenses			Income		
Extra Expenses	Year 1	Year 2 to Year 4	Extra Income	Year 1	Year 2 to Year 4
Sub-Total	€146,421	€46,050		€56,117	€91,757
Hidden costs recycling into value added			Income decrease		
Hidden costs estimated in the diagnosis or not					
Decrease of the temporary work 750h	€−15,000	€−15,000			
Cancelling of the machine maintenance	€−500	€−500			
Sub-Total	€−15,500	€−15,500		€0	€0
Total Expenses	€130,621	€30,550	Total incomes	€56,117	€91,757
			Result Year 1	€−74,504	
			Result Year 2 to year 4		€61,207
					€170,325

TABLE 14.6 Example of Outstanding Work by Basket

Basket	Vertical Diagnosis Site C	Vertical Diagnosis Site P
1	• Developed internal and external cooperation and teamwork • Upstream involvement carpenters-installers from the costing of projects and systematic implementation of a single contact for subcontractors.	• Developed synergy and communication-coordination-cooperation between the various sites, services and subcontractors • Defined and structured internal means of communication, coordination, cooperation (3C)
2	• Improved monitoring and performing tools • Simplified billing procedures and integrated training to client-related procedures	• Reliable planning and programming activities that improve the quality of service • Implementation of an work plan for each site
3	• Improved management of human potential • Internal seminar for business areas presentation (1 day)	• Strengthened responsibility and autonomy of the management and personnel management functions • Managers participation in job interviews
4	• Improved material conditions of work • Purchase of a numerical control manufacturing machine for the workshop	• Encouraged decentralized implementation of the strategy and of the company policies • Renovation, upgrading local and Creating a Company Savings Plan (PEE)

Main Issue and Research Hypothesis

Our research problem was that the cooperation practices between the stakeholders of a general contract project is a vector of more and more serious dysfunctions which reduce the social performance of all of these stakeholders from an internal and an external perspectives, from the design, construction, and use phases (Ruat, 2012).

Our main assumption was that improving cooperation practices through the development of a partnership management between the contract project stakeholders would enhance the socio-economic performance of these stakeholders, and also meet a social issue by improving the integral quality of the buildings. The first results of this intervention-research confirmed the importance of the cooperation issue and allowed us to validate the idea that the synchronization between and within the different stakeholders in a building project was deficient and/or poorly structured, considering that synchronization deficiencies represent more than half of the hidden costs in the case study. This intervention-research allowed us to validate the hypothesis that synchronization errors impact on the stakeholders' social performance, although the indicators on the environmental impact are to be refined.

The impact of the synchronization deficiencies identified during the intervention is great.

- *Economic.* $3,393,500 (€2,468,000) of hidden costs
- *Environmental.* $852,500 (€620,000) of overconsumption, consisting in leftover discarded or re-made materials due to quality deficiencies, resulting in energy and resource consumption, but also pollution related transport and waste treatment.
- *Social.* To illustrate the impact on social performance, here are the words spoken by a business officer in December 2012. "Last year, while waiting for my son to leave school, I began a conversation with another student's father. After a few minutes of a very friendly exchange, he comes to ask me what my job was. When I mentioned the name of the company where I work, he became all red; he took me by the shirt collar and tried to punch me. In this moment of anger that father told me that because of our company, his own company sank, he had to dismiss all his guys, his property was seized to pay off debts and afterwards, his wife left him... Telling these facts the next day to my manager, he began to laugh, "That shows the relationship we have with our subcontractors!"

Many stakeholders in this company have expressed concern about the bankruptcy of many of their subcontractors due to a lack of synchronization (e.g., between pilot actors in the projects such as work foremen and support services, accounting or legal services departments, that is to say between internal direct and indirect stakeholders).

The Study of Root-Causes of Problems

Our ongoing research and the data from this research-intervention, from 212 interviews, documents collected in situ in the organization, as well as 400 hours of collective training carried out with the company stakeholders since October 2012, corroborated the results while bringing new elements of understanding. Indeed, research works led by ISEOR within construction companies in the 1980s already had shed light on the presence of dysfunctions related to synchronization errors (Savall & Bonnet, 1988). The "root-causes" are an interpretation by the interveners-researchers of the actual causes of problems based on the expressed ideas but also on the *non-dit* (unvoiced ideas) perceived by interveners from their field observations. Two root-causes were then pin-pointed. The first was the lack of communication–coordination–consultation and the second was related to an excessive focus on the short term, leading to a disinvestment on the indirectly productive tasks (preparation, coordination, control) and to disorganization due to a lack of anticipation.

The results of this intervention-research confirmed these root-causes and discovered new ones.

- Root-cause 1: Lack of integration of some stakeholders upstream projects. This root-cause highlighted a persistent barrier, introduced by classical theories of work organization such as Taylor's, which creates a separation between the design and execution. Indeed, our results show that the lack of integration of certain actors stakeholders upstream projects increases the number of dysfunctions and of conflicts that affect a large number of stakeholders, primarily internal then spreading to external stakeholders.

- Root-cause 2: Too strong specialization of the stakeholders. The work organization in the contract project, and more generally the organization of a construction project, is split between different professions: designer, surveyor, economist, purchaser responsible for the architectural study, carpenter, mason, electrician, safety controller, business officer, accountant, etc. These different professions do not use the same technical language as each one is a specialist in his field. A separation persisted between the functions which induced lack of synchronization of the stakeholders. This disconnection explains the disorganization of the cooperation practices and as a result the managers' control appears to be nonexistent.

- Root-cause 3: Lack of managerial skills of the pilots. Beyond the difficulties of team management, that slow the employees skills improvement and the development of medium and long term strategies, the poor managerial skills of the managers in the contract project management weakened the projects' profitability. On the financial aspect, a project is sometimes a loss before it starts because of a lack of control indicators by the managers and the project managers. Thus, we hypothesize that improving the synchronization function is partly based on improving the managerial skills of managers and supervisor and their monitoring role.

- Root-cause 4: Depreciation of certain functions and activities. The lack of synchronization means integrating the functions of manufacturing/construction, such as carpenter-installers with design function upstream projects, can be explained by the lack of consideration of the manual professions within the companies. The diagnoses revealed that these persons do not feel recognized by the other players and they have the feeling of being denigrated and excluded from the life of the company.

In construction projects, a function lacks for coordinating the different stakeholders. The architects could play this role, however their lack of management skills (Zardet, Delattre, Petit, 2010) does not allow them to monitor the different actors. In addition, only 30% of the buildings are built with the help of an architect in France.

CONCLUSION

This intervention-research represents 300 days of work for the interveners-researchers team. From the identification of dysfunctions experienced by the company stakeholders in the company, including those related to synchronization errors between stakeholders, this intervention allowed the fostering a dynamic of organizational, managerial, and strategic changes.

The first difficulty was to intervene in a difficult economic environment for the company, because when we started the first diagnosis, the company lost $6.2 million (€4.5 million). The company's survival was threatened. Thus, a pressure for immediate results led us to accelerate the pace of change. We had to face the dynamic differences between the various clusters and sites. Thus, the two project groups have not fostered similar dynamics of change.

Work on synchronization methods and implementation through the project groups, and the collaborative trainings, allowed developing internal cooperation. Using the tools of time management, such as agendas and Operations Scheduling Sheet (workplan) strengthened the organization and time management by the managers. Actions to reduce dysfunctions also allowed the company to reallocate time to team management. Although all managers are now trained to the tools of socio-economic management, some tools such as the Priority Action Plan and the Strategic Piloting Logbook are not used yet.

The results in 2013, including economic improvements (+€15 million EUR in revenue and an increase of €5 million EUR of profit), show that improving the internal organization prompts progress in the external performance. The qualitative improvement of the client satisfaction through the development of partnerships is an example.

We are currently pursuing collaborative training, consultations with 8 clusters of managers as well as 5 new clusters of work foremen that began in October 2013. The architecture of the current intervention consists of 13 clusters of more than 90 persons, trained in parallel. We are carefully orchestrating the work to ensure the progress of the socio-economic change at all the levels of the company.

The current challenge today is that the non-supervising staff became the key motor in the business strategy.

Finally, we note that in a few weeks we can calculate the Intangible Investment in Human Potential Qualitative Development, that is to say, the return on investment of the intervention including exogenous and endogenous cost of actions compared to the recovery of value added on variable cost.

REFERENCES

Freeman, R. E. (1984). *Strategic Management: A stakeholder approach.* Boston, MA: Pitman.

Ruat, T. (2012). *Le management socio-économique d'une agence d'architecture: Quels leviers d'amélioration de la performance globale? [Socio-economic management of architecture agency: The levers for improvements of overall performance?].* Mémoire de master Recherche en Gestion Socio-économique, IAE Lyon.

Savall, H., & Bonnet, M. (1988). *Un potentiel caché de productivité dans le bâtiment: La synchronisation préventive des chantiers* [A hidden potential productivity in the building: Preventive synchronization projects]. Chapitre du Cahier Emploi et valorisation des métiers du bâtiment « gestion de chantier et sources de productivité » - Centre Scientifique et Technique du Bâtiment, 383.

Savall, H., & Zardet, V. (2011). *The Qualimetrics approach: Observing the complex object.* Charlotte, NC: Information Age. (1st French edition, Paris, France: Economica, 2004).

Savall, H., & Zardet, V. (2005). *Ingénierie Stratégique du Roseau.* [Strategic engineering of the reed, flexible and rooted] Préface de Serge Pasquier, 2ème édition, Paris, France: Economica. (First published in 1995.)

Savall, H., & Zardet, V. (2008). *Mastering hidden costs and socio-economic performance.* Charlotte, NC: Information Age Publishing. (First published in French in 1987).

Zardet, V., Delattre, M., & Petit, R. (2012). *Responsabilités sociale et économique indissociables face à la crise: Le cas du secteur de l'architecture* [Inseparable corporate social and economic responsibilities face to the crisis: The case of the architectural sector]. IXème Congrès international de l'ADERSE, RSE, globalisation et normalisation. Nouveaux enjeux liés à la crise, Mars 2012, IAE de Nice.

CHAPTER 15

MANAGEMENT CONTROL PRACTICES IN FOREIGN SUBSIDIARIES OF A FAMILY MULTINATIONAL CORPORATION

Seam Intervention-Research Findings

Laurent Cappelletti and Amandine Savall

CONFERENCE REMARKS:
Chapter Prologue

A very long-term socio-economic intervention-research has been carried out in this family Multinational Corporation for three decades. This longitudinal study enables a second stage in-depth analysis of its management practices. The first stage was highlighted in our last paper written for the first SEAM Conference held in Minneapolis in November 2012. The first stage analysis studied the internationalization process of this MNC, exporting the SEAM system to every foreign subsidiary. This second stage is a

Decoding the Socio-Economic Approach to Management, pages 241–258
Copyright © 2016 by Information Age Publishing
241

second level analysis of what kinds, types, levers of management control, this family food-manufacturing MNC has been practicing to control foreign activities and off-shored employees. The studied company has 4,000 employees on its payroll with more than 10% abroad. The question raised here is, "how a family MNC can grow and still keep good control of its subsidiaries?" "Are the control practices different from non-family companies or from companies that don't implement SEAM?"

Based on our scientific observation in this company since 1984, we assume that the management control practices rely on three incremental levers:

- The management system and the family culture;
- The organizational structure; and
- The information system, mostly including financial information.

The three levers play a big part in the quality of management control of subsidiaries. Since 2011, we carried out 46 interviews with the international activity involved employees to complete the intervention research findings. This enabled us to make a deeper analysis of the specific features of management control.

THE SOCIO-ECONOMIC INTERVENTION-RESEARCH PROTOCOL

The long-term SEAM intervention-research led to a wide knowledge and understanding of the management system the company has developed. Intervention-research is an exploratory and confirmation research technology that consists in really getting into the company, to conduct the change process (Buono & Savall, 2007). This research methodology offers an attractive asset for Management Sciences, in that it is a transformative, non-contemplative, longitudinal research. It is based on organizational immersion and cooperation between scholars and company actors, in order to get reliable experimental materials and data, and lead to organizational improvement. This comprehensive approach was allowed through participating in many collaborative sessions between intervener-researchers and organizational agents, conducting interviews, collecting and analyzing various documents, and closely observing their organizational practices.

The French family MNC has been experiencing a growing international development, reaching almost 20% of the €550-million annual sales. Its international strategy is hybrid: a mix of exportation, and local settlement through endogenous and exogenous growth, according to the target countries.

Forty six interviews have been conducted with about 50 persons, from different hierarchical levels. These people are located in all the foreign subsidiaries of the family MNC and in the French headquarters section that is dedicated to the management of international activities. Most employees were interviewed in their native language (i.e., in French, English, or Spanish). We elaborate the interview guide from the existing literature and our intuition (Savall & Zardet, 2004) in order to grasp the internationalization process of this family MNC through describing, explaining, and recommending some international management practices. It was made up of three general topics with no specific questions:

1. *Strategic decisions about family business internationalization:* decisive factors related to family business, rationality, and decision-making criteria, decision-making process;
2. *Strategic Management family business internationalization:* stakeholders' management, management of international activities, learning phenomena and knowledge management, intercultural management, considering commercial, social, environmental, accounting & financial standards & norms; and
3. *Measurement & Control of family business internationalization performance:* performance measure, management control practices and tools of international activities, factors of value-added creation in internationalization.

Data Processing Through SEGESE© Research Software

The expert socio-economic management system SEGESE has been developed by ISEOR research center in France (Zardet & Harbi, 2007; Krief & Zardet, 2013). This center specializes in intervention-research and action-research methodologies. Briefly, this software enables the researcher to categorize the materials or data into different areas of the research topic. These large themes are identified by the researcher and can be split up into sub-themes or sub-areas, according to a traditional arborescence system. Then, the process is about coding the selected quotes of each interview, following various steps: from selecting the meta-category (area or theme) to selecting the very detailed code, called "key idea." This software has been designed according to an epistemological abduction assumption; the researcher selects an existing code or is able to create a new one to better sum up the quote. In other words, it is a data compression (or concatenation) process, in that the researcher presses down the scientific knowledge in a very dense way. After coding all the quotes selected from the interviews, the software generates the set of "key ideas" that sums up all the quotes.

The following findings have been elaborated through a second stage of compression: we synthesized around 1,500 verbatim spread in around 400 key ideas. Those are divided up into seven themes or areas, which have appeared over the interviews processing (induction), and from the initial interview guide (deduction). These seven areas are: (a) strategic decisions and decision-making process, (b) stakeholders' management, (c) organizational structures and functioning, (d) learning phenomena, (e) intercultural management, (f) consideration of norms and standards, and (g) measurement and piloting performance. The specific findings about management control practices are based on the 7th area "measurement and piloting performance" (i.e., 33 key ideas and 250 verbatim).

GENERAL FINDINGS ON SEAM-BASED INTERNATIONALIZATION PROCESS

The family MNC has two main notable features of its management system: a family-based governance and an original desire for growth.

Family Governance and Top Management

The studied family MNC is a French food manufacturing group which was founded in 1974 by five brothers. Each one owned 20% of the capital. Three brothers were top managers; the two others preferred more operational positions. The elder was a commercial and marketing genius. The second quickly took over the CEO position, and was financial and industrial oriented. The younger brother entered the company with small commercial responsibilities in France, moving up through the hierarchy, from site manager, Business Unit director, to CEO in 2007. The small family business had turned into a multinational company. The company is organized according to four business units: three of them are product lines and the fourth one is 10 years old and overarches all the international activities. Despite this exponential growth along the SEAM intervention-research, the same family still owns 100% of the capital. The company thrives and has no financial problem.

Its market strategy is fully based on the customer closeness. From the very beginning, the five brothers wanted to maintain the quality of the manufactured products. The top managers have always been sensitive to their external environment, in terms of customers' health and ecological aspects of the products. Eighty percent of the turnover is made under their own brand. As a result, the expected level of quality is very high. Their management system rests upon four basic rules, largely resulting from the SEAM intervention-research: in-house training for all staff, human-sized subsidiaries (no more than 300 people) so to encourage management closeness and communication, global comprehensive approach of the organization, and cooperation between industrial and sales operations. The twenty national and international subsidiaries are completely decentralized. This functioning mode underscores the industrial and sales autonomy of every subsidiary.

Internationalization Strategy and Process

Its internationalization strategy began in 1998 and has accelerated since 2007, with the creation of the International business unit. In the 1990s, the brothers thought about going international. They started exportation in 1998. The first countries where they decided to go were Latin countries such as Italy, Spain, and Belgium. This decision was made so they could make durable the already implemented French strategy, according to which "every product directly leaves from each site." Products for Italy consequently left from Eastern France, for Spain from Southern France, and for Belgium from Northern France. The company held a significant asset: Its French customers were already present in the aforementioned countries. Indeed, at that moment, large French retailers were moving all around Europe. The group was also participating to this global movement, opening small subsidiaries in the United Kingdom, Spain, Italy, Germany, and Belgium. The company realized from the very beginning that a sales force should be locally present in order to immerse into the other cultures and consumption habits. So the managers asked employees to go there. Thus, internationalization in this company was falling under integration and closeness strategy. The competitors were doing differently, by using intermediaries, such as sales agents.

In the early 2000's, the company decided to enter the United Kingdom. They rolled out the same strategy as in previous occasions, by transferring people to the United Kingdom. The subsidiary reached €30 million revenue within a decade. So, they plan to build a factory there because of the exponential UK market growth.

In 2001, the internationalization process continued with the acquisition of one Spanish manufacturer and an Italian one. The expectation of both operations was to get industrial entities and to work with local people, not only with French expatriates.

In 2004, the CEO suggested a reorganization of the company: passing from three geographical business units to three product lines and one International business unit. "If I hadn't created the International business unit, I think that we wouldn't be as globally outstanding as we are now" (CEO of the group, July 2012).

As another result of the SEAM intervention-research, after a few years of exportation and internationalization, and more specifically after the Italian market failure, the CEO and the international business unit Director wrote a new business plan: "producing local," "developing international partnerships," and "spreading the management system" (sales and industrial balance, PNAC, business plan . . .) but respecting national and organizational cultural differences. The Periodically Negotiable Activity Contract (PNAC) is a "management tool that formally states the priority objectives and the means made available for attaining them, involving every employee in the enterprise (including workers and office employees), based on a biannual personal dialogue with the employee's direct hierarchical superior" (Buono & Savall, 2007, p. 430) The purpose is to link the company's strategy to individual objectives. This motivating and piloting tool is applied throughout the whole company: from CEO to workers. PNAC is a great tool for managerial authority maintenance, and for financially rewarding the staff. Another crucial resolution was also to promote international development through local subsidiaries, rather than exportation. Moreover, the company's cornerstone of internationalization was to settle strategic partnerships, requiring them to find reliable and effective local partners to become their spokespeople in the foreign countries. This partnering process was implemented with the American Small and Medium Enterprise (SME) they acquired: "We have met them four or five times a year since 2008. We created trustful relationships until we eventually crossed the capitalistic stage. It wasn't only phone calls, but a strong partnership: travels, promotional events, and so on" (CEO, personal communication, July 2012).

In early 2012, the family group acquired this American SME. The negotiation process had started from 2009. This SME was already manufacturing similar products to the French group. Its turnover is $25 million. The American project was aimed at working on existing American products under the American brand name, and marketing one of the French product lines under the French brand name.

Specific Findings on SEAM-Based Management Control Practices

Processing the 46 interviews showed that different kinds of controlling the foreign subsidiaries were implemented. This complementary process shed light on the scientific observations the intervention-research team had made since 1984.

The management control practices (i.e., measuring and piloting the foreign subsidiaries' performance, implemented by the family MNC, are both formal and informal). Three types or levers were considered: the management system and the family members, the organizational structure of the international business unit and its subsidiaries, and the information system (mostly regarding financial information) (Savall, 2014).

We must say that very few verbatim from the French interviewed persons were about control and piloting practices of the subsidiaries. The following findings are mostly based on the delocalized staff voices (i.e., the Belgian, Spanish, UK, and U.S. subsidiaries). Appendix 1 presents the set of key ideas (column 2) emerging from the 46 interviews and classified in the "measurement and piloting performance" area. This area is compounded into 4 sub-areas (column 1): Performance Measurement & Steering (it-selves), Budgetary & Financial Control Tools & Practices, Information System, Performance Indicators & Tools, and Key Individuals in Performance Steering & Assessment. Columns 3, 4, and 5, show which type/lever of control the key ideas were priory attributed (Savall, 2014).

The Management System as a Lever for Management Control of Foreign Subsidiaries

This first type of control practices is revealed through management tools, and the moving-abroad of family members to key management positions in the foreign subsidiaries.

In each and every foreign subsidiary, a family member, previously working in the French sites of the MNC, takes part in the top management of the subsidiary. The UK subsidiary CEO is one of the group CEO nephews. Another nephew left a year ago to the American subsidiary, to increase sales in the imported French products. This person was previously managing the Italian subsidiary for 8 years. A third nephew is currently managing the Asian market and lives in Seoul. Other very experienced non-family members have taken big responsibilities in the Belgian and Spanish subsidiaries. These kind of experienced and trustworthy employees, living abroad, are a very powerful way to guarantee soft laws and values of the family MNC, such as they are alive in the French subsidiaries. These people are controlled development factors of the MNC.

The integrated comprehensive approach of the organization was also a performance lever of the corporate international strategy. Employees' skillfulness and participative management practices give sense to work for the employees, and enriches jobs and functions. This generates better performance. Looking for both social and economic, both short and long-term, both result-based and method-based, performance is successful.

> I went through various integration processes at my providers? Each time a company is acquired by an investment fund, the quality of service decreases and the communication becomes more complicated, deadlines are not respected and we lose some effectiveness.

The management system is completely broken down to each and every foreign subsidiary. The MNC top management team considers that the management tools (SEAM tools) and rules (SEAM theory) constitute a real lever for team cohesion, thus for performance. A common base for both kinds of organizations, headquarters, and subsidiaries, makes professional relationships easier and more effective, despite cultural differences.

> With CAP now everyone shares their goals and we're working together. So it's a good change. There is more a sense of direction. (translated from the French)

The collective and individual assessment of foreign teams relies on the same French system of people control & support: PNAC, business plan, one-to-one meetings... The assessment process is intended to make employees more responsible for obtaining the expected performance. While the foreign subsidiaries' top managers have mostly financial goals (profitability, sales...), other employees are rather assessed on their capacity and the way they pilot and manage their day-to-day activities and teams. Most interviewees claim that the management system breakdown makes them more responsible, especially in the self-assessment of their individual performance.

However, several interviewees shed light on the fact that the individual assessment system is not fully spread to all foreign employees. Indeed, the system is not as effective as in the French subsidiaries, and the financial bonus is not applied to any kind of employee in some countries.

Finally, the management control of subsidiaries relies on several specific individuals. The international director is responsible for the strategic implementation in all the foreign subsidiaries. The off-shored family members are responsible for their own assignments in the local subsidiaries, as well as supporting the local employees, and rising up some information to the MNC top management. Nonetheless, nobody dared to express any kind of over controlling feeling from the family members.

As a conclusion, we may say that the active piloting and management of all the employees, and from all of them, encourage effective, efficient, and profitable cooperation between headquarters and subsidiaries.

The Organizational Structure as a Lever for Management Control of Foreign Subsidiaries

The main idea of the family MNC top management team was that "the more the organization is decentralized, the more people will be involved, the more the company will be thriving and be performing." That is the reason why most functions are locally operated. Every subsidiary is or will be provided with production, sales, logistics, human resources, accounting and finance functions. Decentralization does not mean losing control, only if the high level of cohesion is maintained. Informal control is more powerful and more effective than traditional formal control, through a supposed powerful IT system for instance.

There are many interactions between operational and support teams, both from headquarters and those from subsidiaries. Those coordination and communication flows are respected during the decision-making process and implementation and assessment process. These interactive relationships between headquarters and subsidiaries' staff enable better understanding of the financial results. The finance manager of a foreign subsidiary holds a monthly meeting with the international finance manager and the corporate finance director. If the subsidiary is too far from the headquarters, the meeting is held by visio-conference. This meeting is aimed at explaining and understanding what were the origins of last month financial results, and what are the main actions to implement next month.

> Every end of the month, we have a one-hour video conference call with the financial manager of the business unit, focused on the monthly results and he asks very precise questions to understand our margins.

The internationalization process of the group also leads to a more complex organization. For instance, support function managers from the subsidiaries report to a local direct supervisor, and a support director in the headquarters. Nevertheless, the flat structure of the organizational tree helps in overcoming the double supervisors' consequences for the people involved. "Before, we were accountable to the CEO and the founder, now to a whole team in France."

Appendix 2 pictures the control relationships within the organizational tree of international activities. It highlights the support function relations (spotted line), the informal control practices (dotted line), and the support-training relations (narrowed solid line), far beyond mere hierarchical and formal relationships.

Numerous mutual travels between foreign and French managers have taken place. Less qualified employees are also sometimes traveling to France or to foreign subsidiaries. This travel policy encourages effectiveness of relationships. We may call this a "warm training and support policy." It generates efficiency and effectiveness in integrating common working practices and cultural differences. It promotes a better sharing of best practices between countries, and employees.

> I meet with the finance manager twice a month through visio and we have emails back and forth throughout the month. Except with the language part, he is a sweetheart, very courageous, very friendly, and respectful.

> The production manager, the engineering plant guy, the R&D guy and me, we went to France while the production line was still there. The French team

came over here when the line was here too. Then, we've been training the workers on the line.

We've had 8 employees going to France last year. It has been great for the integration. I think it's important to keep doing that. That builds a lot of comfort between our employees.

The Information System as a Lever for Management Control of Foreign Subsidiaries

Information system refers to all the system (mainly IT) of formal information: management information (inventory of business plans, PNACs, reports of 1-to-1 meetings...), sales information (inventory of daily sales), and financial information (general, analytic, and financial accounting IT system access). This IT system is the same for all the foreign and French subsidiaries, except those that were recently acquired (such as the U.S. one).

For the American staff, the integration of such a new IT system stirs apprehensions up with regards to their independence, the adaptation to local law, the time devoted for the transfer, etc. For instance, the discrepancies between European and American accounting systems require additional time to undertake the daily accounting activity and additional reporting to headquarters.

But, the integration of the new IT system in all the subsidiaries still constitutes a big expectation for reporting and formal control from headquarters. Budgetary control, management control, and reporting practices have much developed within the subsidiaries. These piloting activities are under the headquarters and the subsidiaries' responsibility. This requires mastering accounting-financial skills and foreign languages. However, employees have different opinions on budgetary control practices and management control practices. Subsidiaries had to increase the staff of finance-control departments in order to provide the workload, or to standardize processes.

Foreign subsidiaries' employees also seem to better pilot the economic results than French employees. The reason would be that the MNC's products and brand are much more renowned in France than abroad. Thus, there is a greater risk abroad, to damage local gross margin and economic results. It must also be the reason why local top managers have financial goals in their PNAC (profitability, sales...).

We set up objectives to the different CEOs [of BusinessUnits and subsidiaries] in terms of EBITDA [Earnings before Interest, Taxes, Depreciation, and Amortization], sales revenues, and profit according to the investment made. The perspective is set on a 3-year period and every year we discuss the objectives based on two organizational levels: business unit and site. These objectives are translated through the decisions made by the business unit. Regarding the reporting, we analyze once every 3 months, during the Group's

Board of Directors, these different indicators and the strategic topics for each business unit, in business units' directors' presence. The link between the management, the governance and the shareholders is ensured by the CEO.

CONCLUSION

The findings of the 46 interviews within the family MNC confirm and shed light on the previous observations that we have been making since 1984, among the intervention-research teams.

The findings show the three management control levers through the management system, the organizational structure, and the financial information system. A very specific feature of a family business, family members are great vectors of informal control, in each of the three levers. Family members enable informal control, through their key management positions in the foreign subsidiaries, the easier communication with headquarters, and their participation to financial reporting practices.

The findings also show that the family MNC has a distinctive taste for informal control based on supporting and managing employees, beyond traditional reporting. Aiming at grasping the hierarchy of the three control levers, the SEAM general idea, before anything else, is that management control (i.e., managing people) enables better control of organizational functioning, to better analyze the financial reporting reliability.

The proactivity of control is also much highlighted. "Management control" gets back to its original meaning about "piloting" subsidiaries, beyond the generally accepted idea that control is about "follow-up."

APPENDIX 1

Primary Results From Interviews (Processing Through @SEGESE)

Theme	Key Ideas	Management System	Organizational Structure	Financial Information System
		Management Control Levers		
Performance Measurement & Steering	1. Foreign subsidiaries' employees have a better economic steering of business than those of the country of origin			X
	2. Internationalization drives growth of the subsidiaries			X
	3. Sales foreign policy of imported products from country of origin is successful	X	X	X
	4. The subsidiary integration in a manufacturing MNC transforms the accounting structure			X
Budgetary & Financial Control Tools & Practices	5. Employees have different opinions on budgetary control practices			X
	6. Finance-Control department of the subsidiary had to increase the staff			X
	7. Management control practices of the subsidiary have changed since the merger			X
	8. The subsidiary has a budgetary and financial monthly follow-up	X		X
	9. Management control operations of the subsidiary are both the business unit and the subsidiary's responsibility			X
	10. Management controller of the subsidiary is expected to make the information clear and reliable for the parent company			X

(continued)

APPENDIX 1

Primary Results From Interviews (Processing Through @SEGESE) (continued)

Theme	Key Ideas	Management Control Levers		
		Management System	Organizational Structure	Financial Information System
Information System, Performance Indicators & Tools	11. The top management team of the subsidiary has financial goals set by the parent company (profitability, sales . . .)	X		X
	12. The assessment system of employees is supported by a set of management and steering tools	X		
	13. The bonus system of overseas salesmen is exactly the same than other foreign employees	X		
	14. The individual assessment tool of salesmen is consolidated in a collective tool	X		
	15. The assessment system of overseas employees is the same than those of the country of origin	X		
	16. The group individual assessment tool is not broken down to all overseas employees	X		
	17. The integration of the parent company IT system into foreign subsidiaries is complex			X
	18. The lack of common IT system has negative impacts			X
	19. Transferring the management system to foreign subsidiaries makes local employees more responsible and involved	X		
	20. The individual assessment system is not as alive in the foreign subsidiaries as in the parent company	X		
	21. The individual assessment tool enables setting cross-collaborative goals	X	X	

(continued)

APPENDIX 1
Primary Results From Interviews (Processing Through @SEGESE) (continued)

Theme	Key Ideas	Management Control Levers		
		Management System	Organizational Structure	Financial Information System
	22. The individual assessment tool enables setting integration-oriented goals	X		
	23. The financial compensation of the individual assessment system is not broken down in every subsidiary yet	X		
	24. The lack of common IT system ensures the subsidiary independence towards the parent company			X
	25. Implementing a common IT system in the subsidiary is a challenge for its independence			X
	26. The assessment system of the subsidiary has changed along with the merger			X
	27. Powerful IT tools are needed to enhance the subsidiary performance			X
Key Individuals in Performance Steering & Assessment	28. The international director is responsible for the foreign subsidiary strategy implementation	X	X	
	29. The management system of the parent company makes local managers and employees more responsible for their self-assessment	X		
	30. One of the family members works in a foreign subsidiary	X		
	31. A subsidiary employee is in charge of assessing and supporting trainees	X		
	32. The integration of the parent company IT system must be managed by a local employee as well	X		
	33. The interactions between the parent company employees and those from the foreign subsidiaries enable a better understanding of the subsidiary economic results	X		

APPENDIX 2: Representation of Management Control Relationships Between Headquarters and Foreign Subsidiaries

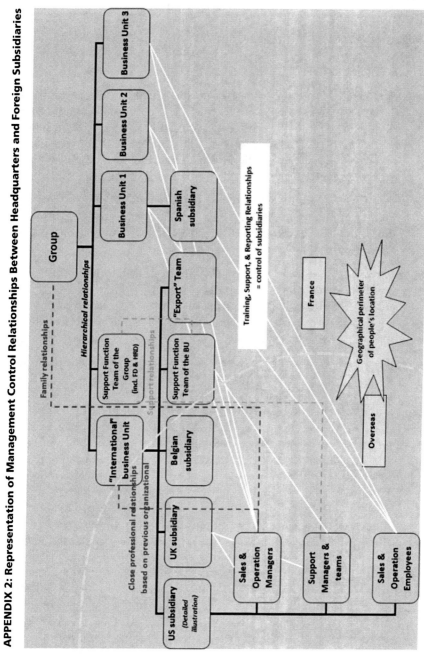

APPENDIX 3:
Conference Dialogue

Conference Participant: I have a question about the American subsidiary. How do they apply SEAM? Do you, at ISEOR, work with them or their headquarters?

Amandine Savall: Not yet. They have done it internally, sending experienced SEAM employees from France to train them in the management system with management tools, such as learning how you take care of people, how you run a meeting, and so on. But I presented the results of my research to the CEO and the International Director, and they want me to present this in front of all the international subsidiaries' CEOs.

Conference Participant: I was wondering how, over time, the strategy of an organization may change after a SEAM intervention? What direction the company is going and if there is sort of a common evolution that happens with that?

Henri Savall: Yes, we have more than 1,000 cases which demonstrate that when the firm is learning how to calculate hidden costs and value added, what we call strategy strengths, then the ambition of the strategy grows. And that is an effect, a very positive effect of SEAM. It is a resource based strategy.

Véronique Zardet: Our position, when we are negotiating for the first time with the client, we have done research revealing that SEAM in an organization. Once we have convinced the CEO to buy the intervention and to initiate the SEAM process, then there is still a huge challenge to convince the management team, the middle management. Another point is how to assure sustainability of the intervention towards the higher level and there is another person we have to sell. The CEO has to sell the project to the board, to his/her governance; it remains a long term project with high performance in case of change of roles, change in leadership. For example in the case of the public Mexican organization, which was presented in the first conference last year, the CEO had an action towards his secretary to present the intervention and the assessment of the intervention and the assessment of his subsidiary. After the elections in the federal government, he had to leave because he was governor, but the new CEO of this organization continued with the SEAM. He was former director and he continued because there were the majority of managers who were convinced and were applying SEAM in their work day-to-day. After one year of implementation, SEAM converts itself in a new way to do the daily work. It is not a project anymore. It is a new way to work.

Henri Savall: May I complete the completion of Véronique? The key factor for successful SEAM is selling. The maintenance of SEAM requires constant negotiation and conviction. We can tell from our learning of 40 years of SEAM that SEAM maintenance in an organization requires constant amount of selling because resistance to virus is very high, very implemented in our minds and we need selling. We had 95% of the people in the organization, 5% will try to convince and they will never be convinced and implement SEAM. We have 95% to convince to win. So it is all about selling. You need somebody to sell SEAM. You need your subordinates to do so because SEAM is very efficient but it is not natural. We need to sell constantly. And when implementing SEAM in an organization, we must convince the people who are going to sell SEAM to others. People around are blind. They don't want to see the positive results. I think that is the main recommendation we can tell you for implementing SEAM.

REFERENCES

Buono, A. F., Savall, H. (Eds.). (2007). *Socio-economic intervention in organizations. The intervener-researcher and the SEAM approach to organizational analysis.* Charlotte, NC: Information Age.

Krief, N., & Zardet, V., (2013). Analyse de données qualitatives et recherche-intervention [Qualitative data analysis and intervention research], *Recherche en sciences de gestion-management sciences-ciencias de gestión, 95,* 211–237.

Savall, A. (2014). *Étude du processus d'intégration d'une filiale américaine dans un groupe industriel familial français* [Study of the integration process of a US subsidiary in a family French industrial group]. Association Francophone de Management International (ATLAS-AFMI). Marseille.

Savall, H., & Zardet, V. (2004). *Recherche en sciences de gestion: Approche qualimétrique. Observer l'objet complexe.* Economica [*The qualimetrics approach: Observing the complex object].* Charlotte, NC: Information Age.

Zardet, V., & Harbi, N. (2007). SEAMES (SEGESE): A professional knowledge management software program. In A. Buono & H. Savall (Eds.), *Socio-economic intervention in organizations. The intervener-researcher and the SEAM approach to organizational analysis* (pp. 355–372). Charlotte, NC: Information Age.

PART III

FURTHER REFLECTIONS ON SEAM

CHAPTER 16

IS INTERVENTION-RESEARCH A RESEARCH METHODOLOGY OR SCIENTIFIC-BASED CONSULTING?

Henri Savall and Véronique Zardet

CONFERENCE REMARKS:
Chapter Prologue

A few management researchers in France are also consultants, and many in the United States. But most keep their consultancy work completely separate from their research. In academic management community jargon, consultancy means activities carried out in corporations, at their service, generating income, whereas research is synonymous with the production of publications, usually academic articles, generating academic recognition and fame—and to a lesser extent, promotion and extra income—a little in France, more in the United States. However, we have noted that some consultants enter research to obtain a doctorate and then continue as post-doctoral students. The activities of the Academy of Management, Management Consulting Division closely mirror this two-way flux: research professors attracted to consultancy and consultants attracted to research.

Decoding the Socio-Economic Approach to Management, pages 261–274
Copyright © 2016 by Information Age Publishing

The purpose of this article is to present and analyse an alternative way called intervention-research, or "scientific consultancy" practised by a European management research team. We review the specificities of intervention-research vs. consultancy as a research method that is scientific in nature, clearly different from the practices of consultancy and action-research (Savall, Zardet, Péron, & Bonnet, 2012) and examine its benefits and limitations for corporations and researchers. This chapter aims to analyse research practices rather than develop an academic theory.

The ISEOR research team was set up in 1975 in Lyon, France to apply the intervention-research concept, generate scientific knowledge about management and, simultaneously, help corporations introduce change, improve performances and solve problems (Buono & Savall, 2007). To date over 600 researchers have worked on this team, more than 150 theses have been defended and several thousands of research reports, works, and articles have been published. This research model is rare and innovative, at least in Europe and in our discipline, but has not as yet been fully recognized.

After examining the specificities of the negotiation of an intervention-research contract with a corporation and comparing them with the negotiation of a consultancy mission, we address the characteristics of scientific consultancy and then clarify the articulation between intervention-research activities and publication.

We conclude on the requirements of intervention-research and give details about the economic model used by our research centre which opens new horizons at the moment when public research budgets are increasingly limited.

INTERVENTION-RESEARCH CONTRACT NEGOTIATION: A HIGHLY SPECIFIC TECHNIQUE

Like consultants, intervention-researchers contact corporations in several ways—canvassing, frequently by recommendations from past or present customers or, in the case of the ISEOR, an unsolicited call by a corporation to the research centre. After this initial contact, the negotiation of an intervention-research contract is a long process which determines the success of the intervention itself. To define success, we initially propose to consider that a successful intervention-research has achieved two sets of goals:

- the goals pursued by the corporation and formalized during the negotiation phase; and
- the goals pursued by the researcher, i.e., changes in the company, improvement of its economic and social performances–but also new scientific knowledge.

These two goal sets precisely summarize the definition of an intervention-research (Savall & Zardet, 1996, 2011; Plane, 2000; Moisdon, 1984; David, 2000).

Specificities of the Negotiation Process

The negotiation of an intervention-research contract is a process which comprises specificities, the most important of which are:

A Successive Iteration Process

At least three to four meetings with the initial contacts (called introducers), then with the decider-payer, i.e., the person empowered to sign and pay the intervention-research contract. The negotiation process takes at least four months whatever the size of the company and 6 to 12 months in the cases of complex negotiations. Negotiation quality is a success factor in scientific consultancy, as it is during this phase that mission contents and methods are precisely defined and the degree of management's commitment to change tested. On the opposite, rare cases exist where a quicker negotiation process led to failure, i.e., refusal to sign the contract or interruption after the mission had begun.

The Negotiation Listening Phase is Very Important

Intervention-research negotiations begin with one to two hour "listening meeting" during which we listen to the "introducer" who called in the researchers before we discuss an offer of service, a method of intervention and costs. Strangely enough CEOs, for example, talk very openly during this first contact and provide information and opinions that they would probably not voice subsequently. This listening meeting, in addition to the fact that CEOs express problems to an "unknown" third party, also reveals expectations and challenges which later become intervention-research objectives. Usually all the problems evoked are challenges, strategic objectives and goals for the corporation expressed in the natural vocabulary of the interlocutor. For example, the CEO of a small building finishing company explained during this first interview that he was in very precarious economic situation as his associates and president did not fully assume their responsibilities and that his objective was to consolidate the role of the managerial staff and redefine his associates' roles in the corporation.

About fifteen days after the "listening meeting", we present an intervention-research project to our initial interlocutor to produce a "mirror effect." In fact the project is formulated as a product-objectives/product-methods/product-services triptych (see below), the intervention-research project perhaps addressing services (or intangible products) formulated in terms of goals to attain, or methods developed to achieve these goals, or services implemented to enable the adoption of these methods. Product-objectives are formulated starting from the problems expressed in the first "listening meeting" with the CEO, "mirroring" his statements. This intervention-research project does not even have an indicative *price tag* to avoid any form of bargaining about the contents of the project and this despite any pressure from the partner company CEO.

A third, and even fourth, meeting finally makes it possible to agree an adapted and validated intervention-research mission with the CEO, with a provisional budget. If this estimate is much higher than the company can afford, an additional iteration scales down the mission.

The Negotiation of Methodological Specification

The intervention-research project is presented in a three tier structure:

- *Product-objectives*: the objectives the corporate partner hopes to attain through scientific consultancy, generally formulated in terms of *improvements* to profitability, effectiveness, cohesion, and strategic pro-activity . . .
- *Product-methods*: methodological specificities proposed to achieve the predefined goals using the scientific expertise of the intervention-research team;
- *Product-services*: interventions by the research team inside the corporation and at the centre. These services are time-consuming and must be calculated to estimate a budget.

The contents of each mission and each corporation are different but always include non-negotiable elements which it is advisable to explain and justify to the corporate partner. In the event of refusal, the negotiation stops and the mission will not take place. This is a vital difference between intervention-research and classic consultancy, in which, usually, the consultant adopts the request and expectations of the customer to conserve the mission—and the fees.

Here are two examples of negotiations that were interrupted because of these non-negotiable elements.

Case 1

An industrial company with approximately 300 employees, a subsidiary of a major international group, contacted our research team, because it had recently introduced ERP and a "lean management" approach. Corporate HQ required it to improve its productivity and reduce occupational accidents. The CEO reviewed the current organization of the industrial facility and his strategic planning for the two years to come during an initial 90 minute "listening meeting." A few days later he called the intervention-research team to say that he did not want them to include the production sector as it had already been impacted by frequent changes in recent years and required us to restrict our research to the support services. Considering that the productivity and occupational accidents performance improvement objectives could not be attained *without changes in the production sector* and after discussions with the CEO, the intervention-research team decided to cancel the project.

Case 2

A major medico-social association, with 900 employees, called in the intervention-research team to introduce change, required in a tougher economic climate. The objective was to develop the managerial role and pilot the 80 managers in making changes. The human resources director —our contact—wanted *management training for the managers.* However, the intervention-researchers knew by experience that training alone could not achieve the goal and that a more thorough approach to change introduction, not only of executives but the whole training personnel was necessary. The intervention-research team refused this mission–and the $214,000 fee.

To conclude, intervention-researchers stop intervention-research missions if they believe they will fail, i.e., when they know in advance that the product-methods and product-services requested by corporations will not achieve the goals they themselves have set.

Running an Intervention-Research Mission

Scientific consultancy is an *in vivo* research methodology which proposes to generate knowledge by transforming the object studied (Savall & Zardet, 2011). This parallels clinical research methods in medicine (Savall & Fière, 2007, 2014), in which medical researchers care for patients and, by observing the effects of the therapeutic protocols deployed, formulate conclusions and publish their results in science magazines. Medical researchers thus simultaneously conduct diagnosis-regulation-evaluation processes on the patients in their care and research which aims to produce results replicable on other patients (Kwesiga & Pattie, 2006).

Scientific consultancy is a longitudinal research method, i.e., which observes and analyses a given company over a long period of time. An intervention-research mission effectively lasts from one year to three decades in the case of long-term corporate partnerships (Savall & Zardet, 1995, 2005). Intervention-research missions induce and manage change in corporations and simultaneously pursue two goals to

- bring new knowledge to the researchers, both with regard to initial diagnosis of situations, "remedies" and their effectiveness. This new knowledge makes it possible to deduce descriptive, explanatory and prescriptive assumptions (Savall & Zardet, 2011);
- accompany the corporation in planned change so that it achieves its goals better, for example to improve profitability, bring off a managerial plan, facilitate a merger-acquisition, turn the company round to prevent its short-term disappearance. To put it another way, cure the "patient" or, at the very least, improve his/her health, generating internal dynamics in the company (Coghlan & Brannick, 2005).

The difficulty in intervention-research is to keep both objectives on the same level (i.e., to ensure that the time spent on research for the acquisition of knowledge is not separate from the time spent caring for the patient). From a cognitive point of view, the two activities are simultaneous—better knowledge and understanding make it possible to help everyone involved to define and apply adapted care protocols better.

Leading an Intervention-Research Team

Unlike consultants who often intervene alone, intervention-research missions are carried out by teams. The reason is to achieve several objectives:

First, intervention-research is an apprenticeship for young researchers. An intervention-research team has members with different skill sets and levels of qualification from the most experienced (10% of the time spent on scientific consultancy) to the least (60%) and senior investigators (30%).

Scientific consultancy, whatever the size of the company concerned, takes place at a fast pace. When several researchers intervene simultaneously in the same corporation, in different sectors, the pace of scientific consultancy can be very rapid indeed. *But there is a fundamental difference in the way companies and researchers think of time.*

Team work enables comparisons of different views, interpretations and analyses, as scientific consultancy plunges researchers into the very heart of a corporate entity with the risk of losing the cognitive and emotional distance needed for interpreting and decoding the discourses and practices of everyone involved (Boje & Rosile, 2003). Interactions between the field and the research centre and weekly team meetings "depollute" researchers by enabling them to confront their information and their points of view with other members to improve the decoding of the situations observed. *Cognitive interactivity* and *contradictory intersubjectivity* contribute to scientific consultancy, as do basic epistemological and fundamental principles by facilitating detachment and replacing the illusory objectivity of the researcher (Savall & Zardet, 1996, 2011; Voyant, 2005; Krief, 2005).

The Generation of Knowledge

One of the challenges of longitudinal research is the traceability of the results. Indeed, to generate knowledge that can be published later requires rigorous and homogeneous work protocols between researchers concerning the quality and exhaustiveness of note-taking during the many in-company working sessions, the production of documents intended for the corporation for intermediate exploitation by intervention-researchers and the collection of documents produced by the corporation itself.

Collective team work by the investigators implies taking great care when collecting information and archiving it in a structured way accessible to every team member. In addition, if the research is cumulative, following the example of researchers in medicine who must accumulate a certain number of observations on different patients before being able to claim the validation of new knowledge, it is advisable to develop work methods common to different intervention-research missions. For example, the ISEOR team stabilized a replicable methodology in the 1980s to carry out socio-economic diagnoses of corporations or organizations. This means that today our knowledge base contains over 1,350 diagnoses. Starting from semi-directive interviews led according to a shared interview guide, this method consists in extracting field note quotes, classifying them by topics and sub-topics, then formulating generic key ideas illustrated by the key phrases.

The key ideas, classified in topics and sub-topics, are capitalized in an expert software system built up since 1988. Transversal, thematic and even by-sector analyses can thus be made *a posteriori* thanks to this material obtained using homogeneous protocols. For example, we recently published an article on the appearance of the "TFW (Taylorism-Fayolism-Weberism) virus" in 36 medico-social establishments, based on the transversal exploitation of 36 diagnoses made by different researchers on the team.

Introducing Change

By definition, every intervention-research mission inside a corporation is a set of activities aiming to help the company introduce and then consolidate change. These activities require skills relatively different from those of researchers as publication authors. Indeed, they must deploy an *energy of change* (Lacey & Tompkins, 2007), help convert theories into actions and, to do this, develop a relationship of trust with everyone in the company, from the CEO to the humblest employee.

Researchers plunged into the organisation must, for this reason, express themselves simply, as partners respectful of the people they are talking to. But, simultaneously, introducing change requires firmness by the researchers to ensure respect or, if necessary, concerted adaptation of the initially agreed methodological specifications. For example, corporate managers sometimes need to be reminded and have the principles of the composition of a task force or the interview methodology used in socio-economic diagnoses, which appear explicitly in the initial specifications, re-explained to limit inopportune pseudo-innovations in methods likely to have a negative impact on intervention-research quality and traceability.

A Commercial Relationship

An intervention-research contract is also a commercial relationship: the services provided are charged for. The vocation of the intervention-research team must not weaken this relationship. On the contrary, ensuring that the financial clauses of the contract are respected is key to establishing a balanced partnership between the corporation and the research team. To guarantee the researchers' independence no intervention-research mission starts until the initial down-payment has been paid. Every month it is important to check that invoices have effectively been paid; in the event of non-payment, this question is explicitly discussed at a meeting with the corporate partner. If the company has financial problems, new due dates can be negotiated but if it seems that the company does not intend to honour its commitments, services are cancelled.

Intervention-research contracts finance intervention-research centres and, in particular, pay the investigators. It is an alternative to State funding and the still widespread idea that research should be free for businesses as financed by taxes.

Publications

In the academic universe, researchers become known and recognized through their publications. So the question is how to alternate between the intervention-research mission and writing up the research for publication. There are many difficulties. First of all, the rhythm and duration of an intervention-research mission are very different from those of a publication. Researchers then have to identify problems likely to interest collective publications from an academic point of view. And then, of course, the company or organisation under investigation must agree to the publication of the findings.

The Rhythms of Scientific Consultancy and Publication

Intervention-research missions consume a lot of time and human energy. Publications have deadlines which must be respected, in particular when they are proceedings of congresses. Publication requires careful planning of the time devoted to writing, more especially if articles result from a team effort by at least two researchers as it is most often the case.

Identify the Problems and Write in a Team

Intervention-research missions involve examining a wide range of problems observed in the field, all of which could be the subject of several different and original publications. Nobre (2006) highlighted this phenomenon by stating that the problems evoked when initiating a mission are only the visible tip of the iceberg. After working in a corporation for several months, a wide range of new problems emerge, likely to lead to analyses supported by longitudinal observations. The difficulty lies in extracting generic problems from specific cases. This can be surmounted by the method which consists in analysing the contents of materials resulting from the mission and comparing them with what already exists in the literature. Compiling intervention-research cases in a knowledge base constitutes an inexhaustible resource for validating results from a single case by comparison with a bigger sample. Intervention-research team members can thus produce transversal publications, subjective and quantitative analyses and monographs relating to cases with high subjective input. The essential condition is to define ethical rules for the use of intervention-research materials. This is to ensure that while some researchers expend their energy on intervention-research, others, more comfortably, write publications based on the materials accumulated by the investigators. Rules of equity must be elaborated, for example the fact that no researcher can access the materials of a mission without having inserted original material into the collective knowledge base. The principle is pay in/take out. The time, effort, tiredness and personal investment in an intervention-research mission are thus doubly recompensed. In addition to being paid for their time, researchers can access team-produced materials enabling the production of a thesis, a paper, an article or a book—a significant advantage in the academic world.

Authorization by the Client to Publish

Unlike consultants who have singular and *a priori* confidential relationships with their clients, intervention-researchers explain their statute during the intervention-research contract negotiation phase. The corporation thus knows that the investigators will publish results based on the client's case. Contractually, the researchers always undertake to use the results *anonymously*, without mentioning the name of the company. If this were not the case, the information obtained would be skewed, in particular in sensitive areas such as corporate strategy and other confidential data. The guarantee of anonymity facilitates the extraction by the researcher of more authentic information, an important guarantee of the scientific quality of publications.

Methods nevertheless exist to enable checking by in-house corporate experts of accuracy of the results published. For example, a director of the client is systematically invited to take part in the deliberations of the jury judging the validity of a doctoral thesis.

Publication by the Corporation

The presentation of results that are not anonymous is nevertheless possible when the management agrees to have the results of their intervention-research presented in events open to the public, such as professional or mixed academic and professional conferences. Oral presentations of the results by a CEO can be written up and then submitted to the CEO for validation before publishing, which constitutes a non-anonymous public source for the results that can subsequently be used both by the researcher and by the corporation.

DISCUSSION AND ANALYSIS

"Scientific consultancy" is an intervention-research technique. It contradicts the generally accepted idea that consultancy *follows* research, just as many people believe that applied research *follows* pure research. The practice of scientific consultancy is an invitation to continuously explore new, scientifically relevant and credible sectors, businesses, statutes, contexts, countries and problems from a societal viewpoint.

For a Corporation or Organization, What Is the Difference Between Using a Consultant and an Intervention-Research Team?

In the eyes of the corporation, consultants are service providers who must "obey" their clients. One of the challenges when an intervention-research team intervenes in a corporation is to transform this traditional customer/supplier relationship into a *balanced partnership*. Intervention-research teams become real partners as transparency increases between the parties involved. Sometimes the corporation requests opinions and even advice from intervention-research teams, calling on their scientific expertise before making decisions in areas covered by the research. Shared transparency also means that clients forward strategic internal documents to the intervention-research team, contributing to improving the quality of the research. To illustrate this partnership relationship, we will take as an example a corporation with which the Iseor team has been working for 10 years. Recently, our intervention-researchers had to explain to the CEO that it seemed preferable to stop the intervention-research process as our services had very low effectiveness due to the behaviour of some members of the company's management team. This decision surprised the chairman, but made him aware of professional disloyalty and resistance to change by his closest collaborators. By proposing to break the contract, the researcher risked losing the remainder of the $100,000 fee which was needed to balance the research team's annual budget.

What is the Difference for Intervener-Researchers?

Scientific consultancy addresses sets of research topics useful for corporations. The social utility of research is better guaranteed by intervention-research. Another difference compared to other researchers is the satisfaction felt when observing how corporations and organizations succeed in improving their practices and social and economic performances by applying new knowledge resulting from the research mission. One of the main difficulties consists in the "must" shift from one universe to another, from one language to another...Abstruse language is neither understood nor accepted in companies, just as pragmatic language is not tolerated in academic publications–probably truer in Europe than in America. Researchers reporting intervention-research cases are immediately accused of consultancy and "excluded" from the academic community, very often damaging their reputations and harming their university careers.

What Economic Model Should an Intervention-Research Team Adopt?

An intervention-research team is financed by its research contracts, with rates similar to those practiced in the consultancy market although it has a triple vocation: scientific intervention, research and the communication of results for training and academic publications. Intervention-research missions finance non-profit activities such as publications, academic exchanges and team management.

The first consequence of this economic model is that an intervention-research centre must, just like any other business, continuously sell or renew intervention-research and training contracts to generate income to pay for non-profit activities.

The second consequence is that sufficient income is needed year after year. Financial resources are essential, not only to carry out intervention research but also to invest in the design and introduction of new research programmes and self-finance valorisation activities such as academic publications, general communications, the organization of academic and professional international symposiums, etc.

As an illustration, the economic model of the ISEOR team breaks down as follows: Our annual resources of €2.5 million ($3.5 million) come from intervention-research sales to about twenty five corporations and organizations. These resources cover the overheads of administrative, technical, accounting and data processing staff, as well as the intervention-research team made up of eight doctoral students, recruited for three years to prepare their doctorate, sixteen doctors considered as seniors or experts, and doctoral students not paid for by the team budget, but financing the preparation of their theses through jobs or doctoral grants.

The time spent on the main activity families in 2011 is summarized in Table 16.1. 22% of intervention-research time financed, in addition to time spent on in-house management, valorisation missions (conference organization, preparation of conference proceedings) and writing. In 2011, writing activities produced 6 doctoral theses, 6 articles published in academic journals, 45 papers in congresses and 4 books. This economic model proves that research can be self-financing, in particular for doctoral

TABLE 16.1 Distribution of the Time the Research Team Spent on Different Activities

Activities Families	Time Spent (Days)	% of Total Time (All Staff Categories Included)
Intervention-researches	1,280	22%
Training	400	7%
Negotiating and Contract sales	460	8%
Publications (articles, papers, chapters, books, doctoral thesis...)	940	16%
Team management	1,160	20%
Internal missions: organization of conferences, preparation of proceedings	1,100	19%
Research and development	460	8%
Amount	5,800	100%

students preparing their theses, while at the same time training them for interventions and change management, making it possible to develop the researchers' consultancy skills so they can choose to orient their careers differently. It is an alternative solution to face up to reductions in public research financing, but requires leadership, management and corporate research management skills. It also strengthens team work, too rare occurrence in management and other social sciences.

CONCLUSION

This article intends to show that intervention-research is a way to approach reality in corporate universes and a methodology for management sciences. Usually due to ignorance, intervention-research is considered to be consultancy in that it aims to improve corporate practices and obtain budgets to finance research valorisation activities.

The main discriminating factors between intervention-research and consultancy are scientific rigor and the progressiveness of the negotiation process, the negotiation of methodological specifications that are subsequently strictly respected, a team using "tracked" methodologies so that research is "cumulative" and finally, systematic doctoral and post-doctoral publications.

An intervention-research team functions like a *research corporation* which must provide for its financing by the permanent negotiation of new funds to cover the pay of technical, administrative, doctoral and post-doctoral employees, overheads and also the costs of R&D activities and publications.

REFERENCES

Boje, D., & Rosile, G. A. (2003). Comparison of socio-economic and other transorganizational developements methods. *Journal of Organizational Change Management, 16*, 10–20.

Buono, A. F., & Savall, H. (2007). *Socio-economic intervention in organizations*. Charlotte, NC: Information Age.

Coghlan, D., & Brannick, T., (Ed.). (2005). *Doing action research in your own organization* (2nd edition). London, England: Sage.

David, A. (2000). La recherche-intervention, cadre général pour la recherche en management? [The intervention-research framework for management research?] In A. David, A. Hatchuel, & R. Laufer (Eds.), *Les nouvelles fondations des sciences de gestion. Eléments d'épistémologie pour les sciences du management*. Paris, France: Vuibert.

Krief, N. (2005). Le rôle du chercheur en sciences de gestion: Éléments pour une "intersubjectivité contradictoire" [The role of the researcher in Management

Science: Elements for a contradictory intersubjectivity]. *23ème Université d'été de l'Audit Social.* Lille. 12–22.

Kwesiga, E., & Pattie, M. (2006). Is management science built on a shaky foundation? The case of intersubjectivitive certifiability. *Revue Sciences de Gestion, 50,* 33–68.

Lacey, M., & Tompkins, T. (2007). Analysis of best practices of internal consulting. *Organization Development Journal, 25* (3), 123–131.

Moisdon, J.-C. (1984). Recherche en gestion et intervention [Management research and intervention]. *Revue Française de Gestion, 47*(48), 61–73.

Nobre, T. (2006). Pour une lecture en hypertexte des organisations par la recherche-action: Le cas du changement à l'hôpital [To read hypertext organizations by Action Research: The case for change in hospital]. *Finance Controle Stratégie, 9*(4), 143–168.

Plane, J.-M. (2000). *Méthodes de recherche-intervention en management* [Methods of intervention-research in management]. Paris, France: L'Harmattan.

Savall, H., & Fière, D. (2007, June). Analogies entre la recherche médicale et la recherche-intervention en sciences de gestion [Analogies between medical research and he intervention-research in management sciences]. *Conférence Internationale-Academy of Management, Divison "Research Methods" and ISEOR,* Lyon, France.

Savall, H., & Fière, D. (2014). Analogies entre la recherche médicale et en gestion. Cas de la recherche-intervention [Analogies between medical and management research. Case of intervention-research], *Journal de Gestion et d'Economie Médicale, 37,* 160–197,

Savall, H., & Zardet, V. (1995, 2005). *Ingénierie Stratégique du roseau* [Strategic engineering of the reed, flexible and rooted]. Paris, France: Economica.

Savall, H., & Zardet, V. (1996). La dimension cognitive de la recherche-intervention: La production de connaissances par interactvité cognitive [The cognitive dimension of intervention research: The production of knowledge through cognitive interactivity]. *Revue Internationale de Systémique, 10,* 157–189.

Savall, H., & Zardet, V. (2008). *Mastering hidden costs and performance.* Charlotte, NC: Information Age. (1st French edition, Paris: Economica, 1987).

Savall, H., & Zardet, V. (2011). *The qualimetrics approach: Observing the complex object.* Charlotte, NC: Information Age. (1st French edition, Paris: Economica, 2004.)

Savall, H., Zardet, V., Péron, M., & Bonnet, M. (2012). Possible contributions of qualimetrics intervention-research metodology to action-research. *International Journal of Action Research, 29,* 102–130.

Voyant, O., (2005). La production de connaissances d'intention scientifique: Le principe de contingence générique appliqué à l'audit social, *23°* [The production of scientific knowledge intention : The Generic Contingency principle applied to the social audit]. *Université d'été de l'audit social,* Lille, France: IAE. 212–222.

Zardet, V. (1982). *Vers une gestion socio-économique de l'hôpital: cas d'expérimentation* [Towards a socio-economic management of the hospital: a case of experimentation] (Doctoral dissertation). University of Lyon II, France.

CHAPTER 17

SUSTAINABILITY OF MANAGEMENT METHODS IN ORGANIZATIONS

A Case of Socio-Economic Projects

Gérard Desmaison

CONFERENCE REMARKS:
Chapter Prologue

Why do we spend so much time, energy, and money to frequently change management methods in our organizations, while the players are eager to achieve their goals and projects peacefully? This is the question we have been asking throughout our career in companies and that leads us to conduct a research on sustainability of management methods.

By sustainability, we mean continuity, permanence, persistence, durability, and stability. We exclude all references to sustainability as Corporate Social Responsibility. By management method, we mean the set of rational and organized efforts to pilot, plan, develop, and control an organization in all areas of company activity.

Some management methods are called by the name of their "inventors": McKinsey matrix, the BCG matrix, the Deming, the Ishikawa diagram, methods of division of labor Taylor, or the developed concept: Balanced Score Card associated with Kaplan and Norton, and the Socio-Economic Approach to Management developed by Henri Savall and ISEOR.

DESIGN OF THE RESEARCH

This research is the result of observations made in our professional life and academic literature. The management methods are numerous, evolving overtime. In 1995, Alain Chauvet identified 132 methods. Some have disappeared or gone out of fashion: S-curve, OPT, Waenier, Sweet Cherry to name a few. And since 1995, Balanced Scorecard, 6 Sigma, and Lean Management have appeared.

The management methods have a flexible duration of life in companies. With SEAM we managed projects which had a life time of 4 and 5 years. One other company has been working with it for 40 years. We found another one which stopped after six months.

These changes in management methods contribute to the destabilization of organizations and employees. Drawing on our experience, we found that each implementation of new management method generally involves organizational changes, blocking of ongoing projects, pending new guidelines, withdrawal of actors, a period of learning and ultimately a waste of time in the development of organizations. Work is a place where everyone plays one's identity (Enriquez, 2002) and self-esteem (Lenhardt, 1992). Some changes in poorly managed management methods can lead to disaster (see newspapers). In this context, it seems therefore interesting and relevant to study the sustainability of management methods in organizations and answer these questions:

- Which are the factors that impact the sustainability of management methods?
- How do the actors (managers, employees, interveners-researchers, or consultants) react to these moments of changes of the method and after stopping?
- How to improve the sustainability of projects and avoid psycho-social risks for the agents?

Hypothesis

We'll start this research with the core hypothesis as follows. The sustainability of management methods is based on:

- Sustainable methods, process, tools, which could be called "hard."
- Sustainable players reconciling change and pleasure to work ("soft").

Moreover, we assume that management method life cycle in a given organization is similar to a living being with an *official life* whose duration can be improved by the actors as well as a *hidden life*, beyond the official life of methods of management, generated by the change promoters.

It seemed unrealistic to conduct this research on all management methods. We conducted the research in two steps:

1. Observing the sustainability of management methods and effects on the behavior of actors, we chose one method of management: the Socio-Economic Approach of Management (SEAM) in organizations.
2. Generalizing the findings about SEAM to others methods of management.

What Is SEAM?

This section differentiates the various facets of the SEAM approach:

- *Socio-Economic Theory*: created and tested since 1973 by Henri Savall and his ISEOR team. Inappropriate interactions between behaviors and structures lead to dysfunctions in the organizations which generate hidden costs. The theory integrates the social dimension of the enterprise and its economic performance.
- *Socio-Economic Approach of Management (SEAM)*: In order to come back to a right functioning, ISEOR has created a set of technics (process, tools) integrating the social and the economic dimensions.
- *Socio-Economic Change Project*: The change project is the SEAM story of a company. Each implementation in a company is a SEAM project with its context, its actors, its history, including the intervention phase.
- *Socio-Economic Intervention*: The system wide project conducted by ISEOR interveners-researchers from first contacts to maintenance.

Why SEAM? This type of management has existed since 1973, 40 years of existence, and has been implemented in more than 1,350 cases followed by ISEOR and its interveners-researchers. ISEOR is a research center with numerous writings and theories providing numerous research materials. Interventions have a long range of duration: between 6 months and 40 years. Finally, we practiced this method of management in different companies for 25 years, with and without ISEOR.

Research Methodology

This is qualitative research with an historical longitudinal analysis on different companies over more than 30 years. We have led an action-research with a comprehensive interactive approach to sense making between the researchers and the multiple actors to produce additional knowledge. We undertook an inductive approach to generalize from particular cases, observing specific features in several objects of a category, and demonstrating the ability to generalize these characteristics in that category, with phases of observation, analysis, interpretation, and generalization.

We combined both the diversity and complementarity of sources that helped not having a partial view of the problem, based on a specific analysis, to correct our vision related to our subjective experience, and took the distance from the research object by avoiding transfer effects.

We ensured firstly that our findings are justified by a square triangulation of the data, different cross processing of the data, and a calibration or index expression of key ideas. We managed the triangulation data through the use of multiple independent measurements (Usunier et al., 1993); through cross interviews of 3 categories of actors on their relationship with the research object between 1984 and 2010 to analyze commonalities and specificities.

We also explored whether the results are actionable by the actors (i.e., understood and ready to implement by them).

THEORETICAL FRAMEWORK AND CONCEPTS

Theoretical concepts have been refined over time to focus on:

> *Management tools:* Management tools interact with tools routines that play an important role in structuring management methods over time. They stem from a scenario and can be started with minimal effort (Moisdon, 1984). They are key for the capabilities developed by the organization (Nelson & Winter, 1982).
>
> *Organizational sociology—The actor and the system* (Crozier & Friedberg, 1977): This approach allows us to better understand the role of managers in an organization in times of change management method and/or crisis.

The conventionalist theory: The conventionalist approach aims at understanding how actors facing uncertain situations, decide the behavior they will adopt and how from these multiple individual decisions emerges convergence behavior which fit to each other, to come up to an agreement (Boltanski & Thévenot, 1987).

Organizational resilience: Our research is oriented towards organizational resilience after exploitation of field data, including the reaction of the actors in response to changes in management method (Weick, 1993; Poirot, 2007; Koninck & Teneau, 2010).

Human potential theory: The internal energy of each person which could be mobilized (or not) and transformed (or not) in human potential by a company (Savall, Zardet, & Bonnet, 2006).

Field experimentation: The problem of this research has initially appeared through field intuitions (Wacheux, 1996).

Professional experience: Levitt and March (1988) described the experience as an indispensable source of organizational learning. This research followed an experience of over 40 years in business, giving the opportunity to observe the individual and collective behavior of managers and leaders in particular through learning, implementation, and practice under operational positions of SEAM in the business for twenty years.

Field Materials

Our experimental materials consist mainly of cross-interviews of 3 populations:

- *Leaders and managers* having implemented or using the Socio-Economic Management between 1985 and today in their organizations, 35 interventions representative of interventions by ISEOR;
- *ISEOR Interveners-researchers* seniors exercising for at least 10 years as experts of the problem; and
- *Employees* who worked directly with the author on socio-economic projects, having the same experiences at the same times but evolving differently. This category has allowed us to consider the problem from another view.

Operation of Testing Materials

Field note quotes were classified by themes and under themes and imputed to a key idea, with mention of the frequency. We used the ISEOR expert software (SEGESE) as a database to structure the treatment of the verbatim in the form of key ideas.

FINDINGS

We differentiated two types of findings. First, we shall see the findings concerning the sustainability of SEAM projects, then our approach of generalization to others methods.

Finding About SEAM

According to the main results of the field experiment, the sustainability of Socio-Economic Management projects is mainly linked to:

- the achievement of visible economic results,
- an adjustment period necessary to gain trust among interveners-researchers (ISEOR) and leaders,
- a formalized process of intervention,
- a change process led by interveners-researchers, and
- the reference to humanistic values.

What are the specifics of the SEAM when compared to other methods? The Socio-Economic Management is a management method referred to in *cross-organizational development* (Boje & Rosile, 2003). The cross-organizational development is based on a collective history that has been designed and built through a network of participants in the organization where everyone can influence the collective history.

The Socio-Economic Management is an *intervention-research methodology* first developed in France (Savall & Zardet, 1987; Moisdon, 1984; Cappelletti, 2009). Intervention research is part of the current collaborative research stream (David & Hatchuel, 1998; Van de Ven & Johnson, 2006). There is an alternation of field work (immersion phase) with periods of decline and analysis of these studies (distancing phase). It provides the researcher involved with an alternate position to create knowledge (Burrel & Morgan, 1985; McKelvey, 2006).

The qualimétrique approach (Savall & Zardet, 2011): The ISEOR intervention can be qualified as qualimetric intervention characterized because of a systemic approach of the organization and a real methodological conditions of contract (even normative) of the intervention which have the advantage to enhance, to objectivize, and to support the research results.

The connection with humanistic values: The leaders and managers largely refer to human values underlying SEAM. It should be stressed that these values are not frequently put forward by ISEOR, even if they are present in the writings of H. Savall and his mentors (Bernácer, 1922; Savall, 1973, 2012; Perroux in Savall, 1979).

Results Generalizable to Other Methods for Management

After excluding the results related to the specifics of SEAM, we interviewed leaders practicing other management methods to determine the following conditions for sustainable management methods.

A method that does not generate profit on short-term is declining and doomed to failure.

It is the perception of a threat by the leader that generates the choice of a method of management or sustainability. A method of management is implemented to last as long as possible, it is therefore not a project, which by definition has a beginning and an end and is non-recurring in nature. The sustainability of a management method in an organization depends on the leader who decided its implementation, according to his/her conviction, his/her exemplary, and his/her personal qualities. Holding up management methods have often exogenous causes (e.g., merger, reorganization) and result mostly by the departure of manager. If he or she leaves, the method stops.

Sustainability depends on the degree of embedding of the method in the organization. The embedding of a method depends on the knowledge and the mastering, by the greatest number of actors, of four elements: *Values* that support the method and the *theory* of the method which allow the anchoring among actors. *Processes* and *tools* that allow the rooting of the method in the organization. The degree of embedding is generally stronger among leaders who have mastered these 4 elements, while the majority of employees know only the tools. The embedding of the method is favored by a process of continuous maintenance and control driven by leaders and support of the actors.

When the management method stops, and according to the degree of embedding, leaders try to perpetuate the management style *(hidden life)* in the organization or in another. Employees adapt, willingly or by force, to the new dominant method of management in order to save their employability and their survival in organizations *(managerial resilience)*.

Sustainability depends on the development of human potential. Human potential can be defined as the intelligent and active energy which is latent in every person or group of people and which can be used to adapt to the environment, to create goods and services, identify new and innovative needs (Savall, 1973).

The speeding up of human potential of the actors answers the question "What does it take to improve the sustainability and avoid economic and psycho-social dysfunctions associated with change?" At each change of management method:

- The creative energy of each actor or human potential investment is questioned, and thus the motivation, involvement, and commitment. Each is shared between submission and resistance.
- The cards are reshuffled and actors must establish new agreements (or convention as defined by Boltanski and Thévenot, 1987), a time space for the understanding and support of actors.

The implementation of the Human Potential prepares actors to changes in management methods and to become agile managers.

From these results and in order to help the leaders and managers find solutions facilitating the changes of management methods, we worked out a 22 questions auto diagnostic template enabling leaders to: (a) assess the sustainability of the management method with a profile and a sustainability score and (b) define 3 concrete actions to set up.

CONCLUSION

We led a research on a non-common object of research providing actionable answers:

- For all the people working or on the point to work with SEAM; the ways of improvement of the sustainability of each stage of the life cycle of the SEAM projects in their organization.
- For all the people concerned by a management methods (executive, consultant, academic); the main trunk roads insuring the durability of the methods of management in organizations. An auto diagnosis allows these people to decide on actions to be led.

Underlying our work, we also presented an approach of the research in management science which could be useful to the managers or students grounded in the company and enable them to produce an impactful research in management.

Finally, and more modestly, we contributed to complete or develop theoretical concepts such as meta-management, specificities of SEAM, anchoring and rooting of management tools, human potential vs. human capital, and the will to pursue other researches.

REFERENCES

Bernácer, G. (1922), *La teoría de las disponibilidades como interpretación de las crisis y del problema social* [The theory of the availability as crisis and social issue interpretation]. Madrid, Spain: Revista nacional de economía.

Boje, D. & Rosile, G. A. (2003). Comparison of socio-economic and other transorganizational development methods. *Journal of Organizational Change Management, 16* (1), 10–20.

Boltanski, L., & Thevenot, L., (1987). *Les économies de la Grandeur, Cahier du centre d'étude pour l'emploi* [The Economies of the Greatness]. Paris, France: PUF.

Burrell, G., & Morgan, G. (1985). *Sociological paradigms and organizational analysis, elements of the sociology of corporate life.* London, England: Heinemann.

Cappelletti, L., (2009). La recherche-intervention: Une réponse au besoin d'evidence based management en contrôle de Gestion? [The intervention-research: An answer to the need for Evidence Based Management in in management control?] *La place de la dimension européenne dans la Comptabilité Contrôle Audit,* May, Strasbourg, France, CD-ROM.

Crozier, M., & Friedberg, E. (1981). *L'acteur et le système: Les contraintes de l'action collective* [The actor and the system: The constraints of collective action]. Paris, France: Seuil.

David A., & Hatchuel A. (1998). *Des connaissances actionnables aux théories universelles en sciences de gestion* [Actionable knowledge in the universal theories in management sciences]. Retrieved from http://basepub.dauphine.fr/handle/123456789/2345.

Koninckx, G., & Teneau, G. (2010). *Résilience organisationnelle: Rebondir face aux turbulences* [Organizational Resilience: Bouncing back in the face of turbulence]. Brussels, Belgium: De Boeck.

Lenhardt, V. (2002). *Les responsables porteurs de sen: Culture et pratique du coaching et du team-building* [The responsible carriers of meaning: Culture and practice of coaching and team-building.]. Bruxelles. 2e éd. Paris, France: INSEP.

McKelvey, B. (2006), Comment on Van De Ven and Johnson's 'Engaged Scholarship': Nice try, but... *Academy of Management Review, 31,* 822–829

Moisdon, J.-C. (1984). Recherche en gestion et intervention [Research in management sciences and intervention]. *Revue Française de Gestion,* 47–48, 61–73.

Poirot, M. (2007). L'organisant de la résilience individuelle au travail: Premiers éléments d'analyse [Organizing individual resilience at work: First elements of analysis]. In S. Hayward, M. Poirot, & L. Chaine (Eds), *Cahiers du CEREN.* Dijon, France: Groupe ESC Dijon Bourgogne.

Savall, H. (1973). *G. Bernácer: l'hétérodoxie en science économique* [The heterodoxy in economy]. Paris, France: Dalloz, Collection Les Grands Économistes.

Savall, H. (1979). *Reconstruire l'entreprise. Analyse socio-économique des conditions de travail, Préface F. Perroux* [Reconstructing the enterprise. Preface by F. Perroux]. Paris, France: Dunod.

Savall, H. (2012). *Origine radicale des crises économiques: Germán Bernácer, précurseur visionnaire* [Radical origin of economic crisises: Germán Bernácer, a visionary precursor]. Charlotte, NC: Information Age.

Savall, H., & Zardet, V. (1987). Maîtriser les coûts et les performances cachés, Editions Economica, Paris. [Translated in English in 2008 *Mastering hidden costs and socio-economic performance*]. Charlotte, NC: Information Age Publishing.

Savall, H., Zardet, V., & Bonnet, M. (2006). XVIIe Congrès de l'AGRH—Le travail au cœur de la GRH IAE de Lille et Reims Management School.

Van de Ven, A. H., & Johnson, P. E. (2006). Knowledge for theory and practice. *Academy of management review, 3* (4), 802–821.

Weick, K. E. (1993). The collapse of sense making in organizations. *Administrative Science Quarterly, 38,* 628–652.

CHAPTER 18

STRENGTHENING THE SEAM COMMUNITY IN NORTH AMERICA, PART DEUX

A Longitudinal Case Study in Group Dynamics

Eric Sanders and Lachlan Whatley

CONFERENCE REMARKS:
Chapter Prologue

This is a phenomenological case study of the participants in the first two SEAM Conferences held in North America. The purpose of the study is twofold: firstly, to examine Whatley's (2012) Individual "States" Model for Healthy Group Dynamics in an applied circumstance; and, secondly, to document some of the historical events of those first SEAM conferences held in North America as a participant-observer. A more detailed look at Whatley's (2012) model and the events of the first North American SEAM Conference are presented in the OD Journal (Sanders & Whatley, 2015).

Decoding the Socio-Economic Approach to Management, pages 285–298
Copyright © 2016 by Information Age Publishing
All rights of reproduction in any form reserved.

SEAM was developed in France in 1974 by Dr. Henri Savall (Savall, 1981). It is a systemic approach to simultaneously intervene in organizations while researching them collaboratively with their own members. SEAM has been used extensively in Western Europe, and has been used successfully worldwide. Over the past decade, we have seen a growing base of practitioners in North America who are using SEAM to help many organizations, including firms (Hillon & Boje, 2007), government organizations in the United States (Conbere & Oestreich, 2012) and in Mexico (Arceo, 2012), and regional multi-organizational groups (Boje & Gomez, 2008). There is an annual conference for SEAM intervener-researchers held in Lyon, France, but to support the growing base of SEAM practitioners in North America, John Conbere and Alla Heorhiadi (of the University of St. Thomas in Minneapolis) have begun a series of annual conferences here as well. The first was held in November, 2012, and the second conference was held in May, 2014.

The North American conferences involved a multi-national group of about 65 intervener-researchers and allowed them to consider both the theory and practice of SEAM. Participants came from the United States, France, Mexico, Ukraine, and Canada. Given the small size of the group, the participants stayed together for the entire time, sharing ideas, meals, and discourse. Over the days of each conference, the group bonded quickly, following the model of Whatley's (2012) Individual "States" Model for Healthy Group Dynamics through the various phases of Surrender of Self and those of Growth of Self. More than half of the participants attended both conferences, which added to the group development in the second year. We detail that process below, with the participant observations by one of the authors (Sanders) offered in first person as appropriate.

WHATLEY'S MODEL

Whatley also builds on Lewin's (1947) equation showing that behavior is a function of the person and the environment, $B = f(p, e)$, extending this to group performance:

$$GP = f(X1 + X2 + \ldots + Xn) \wedge \pm D$$

where GP = group performance; X = the individual's skills, abilities, and behavior; n = number of group members; D = the dynamics of the group…and D is either > 1 or < -1 (Whatley, 2012, p. 41).

Two key points to this formula are: firstly, that group performance is greater than or less than, but never equal to the sum of individual performance; and, secondly, that group dynamics has the largest impact on total group performance, so it is a critical factor for analysis. Groups need several conditions to develop effectively, notably:

1. proximity—a physical closeness so that all the senses are available;
2. homogeneity—a degree of likeness and agreed upon values;
3. diversity—a diversity of the mind;
4. distinctiveness—an identity and awareness of the uniqueness of the group; and
5. mutual attraction—involving high quality connections, which is the most important aspect to develop (Whatley, 2012, p. 42).

Whatley's (2012) model includes two phases of development that the individual needs to go through as a member of an effective group: Surrender of Self and then Growth of Self. These two phases of development have five sub-phases each. Surrender of Self includes: Awareness, Commitment to Growth of Others, Community Building, Empathy, and Listening. Growth of Self includes: Vision, Conceptualization, Persuasion, Stewardship, and Healing. The model focuses on individual behavior in a group context, and on language as a reflection of reality (see Figure 18.1). Thus, the application of the model to the participants in the SEAM conference is an adaptation of what he saw as the development of a single individual to the display of these characteristics by various members of the group, so that the group as a whole shows all of the Individual States Model for Healthy Group Development.

Method

The North American SEAM group met for approximately 9 hours the first day (including meals) and 6 hours the second day in each conference. Sanders recorded notes for most of the open sessions of the conference, but not the conversations at breaks and during meal periods. Those recordings, plus Sanders' recollections of the events allowed him to offer a phenomenological perspective of the conference as a participant-observer. As such, the balance of this paper describes the conversations, presentations, and general context of the conference; and shows how the individuals developed interpersonal bonds and became a group in just two days together each year through the lens of Whatley's (2012) model.

Analysis and Results

The first phase of Whatley's (2012) group dynamics model is Surrender of Self. There were three such leaders at the SEAM conferences. Most

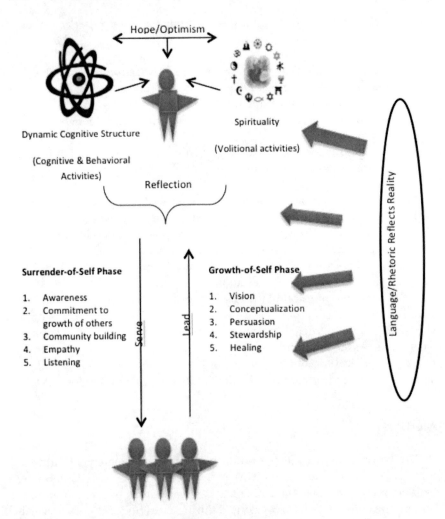

Figure 18.1 Individual states model for healthy group dynamics.

notable was Dr. Savall, but his role was more as a senior advisor than as an active leader of the group. The organizers and leaders of the conference were John Conbere and Alla Heorhiadi, both of the University of St. Thomas (the host of the conference).

Phase 1.1: Surrender of Self: Awareness

In both of the conferences, Conbere's screening of the papers prior to the conference shows an excellent example of personal awareness. He contacted me (Sanders) to review the paper I submitted via Skype, rather than through e-mails or even phone calls to allow for closer personal communication. Throughout the conversation, Conbere was attentive to my thoughts as both a graduate student and fellow professional. He added insight on how to better incorporate SEAM methodology in my presentations, and was reasonable in what he expected of me and my work. In the second conference, he also adjusted the agenda so mine was the last presentation scheduled, which allowed me to recap how we had come together as a group over both conferences, strengthening the impact of the presentation. All of these actions are characteristics of good self-awareness and social awareness (Goleman, 1995). He continued to show that awareness throughout his facilitation of the conference.

Phase 1.2: Surrender of Self: Commitment to the Growth of Others

There were two excellent examples of individuals in the group showing their commitment to the growth of others during the conferences. The first was the design of the conferences by Conbere and Heorhiadi. It was a small conference, with just 65 participants, about half of which also presented sessions either individually or in groups. We met in a single room and stayed together the entire time. During the first conference there was another space for break-out conversations (an elegant, wood-paneled room with a fireplace), but no one ever wanted to use it, so that option was not even presented in the 2nd conference.

Likewise, the scheduling of sessions on the agenda lent itself to the growth of the members of the North American SEAM community, with a mix of case studies, and historical and theoretical sessions about SEAM presented throughout each day. All aspects of the methodology and the theory that supported it were covered, without the pace lagging in either direction. That attention to detail and then effective execution of the design was clear evidence of their commitment to the growth of others.

A second strong example of commitment to the growth of others was shown by Jean Caghassi's (2012) coming from Lyon, France to present a case study of his former company in the 1st conference. He is semi-retired now, with no financial incentive to come to the United States for this conference, but did so out of his commitment to Savall and the growing North American SEAM community. He shared how he used SEAM in his firm, and then when they acquired another firm, he used SEAM to build new policies that would benefit all parties of the new, larger company. They discovered hidden costs of $4.2 million USD ($28,600/person/year), and over just two years eliminated $2.3 million USD of those costs ($17,550/person/year). Through implementation of the managerial practices inspired by SEAM, they increased trust and built a strong, unified company. He also stressed that if a firm achieves a gain, it must distribute it among all the key stakeholders. He recommended dividing gains in thirds: one third to employees, one third to managers, and one third to shareholders, so that all stakeholders are respected and rewarded. He called this respect to all stakeholders the cornerstone to success of the SEAM methodology.

Phase 1.3: Surrender of Self: Community-Building

The third subphase of Surrender of Self is Community-Building. This may be best shown by the very first presentation of the 1st conference, the Bloomington Public Schools Transportation Center Case Study, presented by John Conbere and Tom Oestreich (2012), which was revisited in the 2nd conference to show their continued progress (Oestreich, Conbere, & Heorhiadi, 2014). The review of this intervention shows community-building on two levels. The first was in using SEAM to benefit this unit of a local school district close to Minneapolis. Their successful implementation of a SEAM intervention to improve performance in the school district's transportation system built strength for SEAM in that community. The second was the way in which they shared their process, with both the successes and challenges that came with it, which helped build community among the conference attendees as well.

Conbere personally showed both strength and humility as he acknowledged that this was a learning process for him and his team as well as the client, as they worked through the intervention. Thus, they truly surrendered themselves to the group in this presentation. Conbere and Oestreich focused on the earlier parts of the SEAM methodology, including contracting, HORIVERT (horizontal and vertical) analysis of the transportation center, the Mirror Effect of showing the client the data they had collected in that analysis, and the expert opinion that they added to their analysis, in helping the client see the root causes of the hidden costs they had uncovered. The client liked this holistic approach and the education of the managers, and they especially liked the ongoing coaching for those mangers that was included in the implementation of the SEAM methodology.

Phase 1.4: Surrender of Self: Empathy

There were many examples of empathy shown as our group came together in each conference. Given that presenters came from multiple countries, one was how people listened to each other, and those who spoke multiple languages found a common language (English, French, Spanish, Ukrainian or a combination thereof) to communicate with each other.

To show some understanding of the difficulties of working in a second language, I noted how the first time I heard the term "*HORIVERT*," I thought the French scholar-practitioner had said *haricot vert* (French for green beans), which seemed curious to me. Having worked on a green bean farm as a youth, I went on to relate how green beans and HORIVERT can be compared in the analysis process. When *haricot vert* are grown on a trellis, harvesting them has to be done horizontally across the vine, and vertically at all levels to gather all the vegetables, just as in HORIVERT all voices at all levels should be heard. Everyone laughed at the comparison, and the conscious effort to add elements to which the French and North Americans alike would enjoy was an example of empathy in the group.

Another example of showing empathy from the 2nd conference was when Conbere and Heorhiadi did a role-play acting out the aspects of the TFW Virus (described below), and how SEAM could overcome it. By understanding the content and the attendees, they brought the concept to life and changed the feeling in the room after a lecture-style presentation to keep our energy up.

Phase 1.5: Surrender of Self: Listening

In the 1st conference, Chato Hazelbaker (2012) presented on Critical Theory and SEAM on Saturday, the second day of the program. He opened by describing how it was an honor to present among scholar-practitioners/intervener-researchers whose works he had read and/or with whom he had studied. When presenting in the 2nd conference, Hazelbaker also noted how he had referred to Kennedy's dissertation research on SEAM in his own dissertation and then referred to previous presenters as he made his points. Indeed, throughout both conferences, presenters consciously noted how their work related to each others repeatedly. Savall listened carefully as well, as will be noted below. In his presentation (Savall, Péron, & Zardet, 2014), he used the metaphor of an organization being like a symphony, with the leader as the conductor. In this group, listening helped us all harmonize and perform better together.

Phase 2.1: Growth of Self: Vision

The first sub-phase or state in the Growth of Self phase is Vision. One could argue that there were multiple visionaries in the conference. Most notable of which was Henri Savall. Throughout the 1st conference he listened attentively and spoke only occasionally (seven times in total by my count). The most elegant of his comments came on the second day. Hazelbaker had voiced a concern that Americans would damage SEAM by applying it without respecting and understanding the philosophy that underpins the SEAM process, and thus, it would lose its effectiveness. He then discussed how future research into the core ideologies of critical theory and SEAM would be in order. Savall asked politely if he could add to the discussion, and, of course, the group readily concurred. He wrote on the board for a few minutes, and then spoke for about 5 minutes on the theoretical underpinnings of SEAM.

Savall said that he earned his doctorate in economics in Spain and that, while studying economic theory, he became disenchanted with the classical production function:

$$Y = f(K \times L) + r$$

where Y = Output, K = Capital, L = Labor and r = a residual.

His main concern was that while economists spent great amounts of time and energy deriving capital and labor, those factors only explained 50–70% of total production. The other 30–50% was in the residual. This is a critical error in his mind, so he developed SEAM to uncover and reduce this residual or hidden cost as he developed the concept.

Savall's presentation at this point was a turning point for our group. He had listened and established a connection with the group. Only then, when we were ready as a group, was he able to go beyond his own personal comfort zone in presenting this key background to his philosophy of management in English (which was difficult for him at that time, less so in the 2nd conference). And only then was the group ready to listen to him and appreciate the vision that he chose to share.

In the 2nd conference, since more than half of the attendees had been at the 1st conference and/or in additional SEAM sessions in Lyon or the Academy of Management, Savall set the vision early. His presentation (Savall, Péron, & Zardet, 2014) was the first of the conference, and laid the groundwork for all that followed.

Phase 2.2: Growth of Self: Conceptualization

Whatley (2012) defined conceptualization as where one takes a vision and forms plans to make it a reality. In the 1st conference, two well-known scholar-practitioners of organization development, Peter Sorensen and Therese Yeager, showed a strong example of conceptualization. They presented on "Advancing Research that Makes a Difference" (Sorensen and Yeager, 2012). Sorensen recalled hearing Rensis Likert present his work in the 1960s, and how it moved research in the social sciences forward. He then said that he believed Henri Savall's work may be a similar advance for our work in organization development today. They went on to discuss Appreciative Inquiry (AI), and showed its similarities with SEAM:

- both are based on useful research,
- both apply Action Research,
- both are developed and used by scholar-practitioners, and
- both have global application.

They noted that the core strength of AI is in large-group interventions, especially in strategic planning. Thus, one could begin an intervention using AI and then carry out the application of the ongoing development process using SEAM.

By sharing their background and wisdom, Peter and Therese helped the group see, not just the vision of what SEAM might become in North America, but also conceptualize how they might use SEAM effectively and realize that vision. In doing so, they also brought the group closer together.

In the 2nd conference, Susan Quint (2014) took a different approach to conceptualization, and looked at the differing conceptualizations of cost in standard accounting (using generally accepted accounting principles or GAAP) and SEAM. By considering human factors and the hidden costs they generate, SEAM presents a different and more comprehensive conceptualization of the total cost of running an organization.

Phase 2.3: Growth of Self: Persuasion

Persuasion is the next sub-phase of Whatley's group development model. In this sub-phase, one uses the "emotional bank account" developed earlier in the listening and empathy stages toward moving the group toward some objective. We saw that displayed most convincingly in one of the later presentations of the 1st conference.

Heredia (2012) presented on what he called *IntelliSEAM (SEAM 2.0)*, an adaptation of the SEAM methodology integrating survey feedback to speed up the data collection process. It clearly was designed to persuade the SEAM community to consider a variation in HORIVERT and the overall SEAM process, which requires a significant investment in both time and labor expense to conduct the HORIVERT analysis via a combination of qualitative and quantitative research. It was not successful. A year later, he was not present and indeed has gone in a different direction in his consulting. However, his persuasion and the respectful conversation it engendered, along with the group's solidarity around the SEAM model, built greater cohesion among the remaining members.

In the 2nd conference, a different form of persuasion was used. In this case, Sergiy Ivakhnenkov presented his research on "What is needed for SEAM to work in Ukraine?" (Ivakhnenkov, Heorhiadi, & Conbere, 2014). He discussed how the openness of SEAM would help overcome the culture of corruption and secrecy prevalent in both business and government there today. The core issue was whether SEAM can work in a corrupt society. The argument was that it can, but with limitations.

Phase 2.4: Growth of Self: Stewardship

Stewardship has been defined as "the careful and responsible management of something entrusted to one's care" (Merriam-Webster, 2014). The passing of the baton from one generation to the next is perhaps the clearest example of good stewardship that one could imagine. Such stewardship was shown in the final presentation of the 1st conference by Savall and Zardet's daughter, Amandine Savall (2012). She discussed global work using SEAM, especially her work with a French baking company that has used SEAM for 30 years and is now expanding its global operations into the United States. She talked about how the company is growing by acquisition of subsidiaries globally, teaching them the SEAM methodology, but otherwise letting them work independently. Ms. Savall did a wonderful job of showing respect and strong application of her parents' work, as a good steward of their contributions. During her excellent presentation, it was easy to see the pride on the faces of both of her parents. In the 2nd conference, she re-visited that work, and showed how the firm continues to grow through the application of SEAM.

You might also say that the conferences themselves are another example of good stewardship by Drs. Savall, Conbere, and Heorhiadi; the latter two being stewards of the SEAM concepts they had been taught by the former. Savall was an effective mentor in giving these stewards the opportunity to succeed and through his support in attending and presenting at the conferences.

Phase 2.5: Growth of Self: Healing

The final subphase of Whatley's (2012) group development model is healing. For the individual group member, this may mean making up for hurting another group member (intentionally or unintentionally). Like persuasion, it involves making withdrawals from your emotional bank account to improve others. There was no apparent need for such healing during the conferences themselves. However, there were some excellent presentations related to healing. Three used a virus as a metaphor and another discussed helping heal a community by using SEAM with a non-profit organization.

Vincent Cristallini (2012) presented on "The TFW Virus." TFW stands for Taylor (the American engineer) Fayol (the French engineer) and Weber (the Austrian sociologist). Taylor contributed the underpinnings of *Scientific Management* in which work processes and incentives are optimized to give the maximum performance from both workers and capital. Fayol developed a model of general management tasks which are still taught today: Plan, Organize, Lead, Coordinate, and Control. Weber developed the basic organizational design model for bureaucracy which is widely used in organizations of all sizes.

Cristallini asserted that over-application of these management methods (Taylorism, Fayolism, and Weberism) attacks the organization like a virus— the TFW virus—which results in hyper-specialization, depersonalization, and inefficient processes for firms. Clearly that is the opposite of optimal performance by human beings in firms, so there must be a treatment for this TFW virus, and there is. It is called SEAM. By liberally and effectively administering SEAM, the client can heal from the effects of the TFW virus. In the 2nd conference, he presented on the topic again, with Conbere and Heorhiadi (Conbere, Heorhiadi, & Cristallini, 2014); and Hazelbaker (2014) presented his dissertation research on the same topic.

In the 1st conference, Alla Heorhiadi and Barbara Milon (2012) also presented a case study of a community center that is working to heal the African-American community in Minneapolis through support of life-long learning. They sponsored a preschool program for children and have a record of 95% successful starts in kindergarten by the children who complete their preschool. Giving children that strong start in life is a wonderful way to heal the community as a whole, as children who succeed in preschool tend to be more successful in education and professionally later in life (Reynolds, Temple, & Ou, 2003).

Heorhiadi and Milon described how they used HORIVERT analysis in the center and discovered total hidden costs of about $77K USD in one part of this non-profit organization with just a $1.5 million USD annual budget (about a 5% loss of resources). They developed informal leaders by the establishment of "SEAM Managers," who were non-managers put in charge of some aspect of the SEAM process for their areas. The director gave these SEAM Managers resources and support but the managers themselves were to analyze and solve problems. Mangers and others were coached using competency grids from the SEAM process, and within a year into the SEAM development process, the community center had eliminated some of those hidden costs, and was continuing to serve the community. By helping to heal the community center and sharing that success with us, Heorhiadi and Milon helped build and heal this conference SEAM community as well.

CONTRIBUTIONS TO THEORY

The other purpose of this article was to apply Whatley's (2012) Individual "States" Model for Healthy Group Dynamics in a group setting, across time. The initial results after the first conference suggest the model holds (Sanders & Whatley, 2015). Evaluating the SEAM community again through this lens after a second conference provides additional evidence of the validity of this model.

As a participant scholar-practitioner/intervener-researcher, I was drawn to the discovery of both the SEAM process and the people who employ it through the conferences. Since SEAM is a very humanistic process, it truly is impossible to separate those two elements, which is why Whatley's group development model is so applicable in this context/case. Progression through the individual states by different members of the group seemed to explain and describe what was going on for each individual within the group, and strengthened us as a community.

As individuals who come together on an infrequent basis, the SEAM community presents an interesting context for this analysis. We have shown that each of the phases and sub-phases or stages of the theoretical model can be applied to the individual's states as experienced by a participant within this specific case. As a result, this study has shown examples of each of the characteristic behaviors/states Whatley asserted were necessary for effective group development: First, the study has shown the Surrender of Self via awareness, commitment to growth of others, community building, empathy, and listening. Then the study has shown the Growth of Self through vision, conceptualization, persuasion, stewardship, and healing. We have also shown what it was like as an individual participant to be actively involved in the development of a healthy group/team who was aware (cognitively) of the model and the importance of their individual states discussed within the model. That was especially true at the end of the 2nd conference, when this material was presented to the group as a whole.

Contributions to Strengthening the SEAM Community

Additionally, and importantly, this study represents in part an historical record of some of the highlights of the SEAM conferences in North America, and how they have strengthened the SEAM community in the Western hemisphere. There were many excellent presentations that are not included here as they did not correlate with Whatley's group development model as well as those selected. Please see conference proceedings for them and the full record of those summarized here.

From my (Sanders) initial e-mails and then conversations with John Conbere, to participating in all of the activities detailed above, I felt welcomed into and eventually a part of the SEAM community. That has been further affirmed as I have met with our SEAM colleagues at other conferences in France and the United States, and in other interactions. There is a bond between us that the process in Minneapolis helped build and strengthen. Others also continue to learn and develop professional and personal bonds in the SEAM community.

Limitations and Suggestions for Future Research

One key limitation of this study is that it chronicled the group development events of a limited number of group interactions (2 conferences, or 4 days of interaction). Although I (Sanders) have had frequent contact with the French SEAM community since the conferences, my interaction with the North American SEAM community has been much more limited. That may be evidence that group members truly do need to spend more time together or, perhaps, there are other interactions between the other attendees during and after the conference we are not privy to.

Future research applying Whatley's (2012) model could further confirm it through application on a longitudinal basis with a single team (either a new team or an existing one), cross-sectional analysis of multiple teams in the same organization, or repeated application in similar conferences (perhaps including future North American SEAM conferences).

REFERENCES

Arceo, R., (2012). Mexican case study. Presentation at the SEAM Conference, Minneapolis, MN: University of St. Thomas.

Bennis, W. & Shepard, H. (1956). A theory of group development. *Human Relations, 9* (4), 415–437.

Boje, D. M., & Gomez, C. (2008). A study of socioeconomic interventions of transorganizaiton storytelling among New Mexico arts organizations. *Revue Sciences de Gestion, 65,* pp.199–220.

Caghassi, J. (2012, November) French case study, Presentation at the 1st North American SEAM conference. Minneapolis, MN: University of St. Thomas.

Conbere, J., & Oestreich, T. (2012, November). Bloomington Public Schools Transportation Center case study, Presentation at the 1st North American SEAM Conference. Minneapolis, MN: University of St. Thomas.

Conbere, J., Heorhiadi, A., & Cristallini, V. (2014, May). *An American understanding of the TFW Virus.* Presentation at the 2nd North American SEAM Conference. Minneapolis, MN: University of St. Thomas.

Cristallini, V. (2012, November). The TFW virus. Presentation at the 1st North American SEAM Conference. Minneapolis, MN: University of St. Thomas.

Goleman, D. (1995) *Emotional intelligence.* New York, NY: Bantam Books.

Hazelbaker, C. (2012, November). *Critical theory and SEAM.* Presentation at the 1st North American SEAM Conference. Minneapolis, MN: University of St. Thomas.

Hazelbaker, C. (2014). *Looking for Evidence of the TFW Virus: A Case Study.* Presentation at the 2nd North American SEAM Conference. Minneapolis, MN: University of St. Thomas.

Heorhiadi, A. & Milon, B. (2012). *Community Center case study.* Presentation at the 1st North American SEAM conference. Minneapolis, MN: University of St. Thomas.

Heredia, V. (2012). *IntelliSEAM (SEAM 2.0).* Presentation at the 1st North American SEAM conference. Minneapolis, MN: University of St. Thomas.

Hillon, M. E., & Boje, D. M. (2007). The social ecology of action research. *Management Research News, 30*(5), 359–367.

Ivakhnenkov, S., Heorhiadi, A., & Conbere, J. (2014, April). *Case study: What is needed for SEAM to work in Ukraine?* Presentation at the 2nd North American SEAM conference. Minneapolis, MN: University of St. Thomas.

Kennedy, A. (2014, May). *Rethinking Lean. Combining Lean and SEAM for Improved Profitability and the Support of Cultures of Continuous Improvement in Organizations.* Presentation at the 2nd North American SEAM conference. Minneapolis, MN: University of St. Thomas.

Merriam-Webster Dictionary (2014). Stewardship. Retrieved January 31, 2015.

McKnight, L. L. (2014, April). *The Convergence of Lean Six Sigma and SEAM to Maximize Performance in Organizations.* Presentation at the 2nd North American SEAM conference. Minneapolis, MN: University of St. Thomas.

Oestreich, T., Conbere, J., & Heorhiadi, A. (2014, May). *Case study on the SEAM Outcomes at the Bloomington Transportation Department.* Presentation at the 2nd North American SEAM conference. Minneapolis, MN: University of St. Thomas.

Quint, S. (2014, April). *SEAM values, belief,s and conceptualization of costs.* Presentation at the 2nd North American SEAM conference. Minneapolis, MN: University of St. Thomas.

Reynolds, A. J., Temple, J. A., & Ou, S. R. (2003). School-based early intervention and child well-being in the Chicago longitudinal study. *Child Welfare, 82*(5), 633–656.

Sanders, E. (2012, November). The art and science of revealing hidden value through SEAM. Presentation at the 1st North American SEAM Conference. Minneapolis, MN: University of St. Thomas.

Sanders, E., & Whatley, L. R. (2015). Strengthening the SEAM community in North America: A case study in group dynamics. *Organization Development Journal,* In press.

Savall, H. (1981). *Work and people: An economic evaluation of job-enrichment.* Oxford, England: Oxford University Press.

Savall, H. (2012, November 30). *The theoretical foundations of SEAM.* Presentation at the 1st North American SEAM Conference. Minneapolis, MN: University of St. Thomas.

Savall, H., Péron, M., & Zardet, V. (2014, April). *Human potential at the core of Socio-Economic Theory (SEAM).* Presentation at the 2nd North American SEAM conference. Minneapolis, MN: University of St. Thomas.

Schutz, W. C. (1955). "What makes groups productive?" *Human Relations, 8* (4), 429–465.

Sorensen, P.F., & Yaeger, T. (2012, November). *Advancing research that makes a difference.* Presentation at the 1st North American SEAM Conference. Minneapolis, MN: University of St. Thomas.

Whatley, L. R. (2012). Individual "states" model for healthy group dynamics. *Organization Development Journal, 30*(3), pp. 40–53.

—

CHAPTER 19

THE THIRD INDUSTRIAL REVOLUTION AND SEAM

Alanna G. Kennedy

CONFERENCE REMARKS:
Chapter Prologue

Alanna Kennedy

Well, I'm back and I debated about whether I would do the stretch and do this presentation for you but I just had to. I read the *The Third Industrial Revolution* by Jeremy Rifkin (2012). It was so interesting. It really captured my imagination. I set it on the corner of my desk and I go in and out of the office and then one day I'm looking at the book and this big question races through my mind, you know, all this stuff about the third industrial revolution but where are the social sciences in all of this change? You know, recognizing the history that, through time, there's the first and the second industrial revolutions, we weren't really able to stem off the virus. So the question is in the third industrial revolution, can we kill it?

So I decided that this needed a closer look and I knew the conference was coming up but in order to get you up to speed on the third industrial revolution or IR3, I'm going to have to take you very quickly through the first and the second. I'll sometimes refer to the first and second industrial revolutions

Decoding the Socio-Economic Approach to Management, pages 299–316
Copyright © 2016 by Information Age Publishing
All rights of reproduction in any form reserved.

as IR1 and IR2. One of the things about the first industrial revolution to focus in on is that through each industrial revolution, there's a change, a major change in energy usage, the type of energy we use and also a change in the way we communicate. Okay, so in the first industrial revolution, it was steam. We used steam powered engines for printing presses. We put together public schools and more complex work organizations because this is when the first factories started to come on the horizon. This is when the virus really starts to appear. Now I thought that the first industrial revolution was null and void of any type of controversy of social science. I don't know about you, but I hadn't really looked at it since I think undergraduate. But here's what I found. The controversy about the virus even raged back in the first industrial revolution and it took the form and shape of what they called the factory question. And essentially there were three major debates. There was the school of thought that said, "This industrial stuff is really great because again we're prospering, and we're getting richer. We can live with it." There was another school of thought that said, "It's really nothing more than slavery, called factory slavery." And then there was a third school of thought that said, "Well, how can we blend the two together? How can we get comfortable with the idea of creating value and human potential and these machines that are coming on board—obviously this isn't going to go away."

THE FIRST INDUSTRIAL REVOLUTION

And so you have this substantial economic gain and really the iconic event of the first industrial revolution was the Great Exhibition of 1851. Figures 19.1 and 19.2 are pictures of the Crystal Palace, for those of you who have never seen this. This was billed as an iconic event to symbolize these new machines, this new era of prosperity. And so to give you an idea of just how expansive it was, Figure 19.2 is a picture of the inside and if you notice, there's a tree growing in it. A beautiful, beautiful building and it lasted for quite a long time. Just to let you know what happened to it, it burned down but it burned down in the early 1930s. So it really lasted quite a long time. So again, the energy change was we started to use steam and we started to print, we used that steam power for printing presses and we were communicating more. And you see the factory question starts to appear.

THE SECOND INDUSTRIAL REVOLUTION

For the second industrial revolution, you have your transition period beginning about 1870. So what were the changes in energy and communication? Well, we begin to use fossil fuel for electricity, so the change was to fossil

Figure 19.1 The first industrial revolution: 1851, The Crystal Palace.

Figure 19.2 Interior of the Crystal Palace, showing trees.

fuels. We start to use combustion engines. We invent the automobile. We invent phones. We invent the telegraph. So we're communicating. Arriving on the scene, we have continuous improvement methodologies. We pursue

TABLE 19.1   The Second Industrial Revolution

Continuous improvement methods

- **Lean**
- **Six sigma**

Pursue worker cooperation based upon work organized by engineer

More complex work organization

Assembly line and mass production systems

Debate about "the factory" question continues

- De-skilling of the worker
- Degenerative work

worker cooperation. All the issues we've talked about during this conference. But we're still debating, even though it's a couple hundred years later, we're still debating the factory questions, right? Even here today and this week at this conference we have debated the issue. As we continue to de-skill workers, we continue to debate about the degenerative work of the industrialized world. What is the iconic event for IR2? Probably the world wars I and II. We killed about 75 million people with all the stuff that we made. That's a lot of bombs. We probably couldn't have done that unless we had developed factories and were able to gain somewhere in efficiency (see Table 19.1).

THE THIRD INDUSTRIAL REVOLUTION

And so now that brings us to IR3 and so I'm going to set up a video here because this little video clip I'm going to show you, it's about 4 minutes. It's going to take you through the change. It's going to explain it much better than I could. (At this point the video *The Third Industrial Revolution* by Ballard (2013) was shown: http://vimeo.com/79782365). Dramatic, huh? So then the question becomes, with this shift in communication and energy for IR3, a shift very similar to what we saw during IR1 and IR2, how's that going to change organizational development and what does that mean to SEAM? And what does that mean for the virus? I don't have the answers but the idea of asking the questions were so intriguing. There's more to the shift than we can see. The changes are pretty much out there and happening. There are new concepts in living more integrated with the earth. There is more of an emphasis on biospheres and green spaces and industrial spaces and community planning. So when you read the book, remember this is happening around the globe now. There are governments that are contracting with Rifkin or working with him to design these biosphere spaces in the cities around the world—Spain, New Orleans. So it's actually happening, it's not something that's just out there.

A couple other important changes as we get into IR3 and that is access rights become more important than ownership. It is the idea of having access to things. Last year I was reading books about people who like the idea of access to a thing. You don't need to own the thing anymore. You're access rights become more important. They no longer talk about globalization in IR3. They talk about continentalization and a lot has to do with the way the energy is distributed. So what they're saying is look for big changes in government and in government structures. Social capital, because if everything is integrated, becomes more important. And so the role of financial capital we'll see as we get deeper into the democratization of manufacturing, is also . . . the need for capital becomes diminished. So part of this is the idea of energy feedback loops based upon biomimicry of ecosystems. What they're saying is that if we pay attention to nature, if we pay attention to some of these ideas and the way things work in the universe, and we get more in alignment with that, things will go better and we won't have to destroy our environment. So the biosphere conscientiousness is very much a part of this as well as the idea of the continentialization.

I think I told some of you I track Detroit. I like to figure out what's happening in Detroit. And one of the things about Detroit is just exactly that— they actually went to a biosphere consciousness. The idea of the gardens, the ideas of the spaces in Detroit and the way they're laying them out. So you see, I thought that was an interesting correlation. The democratization of manufacturing concept is just astounding. So because of the dawning of the digital age and because of 3D printers, you no longer need a big factory to make stuff. You can make as many as one of a thing, 500 of a thing, 5000, and 5 million. It's all a matter, now, of using your CAD/CAM system. You upload your digital file. You don't even need to step foot in the factory. You upload it to some factory somewhere that makes it. Because of the economies of scale no longer apply, things are cheap. We no longer need the big industrial base that we had in the second industrial revolution. It changes. Furthermore, what changes, or so they're saying, is that somebody like me . . . I could take a couple thousand dollars, I could take and download free CAD/CAM software from the internet, and I could design my widget. I never need to leave my office. I can upload the digital file to a computer somewhere and have the item shipped somewhere and sell it over the internet. I don't need big money anymore to manufacture a thing. I don't need a lot of capital anymore to manufacture it.

This is a hallmark, one of the hallmarks of the third industrial revolution . . . the idea of smaller footprints factories, and the idea of the democratization of manufacturing. Because the thinking is that now anybody can make a widget and make it a real thing. Anybody can do it and many people will and this will dramatically change our economic landscape and society. 3D printers, they call that additive manufacturing because if you've ever seen it, it just takes a little bead of plastic and it builds a thing, layer by layer by layer it builds a thing. Versus subtractive manufacturing which leaves waste. Again this is the separation of the design from the actual building of the unit because I can design it on free CAD/CAM software and then upload it anywhere in the world.

Another trend during the third industrial revolution is mass customization and then, strangely enough, even custom-made manufacturing. Now we've got this widespread of the idea of making things, so we, theoretically, don't need the type of infrastructures that we have supported during IR2. During IR3 we could be more targeted. We could be more judicious. We could be more customized.

The other thing is open source design and open innovation. This one just blows my mind because the trend in IR3 is not about the idea of rights or owning a thing. It's the idea of going in and making a contribution. So on the internet today you could go out and you could find people all over the globe to contribute. Some guy in China, some guy in India, designing, maybe, it's a circuit board, because he's interested in it. There's no ownership. It's just the idea of contributing because I really love to do it. And the thing is . . . the trend with that is that the products are better, faster, more accurate, and more dead-on. So economies of scale no longer apply the same as they did in IR2. Variety is free. Complexity is free. Flexibility is free under the new paradigm shift.

So this changes the world substantially from one that we've been talking about today; SEAM and IR2. So what are the advantages of SEAM and what could be the disadvantages of SEAM in the third industrial revolution? One of the things that is telling is I started out with the wrong assumption, that there were no social sciences in the first industrial revolution and that the social debate wasn't there, but that's not true. The social debate about the organization of work in human societies and value added activities has followed us for the past 250 years. It seems the TFW virus has been with us all along. The argument may have gotten more sophisticated but it's certainly there. It didn't begin with Taylor. It really began back with the factory question in IR1.

How do we live with this? How do we balance the organization of work in human societies to create value and wealth but still respect human dignity and potential? At this point I do not have an answer. I'm playing with this in my own mind because this is sort of new for me too, and the thing is that the organizations that will exist will be more complicated. More complicated than probably we can even imagine. Also, how much of our social sciences will be obsolete in IR3 because they were developed for the organizational structures of IR2? I'm sure some of it will be obsolete by the new organizational structures, under the new way work is organized. However, SEAM should be a nice fit. SEAM is collaborative, distributed, shared interest, collective trust, and transparent: All of those trademarks and hallmarks that they're saying are big in the third industrial revolution. What could be some of the disadvantages? Well, perhaps more training and the competency grid maybe, because organizations are going to be more complex, supposedly. If that's the case, then maybe we need to look at training a little bit more in the SEAM model. Maybe we need to rethink the way we approach training. And as far as training, the flexibility of the workforce, new organizational structures, the idea of the supply chains and the biospheres' influence. I can't stress to you enough. How much I...I mean I have seen this proliferate and I think one of the things about organization development is the idea of if we're going to be successful in managing a supply chain, from the manufacturing of a thing to the de-manufacturing of a thing, then we have to work across a supply chain. What that means is a coordination of efforts. Supply chains are created organization to organization. It's the idea of being structured within your own organization and being able to communicate and being able to function with other organizations. Being able to undertake your continuous improvement activities as well as being able to talk to the next organization in the chain and improve together. I think that one ultimate result of IR3 will be the idea of being able to develop new organizational structures around supply chains. What that looks like, I don't know. I can just see where it becomes very useful. I know that the productivity improvements over the last decade have been mostly in the area of supply chain management because of the work that I do.

The reorganization of work and the flexibility of SEAM are a factor. When you compare SEAM, I don't think that Lean or Six Sigma would survive very well in this environment. You may use them as tools, but as far as continuous improvement is concerned, because of how fast IR3 promises to be based upon the dawn of the digital age and how these organizational structures may be more complex, I don't think that Lean or Six sigma do the job. So I think that SEAM is in a good place. I think that there is the potential that, going forward, we'll see more people being interested in SEAM as we get deeper into the third industrial revolution. The third industrial revolution is just not an idea. Trust me, it's already happening.

So, I wanted to share with you one last thought. We talk about the virus starting during the second industrial revolution but the virus seems to have also been present in first industrial revolution. What if the virus is really here to stay and it is a natural element of the human condition and societies? Will a version of the virus develop during IR3? Is it possible that one of the larger dynamics that is always present in human societies is a constant rebalancing between the organization and reorganization of work to create perceived value and wealth? What if the process of selecting value added activities is ever present? The intent to achieve improvement in the condition of human populations through improving and achieving value and creating wealth but at the same time attempting to retain respect for human dignity and the creative potential and rights of the individual? Perhaps there is a constant and never-ending dynamic that is always present in human societies. Perhaps the virus is really a reflection of this dynamic process.

THE THIRD INDUSTRIAL REVOLUTION AND SEAM

Today as we embark upon the digital age, those who study invention and innovation believe a third industrial revolution is emerging (Rifkin, 2013; Hassan, 2014). In the future, the technocratic approach and top down model of the second industrial revolution so focused on strategic and business planning will no longer meet the business needs and challenges of the new period. Substantial changes in the organization of work and organizational structure are being forecasted. The new trend is toward organizing work to take place in clusters of workers rather than assembly lines and toward collaborative problem solving and outcomes taking place within the group rather than by a select few (Hassan, 2014, p. 90).

For this paper, we will review similar occurring patterns of change in the source and use of energy in the three industrial revolutions. In each of the industrial revolutions, a change in the source and use of energy occurred which influenced the development of a new economic paradigm which allowed for increase in productivity and changes in the creation of value and wealth for society.

In addition, we will review the resulting societal conflict about the individuals who are in some way hindered in their personal freedoms and liberties due to the new economic paradigm. In conclusion, we will attempt to understand SEAM's potential contribution to organization in the third industrial revolution.

The Third Industrial Revolution

Today as we embark upon the digital age, a new industrial age is dawning. Many are calling the emerging digital age the third industrial revolution (IR3). One of the promises of the new industrial age is new economic freedoms and wealth for each individual (Rifkin, 2013). With the use of tools as simple as a computer and an internet connection it is possible for almost any individual to design and manufacture their idea for substantially less cost and in matter of days (Brynjolfsson & McAfee, 2014). With access to free software programs such as the social softwares and computer aided design (CAD) anyone can easily draw up their design and upload the digital file to anywhere in the world for the item to be made (Anderson, 2012). The internet can then provide a cost effective market place where new designs and products can easily be sold (Flynn & Vencat, 2012).

In IR3, gone are the economic barriers created in the past by the lack of substantial amounts of capital. The barriers to manufacturing a design are quickly coming down. The new catch phrase of the emerging third industrial revolution is the democratization of manufacturing. By most accounts, for a mere $5,000.00 USD it is now possible to design, manufacture, market, and sell an item (Rifkin, 2013, p. 118).

The democratization of manufacturing is also changing the landscape of the standard business model (Rifkin, 2013). No longer is the Max Weber style of a pyramidal business bureaucracy with authority flowing top downward the most favored model. Rather to accommodate the new trend of the democratization of manufacturing a more distributive and collaborative business model with wider participation is being advanced (Hassan, 2014). The third industrial revolution because of its lateral paradigm flourishes in borderless open spaces. However, the democratization of manufacturing and changes in the basic business model is only one of many emerging trends of the third industrial revolution.

In IR3, continents are now becoming the new playing fields and focus of development. The concepts of globalization and working internationally are slowly dying (Rifkin, 2013). Business and commerce are being drawn to developing continental markets due to an increase in profits and energy constraints. The rising cost of energy makes it increasingly problematic to send goods across oceans.

Further, influencing the trend toward continentalization is a new focus on designing human systems to be more sustainable and resilient (Zolli, 2012). Increasingly, it is being argued that continental economies are more sustainable and that the political landscape needs to adapt to the change as the continents continue to develop. Jeremy Rifkin (2013) predicted the formation of political unions to better support continental economies and their continued development.

It is also believed that the rise of continentalization will promote the continued rise of biosphere consciousness (Rifkin, 2013). As science progresses and the IR3 continues, it is believed an emphasis toward protecting all life within the earth's biosphere systems will continue. Further, the development of designed biosphere communities that attempt to integrate with the rest of the living earth will become more common place.

In the shadow of growing biosphere consciousness, working on a geopolitical scale promises to take a back seat to the concept of biosphere politics.

International relations are forecasted to trend toward centering on shared ecological thinking (Rifkin, 2013).

As meaningful as these emerging trends are, the foundation of major change in the third industrial revolution will be changes in the source and use of energy (Rifkin, 2013). Renewable sources of energy such as wind and solar have become a frequent alternative to conventional fossil fuels and nuclear energy. In the future, it is possible, that every building will use solar, wind, and geothermal sources of energy as existing buildings will be converted to capture these forms of renewable energy. Companies like GE and IBM believe that in the short span of time of a few decades, 50 % of all homes will generate their own electricity (Zolli, 2012). We currently possess the technology to collect and store excess energy by using hydrogen and distributing the excess energy via the internet (Rifkin, 2012). This means that energy will potentially be virtually free. Many believe that in the not too distant future each individual may have the capability of generating their own energy.

Similarities in The Patterns of Reorganization of Work and the Creation of Wealth

Changes in the Source and Use of Energy

Similar to the third industrial revolution, historically we see a pattern of change in the source and use of energy in the first and second industrial revolution. In the epoch of each industrial revolution, new sources of energy were developed and used. Historically, changes in the source and use of energy in both industrial revolutions had profound and far reaching economic incentives for the development of new inventions and subsequent innovations (Deane, 1995). In turn, in both instances, this led to a new economic paradigm. During both industrial revolutions there were substantial gain in productivity, a steep decrease in the cost of goods sold, and a substantial increase in profits. These factors led to an increase in wealth for the overall population.

During the first industrial revolution (IR1) which spanned a little over a hundred years from 1760 until approximately 1870 the source of energy changed from the use of water power to the use of steam and steam engines (Deane, 1995). The development of the steam engine meant that factories were no longer limited to locations based upon their proximity to sources of water nor were factories limited in their ability to produce based upon the seasonal influences on water sources. As a consequence, there was a profound and wide scale shift in the economic paradigm. For the first time in human history, the factory system was developed and industry began to thrive. More and more factories came into existence and dotted the landscape.

During IR1, two industries that experienced significant change due to the new economic paradigm were the textile and iron industries (Deane, 1995). These industries had substantial economic influence on other sectors of the economy. English society changed dramatically. Overall, the English people became wealthier as changes in the source of energy led to invention and innovation which led to an overall increase in productivity for English society (Morris, 2012).

Historically, it is calculated that at the beginning of IR1 England's national income per head of population was 12 pounds per annum. However, by the end of the eighteenth century the national income per head was 22 pounds per annum (Deane, 1995). Although these are only rough measures and do not account for inflation, they help one grasp the dramatic changes in prosperity and increase in wealth of the English population.

Curiously, during IR2 we once again see the emergence of a similar pattern of change. In IR2, changes in the source and use of energy created a new economic paradigm. Just as in IR1, the new economic paradigm in IR2 had a profound impact on productivity and the creation of wealth. In IR2, changes in the source and use of energy influenced the productivity and creation of wealth in both England and by this time the United States.

During IR2, the source and use of energy changed from the use of steam and the steam engine to the use of fossil fuels and the combustible engine (Deane, 1995). The new energy source allowed England and the United States to continue to experience an overall decrease in the cost and price of goods sold and an increase in profits. IR2 was marked with inventions and major innovations in steel, railroads, petroleum and chemicals and electricity.

Overall wealth and prosperity are thought to have continued to increase until the post WWII period (Rifkin, 2013). By some accounts, IR2 continued until the 1980's which marked the beginning of the third industrial revolution and the digital age. In the later twentieth century personal computers and digital files were perfected and sources of renewable energy began to be explored as an alternative to fossil fuels and combustible engines (Anderson, 2012; Hassan, 2014; Rifkin, 2013).

In general, the three industrial revolutions are closely connected to and influenced by significant changes in the source and use of energy. Based upon changes in the source and use of energy each revolution appears to foster a significant reorganization of work which adds significant value to the production process. This in turn influences the development of a new economic paradigm that allows for an overall increase in productivity and makes possible an overall decrease in the cost and price of goods sold but yet an increase in profits and the creation of wealth.

Those Industrial Revolutions Leave Behind

Overall the source and use of energy shapes the organization of work in human societies (Rifkin, 2013). During the course of the first and second industrial revolution, work was reorganized based upon the changes in the source and use of energy and the creation of new economic opportunities and wealth. However, not all members of society participated equally in the new economic paradigm. Some groups, although their economic situation was improved, were exploited (Bizup, 2003).

During the first industrial revolution, women and children were the largest group that did not fully participate in the new economic paradigm and creation of wealth. Although they earned a wage and were economically better off than before, as a group they were forced to work long hours in poor and unsafe conditions. In comparison to most other groups, they were economically worse off. Many entrepreneurs argued if the working conditions and wages of women and children were improved then productivity would be ruined and they could not compete. In opposing such arguments, many believed that based upon the exploitation of others that the factory system was inhuman and evil.

The debate about the virtues and evil of the factory system permeated deep into the fabric of English society and culture. The debate raged for the duration of IR1 (Bizup, 2003). Reflected in the open discourse and public debate was English societies' struggle to co-exist with the new economic paradigm of the factory system and still respect human dignity, personal freedoms, and develop human potential. As the debate raged, eventually legislation became a means to ensure economic equality and human dignity for all. Beginning in 1802, the first piece of legislation passed in Parliament to improve the conditions of working women and children. For a period of 80 years, this body of legislation was continuously amended and eventually became known as the Factory Acts (Bizup, 2003). We see a similar pattern of public discourse and open debate surrounding the continued development of the factory system in the Unites States during the second industrial revolution.

By the turn of the century, the center of the second industrial revolution was the United States and the steam engine had given way to the use of fossil fuels and the combustible engine. The factory system had advanced the use of standardized parts and the use of the assembly line. It was also during this time that Fredrick Taylor developed an industrial philosophy called Scientific Management. Taylor's system focused on studying the best way to do a job to achieve maximum efficiency and productivity. From its inception, Taylor's system was subject to debate and controversy (Kanigel, 1997).

Many claimed that Taylor's work and philosophy created an unbearable legacy of the exclusion, submission, and depersonalization of the worker (Copley, 2010; Kanigel, 1997).

Stories abound of men being worked to the point of exhaustion and many more complained about being robbed of independence, judgment, and thought. Further, very seldom did the laborer receive increased pay for his increased efforts and productivity. Many believed Taylor's system was nothing more than a new type of servitude that diminished humanity and stole the souls of workers (Kanigel, 1997).

In contrast, advocates of Taylorism argued that Taylor's system could, if implemented correctly, promote cooperation and harmony between management and the worker (Kanigel, 1997). Many industrialists maintained that a scientific approach to the management of work was a fair and equitable system and in the best interest of all (Taylor, 2006). They argued that the scientific standardization of work not only benefitted management with increased profits, but also benefitted labor with increased wages; and ultimately society benefitted due to the decrease in the cost and price of goods sold and increase in prosperity (Kanigel, 1997). Increased productivity, it was argued, contributed to the good of all and was the best measure of the greatness of a society.

In a pattern strikingly similar to the public debate in Parliament during the first industrial revolution, in 1911 a special committee was formed by the House of Representatives to investigate the Taylor system. The hearings were public and became the catalyst for public discourse and open debate about the evils and benefits of Scientific Management. During the hearings, Taylor was extensively questioned. In its report, the committee concluded that neither the Taylor system nor any other should be imposed from above on an unwilling work force (Kanigel, 1997). However, at the same time the committee ruled that standardization and systemization, both important elements for Scientific Management, were acceptable but that time studies should not be done without the consent of the worker. In its final report, the committee found it neither advisable nor expedient to make any regulation for legislation.

Today, as we embark upon the third industrial revolution, the moral dilemma and debate surrounding modern day production and the factory system has not been resolved. The unresolved dilemma of supporting a production system that creates wealth for many, but exploits the few while minimizing their humanity and personal freedoms, is a morale quagmire that lingers to this day. Although the debate is not as public and as voracious as it has been in the past, the dilemma still exists and daily it influences our working lives.

Today we have learned to accept the moral dilemma and controversy as part of the fabric of the organizations we create. Our morale quagmire has become the back story of our societal systems of production and wealth creation processes for society. As we forged the creation of new economic paradigms for IR1 and IR2, we have believed that there will always be economic winners and losers and some groups will always be economically disadvantaged. Its the way things are. We have no other choice. The SEAM model is built on a different premise and philosophy.

SEAM and the Moral Dilemma Today

Conbere and Heorhiadi (2011) in their article titled "Socio-Economic Approach to Management" pointed out that the traditional approach to management is a fragmented approach. Traditional forms of management are based upon insufficient financial data that leads to a lack of recognition of the people involved. The SEAM model takes into consideration the people and the finances of an organization and does not foster or support the view of employees as a commodity.

Cristallini (2011), in his paper titled "The Importance of Corporate Governance in the Fight Against the World Dissemination of the Techno-Economic Virus," used the analogy of a virus, a concept that was created in 2006 by Savall and Zardet (2009, 2009a, 2010) to describe the prevailing techno-economic ideology that exists in many of today's organizations as a result of treating labor as a commodity. The viral contagion is an ideological pattern of corporate governance and influence that encourages the depersonalization and submission of the individual. In organizations suffering from the virus, it is common place and acceptable to treat members of the organization as if they are intellectually inferior, irresponsible, and untrustworthy.

Long term, the presence of the virus promotes a lack of cooperation and hopelessness amongst members of an organization. Within infected organizations, inclusion and joint participation are viewed as impossible. It is these perceptions that result in the hopelessness that facilitates the creation of the dysfunctions and hidden costs that SEAM theory addresses (Savall & Zardet, 2008; Savall, Zardet, & Bonnet, 2008).

The SEAM model, addresses the creation of value and wealth processes in organizations by caring for the dignity of the individual and recognizing the current and future potential of the human being. SEAM addresses the whole organization by recognizing the dysfunction and is designed to quickly organize and address the inefficient structural aspects of an organization and the human behavior within an organization. The model is intentionally designed to focus on and address the individual and collective behavior of the employees so as to reduce the overall level of dysfunction and to make known and decrease costs that previously have been hidden. It is through the process of addressing the behavioral dysfunctions that hidden cost is reduced and the creation of value and wealth process is improved.

SEAM's Place in the Third Industrial Revolution

As we have summarized in each industrial revolution, a new economic paradigm has developed that was heavily influenced by changes in the source and use of energy. The emerging third industrial revolution seems to be following a similar pattern. A new economic paradigm is emerging that promises to create profound changes in organizational life and design. The SEAM models approach to the development of trust and security among employees is in alignment with the trends and new economic paradigm that is forming (Conbere & Heorhiadi, 2011).

One major change in organizational life and design that is developing and is in harmony with the SEAM model is the global trend toward emergent problem solving. The usage of emergent problem solving models is quickly becoming necessary for organizations to compete in the new developing economic paradigm of IR3. Emergent problem solving is based upon the wide participation and interaction of many people and their sources and flow of information. Participants quickly adapt their behavior based upon their negotiation with each other based upon and influenced by their information flow and sharing with each other. This in turn gives rise to a set of adaptive or emergent characteristics (Hassan, 2014). This type of problem solving does not necessarily have a hierarchy of leader of the group.

There is a growing recognition that the traditional management model with a top down structure and the strategic planning models so prevalent in IR2 are not agile or flexible enough to cope with the rapid flows of information that are becoming more common in the digital age. Further, the top down models are not capable of allowing human groups to quickly adapt to maximize productivity based upon changes in invention and innovation.

In IR3, the generation and sharing of information in a digital format allows information to flow much faster. Due to the faster speeds at which information flows outcomes cannot be predicted or planned. To be successful in IR3, organizational design must promote the flow and use of information and a collaborative business model with wider participation resulting in quick adaptation (Hassan, 2014). In IR3, the SEAM model promises to be effective and supportive in emergent problem solving and highly adaptive in organization environments and organizational design.

First, the SEAM model engages the whole organization and is highly adaptive in its design. The approach to improve the value and wealth creation process of an organization is to intervene and decrease dysfunctional behaviors. Ultimately, a SEAM intervention is designed to be adaptive and create change to improve economic performance by engaging both the human systems and structures of an organization (Savall & Zardet, 2008).

Further, the SEAM model as required by IR3 is a highly synchronized and adaptive organizational design. Design elements that support frequent adaptive behavior is already incorporated into the SEAM model design. The SEAM model is highly coordinated and the entire organization is engaged and all members participate. Large numbers of people are involved with wide participation in a short period of time (Savall & Zardet, 2008).

The SEAM model strives to overcome the moral quagmire so prevalent in IR1 and IR2. The model incorporates the belief that all groups and organizations should advance. SEAM from its inception was designed to address the moral dilemma and the viral contagion so prevalent in organizations IR1 and IR2. SEAM is based upon the fundamental belief that human potential should be developed and that organizations exist to serve society and in particular serve the participants of an organization (Conbere & Heorhiadi, 2011).

Secondly, the SEAM model is highly adaptive by virtue of its design. The SEAM approach has often been compared to a ripple-through process because an implementation always begins with two very formalized and simultaneous actions that engage and encompass the entire organization and its systems (Savall & Zardet, 2013). The first act of the engagement process is a horizontal action which takes place with the executive management team and the second is a vertical action that begins with one or possibly two units within the organization (Savall & Zardet, 2008). These two simultaneous and synchronized, vertical and horizontal actions together are called the Horivert procedure. The Horivert procedure can be viewed as a highly adaptive procedure and process. Ultimately, through synchronizing the engagement and interaction of the vertical and horizontal actions, every member of the organization is quickly engaged and the entire organization can be quickly working to adopt new behaviors and improve selected dysfunctions within the organization.

CONCLUSION

In conclusion we cannot state with certainty what organizational life and design will be like in the third industrial revolution. It is a bold exercise to attempt to speculate about which trends will prevail and dominate and which organizational design elements will be highly prized or die.

However, regardless of the outcome, we must as academicians and Organizational Development practitioners become aware of and engaged in the debate. We must participate fully in the open debate and public discourse. We must do so not only with our intellect but with our hearts. Unlike the open debate and public discourse that took place during IR1 and IR2, we have more social science and knowledge at our disposal.

For the first time in the history of the emergent series of industrial revolutions, we can draw on science to help improve organizations and economic life for many and generations to come. The social sciences and SEAM model did not exist when Taylor invented Scientific Management and the Factory question was asked. Today we are here and we are better prepared to support respect for human dignity, personal freedoms, and development of human potential in the third industrial revolution.

REFERENCES

Anderson, C. (2012) Makers: The new industrial revolution. New York, NY: Crown Business.

Ballard, R. (2013). *The third industrial revolution animation.* https://vimeo.com/79782365.

Bizup, J. (2003). *Manufacturing culture vindications of early Victorian manufacturing.* Charlottesville, VA: University of Virginia Press.

Brynjolfsson, E., & McAfee, A. (2014). *The second machine age.* New York, NY: W.W. Norton.

Conbere, J. P. & Heorhiadi, A. (2011). Socio-Economic Approach to Management: A Successful Systemic Approach to Organizational Change. *OD Practitioner, 43* (1), 6–10.

Copley, F. (2010). *Fredrick Taylor, father of scientific management* (Vol. 2). New York, NY: Harper & Brothers. (Original work published 1923).

Cristallini, V. (2011). *Rôle de la gouvernance dans la lutte contre la pandémie mondiale du virus techno-économique* [The Importance of Corporate Governance in the Fight Against the World Dissemination of the Techno-Economic Virus]. Conference proceedings ADERSE, Paris, France.

Deane, P. (1995). *The first industrial revolution.* Cambridge, England: Cambridge Press.

Flynn, A., & Vencat, E. (2012). *Custom nation.* Dallas, TX: Ben Bella.

Hassan, Z. (2014). *The social labs revolution.* San Francisco, CA: Berrett-Kohler.

Kanigel, R. (1997). *The one best way.* New York, NY: Penguin.

Morris, C. (2012). *The dawn of innovation.* New York, NY: Public Affairs.

Rifkin, J. (2013). *The third industrial revolution.* New York, NY: Palgrave Macmillan.

Savall, H., & Zardet, V. (2008) *Mastering Hidden Costs Socio-Economic Performance:* Charlotte, NC: Information Age Publishing. 1st French edition, Paris, France: Economica, 1987.

Savall, H., & Zardet, V. (2009, June). *Mesure et pilotage de la responsabilité sociale et sociétale de l'entreprise : résultats de recherches longitudinales* [*Measuring and piloting the corporate social responsibility: results from longitudinal research*]. International conference proceedings and doctoral consortium, partnership between the Academy of Management (AOM) and Iseor, Lyon.

Savall, H., & Zardet, V. (2009a, July), *Responsabilidad social y societal de la empresa: Indicadores para dialogar con las partes interesadas* [The corporate social responsibility: Indicators to converse with stakeholders]. Paper, ACACIA's Conference proceedings, UAM–México.

Savall, H., & Zardet, V. (2010). Le non-dit dans la théorie socio-économique des organisations: Situations de management et pièces de théâtre [Unvoiced comment in the socio-economic theory of organizations: Management situations and theatrics]. In R. Ocler (Ed.), *Fantasmes, mythes, non-dits et quiproquo: Analyse de discours et organisation [Fantasy, myths, unvoiced and misunderstanding: Analysis of speech and organization]*. Paris, France: L'Harmattan.

Savall, H., & Zardet, V. (2013). *The Dynamics and Challenges of Tetranormalization*. Charlotte, NC: Information Age Publishing.

Savall, H., Zardet, V., & Bonnet, M. (2008). *Releasing the untapped potential of enterprises through socio-economic management*. Geneva, Switzerland: ILO. 1st edition, 2000.

Taylor, F. W. (2006). *The principles of scientific management*. New York, NY: Cosimo. (Original work published 1911).

Zolli, A. (2012). *Resilience: Why things bounce back*. New York, NY: Simon & Schuster.

ABOUT THE CONTRIBUTORS

Marc Bonnet is Professor of Management at EUGINOV Business School, IAE Lyon, University Jean Moulin Lyon 3, and deputy manager of ISEOR research center. His research in the field of Socio-Economic Approach to Management (SEAM), based on the Qualimetrics Intervention-Research methodology, has been mainly carried out in industrial companies. With ISEOR colleagues, he has published articles in journals such as *Journal of Organizational Change Management, International Journal of Action-Research, Organizational Development Journal, Society and Business Review,* and *Organizational Research Methods.* Prior to the two chapters in this book, he has also co-authored five book chapters in the RMC series edited by Anthony F. Buono and Henri Savall.

Collin Bunch is a counselor at the Columbia office of the Missouri Small Business and Technology Development Center. He is an expert in new media and search engine optimization and is certified by the Edward Lowe Foundation's National Center for Economic Gardening. SEAM thinking informs his work and gives him a complex systemic perspective on his clients' businesses, from early stage bright-eyed startups to older and growing companies. He thoroughly enjoys solving problems with entrepreneurs and is thankful to have one of the most amazing jobs in the world.

Anthony F. Buono, RMC series editor, is professor of Management and Sociology and founding coordinator of the Alliance for Ethics and Social Responsibility at Bentley University, which he directed from 2003 through 2013. He is also a former Chair of Bentley's Management Department.

Decoding the Socio-Economic Approach to Management, pages 317–324
Copyright © 2016 by Information Age Publishing

Tony's interests include organizational change, inter-organizational strategies, management consulting, and ethics and corporate social responsibility. He has written or edited seventeen books including *The Human Side of Mergers and Acquisitions* (Jossey-Bass, 1989, Beard Books, 2003), *A Primer on Organizational Behavior* (Wiley, 7th ed., 2008), and *Exploring the Professional Identity of Management Consultants* (Information Age Publishing, 2013). His articles and book review essays have appeared in numerous journals, including *Academy of Management Learning & Education, Across the Board, Administrative Science Quarterly,* and *Human Relations.* Tony holds a PhD with a concentration in Industrial and Organizational Sociology from Boston College.

Laurent Cappelletti is a Chair Professor of Management Control at the Conservatoire National des Arts et Métiers, University of Paris, where he is the director of the executive training programs and researcher at the LIRSA center. He is also Program Director at the ISEOR Research Center in Lyon. He holds a PhD in management sciences from the University of Lyon. In 2005 and 2009, he received with Florence Noguera and Richard Baker, the Academy of Management best paper award (Management Consulting Division) for his work on human capital and socio-economic management control system. His research is focused on human potential and the improvement of socio-economic performance in companies and organizations, particularly in public services and small and medium sized businesses.

John Conbere is Professor and Co-director of the SEAM International Institute at the University of St. Thomas in Minnesota. He is a primary developer of the SEAM Institute which is a collaborative program between the University of St. Thomas and ISEOR (Lyon, France). He also has been a Fulbright Senior Specialist and Open Society/Soros Foundation scholar, and has taught in the United States, France, and Ukraine. Among his published articles are *Socio-Economic Approach to Management: A Successful Systemic Approach to Organizational Change* (OD Practitioner, 2011), and *Virtue vs. Virus: Can OD Overcome the Heritage of Scientific Management?* (OD Practitioner, 2014). He holds an MDiv from the Episcopal Divinity School and an EdD in Human Resource Development from the University of Minnesota. Conbere is also President of SEAM, Inc., which specializes in consulting using the Socio-Economic Approach to Management.

Vincent Cristallini is assistant professor at the University Jean Moulin Lyon 3. His work focuses on the role of management, people management, change management, and sustainable performance improvement. He practiced intervention research in many companies and organizations for 25 years. He is the author of the book *L'habileté managériale-Réalisme et courage en management-EMS-2009.*

Frantz Datry is a Program Director at ISEOR Research Center. He has been an intervener-researcher of Management Sciences since 1999. He holds a PhD in Management sciences from the Institut d'Administration des Entreprises, University Jean Moulin Lyon 3. His research focuses on SEAM, strategic change management, management control, and socio-economic performance in companies and organizations.

Gérard Desmaison was a Senior Executive at Nabisco/Danone (Belin Biscuits), ACCOR (Lenôtre, Carlson-Wagonlit), and Ferrero (International Headquarters) implementing SEAM for over 35 years. He is now a consultant at +PHOR and a researcher at ISEOR Research Center and holds a PhD in Management Sciences. His research focuses on SEAM, Management methods, Corporate Social Responsibility (CSR), and Human Potential. He published many conference papers. He holds a HEC Certified Coach (member of ICF) and does coaching, training, and conferences for executive and project managers. He is a member of Atelier Du Dirigeant Durable (A3D), a think tank about the reconciliation of "economic" and "human" in organizations, ADERSE (Association for the development and the education of the CSR), and 36000 rebonds (French ONG in charge to coach entrepreneurs after a bankruptcy).

Chato B. Hazelbaker is the Chief Information and Communication Officer at Clark College in Vancouver, WA. He has taught courses in communication, management, and organizational development at Bethel University, Warner Pacific College, and others. He has previously published a book chapter on SEAM and Critical Theory, and the research from his dissertation "Looking for Evidence of the TFW Virus" contributed to an article written with coauthors for *O.D. Practitioner,* "Virtue Versus Virus." He holds an EdD from the University of St. Thomas (MN) in Organization Development.

Alla Heorhiadi, is Distinguished Service Professor and Co-director of the SEAM Institute at the University of St. Thomas, Minnesota. She has doctorates in Organization Development and Economics. She has a vast international experience by having taught and consulted in the United States, Ukraine, France, Greece, and Germany. She is licensed to do Socio-Economic interventions according to the ISEOR's standard in the United States. Since 2010 her scholarly work has been focused on studying effects of socio-economic approach to management. In 2011, the article "Socio-Economic Approach to Management: A Successful Systemic Approach to

Organizational Change," published in *OD Practitioner*, was named the best article of 2011.

Mark E. Hillon has had an eclectic life in civil engineering, international development, sustainable agriculture, strategic planning, and critical management scholarship. The diffusion of SEAM to improve the practice of management in America is the last great challenge of his life. He holds a PhD from New Mexico State University with a concentration in Strategy and a co-tutelle PhD from ISEOR/Jean Moulin University (Lyon 3) in Management Science supervised by David Boje and Henri Savall. His current venture is the Lafayette Institute, a consultancy for strategic performance management.

Yue Cai Hillon teaches strategic management at Western Carolina University in the beautiful mountain valley of Cullowhee, North Carolina. She is an innovator in undergraduate business strategy education, training students in future-oriented data-intensive strategy creation for local business clients. Her graduate students learn the SEAM methodology and work with her to assist local clients of the North Carolina Small Business and Technology Development Center. Her SEAM clients have spanned a wide range of industries including manufacturing, aviation, hotels, restaurants, and education. She holds a PhD from New Mexico State University in Strategic Management, in which she pioneered the study of strategic inflections by imagery deconstruction. Outside of teaching, she volunteers her expertise in strategic planning and performance management to assist local businesses, promote regional economic development, and support the invaluable work of the NC SBTDC.

Sergiy Ivakhnenkov, Professor of Finance at National University of Kyiv-Mohyla Academy, Ukraine. He also worked as the university chief accountant there from 2002 to 2005. Among his books are *Computer-aided Auditing* (2005), *Information Technologies of Auditing and Information Technologies of Internal Control in the Context of Global Integration* (2010), and *Information Technologies in Accounting and Auditing: A Post-Soviet Approach* (2010). His current research interests are connected to audit automation and IT auditing, financial statements and accounting policy modeling, and also industrial organization and managerial accounting. He holds a PhD in Accounting and Auditing and Doctor of Economic Sciences degree from Kyiv National Economic University.

Alanna Kennedy holds an EdD in Organization Development and MBA with a concentration in world class manufacturing from the University of St. Thomas in St. Paul, Minnesota. In addition, she is certified in lean manufacturing at the bronze level by the Society of Manufacturing Engineering and is certified in Production Inventory Management (CPIM) by APICS. Dr. Kennedy has more than 25 years of manufacturing experience which includes over 10 years of "hands on" experience in production management with direct responsibility for manufacturing operations and 15 years of experience in material management operations. Currently, she is employed by Emerson Process Management.

Philippe Lacroix is Managing Director of ManpowerGroup Belgium, Manpower Switzerland and ManpowerGroup Luxembourg. In 2011, he has introduced the SEAM methodology created by the Institute ISEOR to stimulate the economic and social performance of ManpowerGroup BeLux and to implement a change management culture. Philippe Lacroix is member of the AmCham board (American Chamber of Commerce–Belgium). He is graduated in economic and financial sciences at ICHEC, holds a Human Resource Management postgraduate, and a management master.

Leslie L. McKnight is currently the Senior Economic Development Specialist for the City of Peoria, IL and adjunct professor at Robert Morris University and Benedictine University. Her research and consulting interests focus on the use of self in consulting, strategic management, and organization change. She is published in the *Organization Development Journal* and *Journal of Leadership, Accountability, and Ethics.* She recently received the Best Paper Award on Ethical Issues in Consulting from the National Academy of Management, Management Consulting Division. She holds a PhD in Organization Development from Benedictine University, Springfield, IL and a Master of Science (MS) degree in Human Services Administration from Spertus Institute, Chicago, Illinois.

Thomas "Ace" Oestreich is the President of Chance River Vineyards, Inc. Was the Director of Transportation for Bloomington (MN) Public Schools (2004–2015). In the fall of 1999 the school district launched their own Transportation Center to control burgeoning contracted busing costs. Tom was hired as Assistant Director the previous spring and worked as part of a small team to ensure that every student in Bloomington would arrive safely for the first day of school on a bus owned by the district and driven by a highly trained, qualified, and licensed district employee. Tom was promoted to Director in 2004, and the Bloomington Transportation Center continues to grow and thrive as they prepare for their 15th school year launch in September of 2014. Prior to his time in Bloomington, Tom joined the Edina, Minnesota, school district in 1979 first as a driver, then assistant director, and finally transportation director.

Michel Péron is an Emeritus Professor at the University of Paris III Sorbonne Nouvelle. He received his PhD from the University of Lyon. He is a researcher at the ISEOR and the CERVEPAS research centers. His research interests lie in cross-cultural management, corporate ethics, and the history of economic ideas.

Susan Quint is a healthcare industry leader with work experience in organization development, financial analysis, and business analytics. Her current focus is on building new analytic capabilities that improve business performance and add economic value to the organization. Susan holds an EdD in Organization Development from the University of St. Thomas. Her work and research is inspired by the values underlying the Socio-Economic Approach to Management, and the idea that investments in analytics are not complete without corresponding investments in people and readiness of the organization to leverage new information.

Thibault Ruat is a doctoral student at the Institut d'Administration des Entreprises, University Jean Moulin Lyon 3. He is an intervener-researcher at ISEOR, where he has carried out various interventions since 2012, particularly in the building firms and architectural industry. His research interests are SEAM, cooperation practices, strategic management, prime contractor, and qualimetrics methodology. He presented different research papers in international conferences. In 2014, he presented his first research results at the second SEAM conference in United States (Minneapolis, Minnesota). He also teaches management, audit, and quality at the University of Lyon to undergraduate students.

Eric Sanders, MA, MBA, is an organization development economist—a consultant who helps leaders and their organizations achieve measurable results through developing their people. After twenty years in retail, he has worked for over ten years as an OD scholar-practitioner. He has published several articles and book chapters, and has taught economics and/or OD at five schools, including Benedictine University and Loyola University–Chicago. He is currently a doctoral candidate in OD at Benedictine, researching how scholar-practitioners simultaneously help clients and generate new knowledge, and can be reached ateric.sanders@ODeconomist.com

Amandine Savall is an intervener-researcher at ISEOR research center, where she has carried out various interventions in European and American companies. She holds a PhD with a concentration in International Management and SEAM from Conservatoire National des Arts et Métiers in Paris. She teaches at graduate, undergraduate, and doctoral levels at IAE Lyon business school. Her research interests are SEAM, management consulting, management control, family businesses, and international management, using qualimetrics methodology. Amandine has been awarded the best doctoral student paper from the Management Consulting Division (Academy of Management Annual Meeting, August 2014, Philadelphia). She has co-authored the book *Becoming Agile* (in press, Jossey-Bass) with Christopher Worley, Véronique Zardet, and Marc Bonnet. She has also coordinated two books edited by Tony Buono and Henri Savall, in the Research in Management Consulting Series, Information Age Publishing.

Henri Savall is an Emeritus Professor at the Institut d'Administration des Entreprises, University Jean Moulin Lyon, where he is the founder of the EUGINOV Centre (École Universitaire de Gestion Innovante) and the Socio-Economic Management Master's program. He is the founder and president of the ISEOR Research Center. Professor Savall has a multidisciplinary education and his fields of interest include accounting, finance, political science, linguistics, economics, and economic history. His current research interests are socioeconomic theory, strategic management, qualimetric methodology, and tetranormalization. His research methodology is referred to as "intervention research" and "qualimetrics" as it goes beyond traditional action research. Henri (along with Professor Véronique Zardet) has been awarded the famous Rossi Award by the Academy of Moral and Political Sciences (Institut de France) for their work on the integration of social variables into business strategy. He is the founder and the editor of the Revue Sciences de Gestion—Management Sciences—Ciencias de Gestión (Journal of Administrative Science), Paris and Lyon.

Patrick Tabchoury is a scholar-practitioner in the field of Management Sciences. He is an adjunct professor at University of Balamand and at the Lebanese University. He is the co-director with Marc Bonnet of the DBA program at University of Balamand and University of Lyon 3. He is also an associate researcher at ISEOR research center and holds a PhD in management sciences from University of Lyon 3. His current research and consulting interests focus on organizational change in the field of healthcare especially in the MENA region where he made many intervention-researches. Among his publications, one can mention several book chapters and articles focused on qualimetrics researches and Socio-economic Approach to Management.

Lachlan (Lach) R. Whatley is a practitioner/scholar who believes that sound management is based on solid theory and solid theory is grounded in practice. An accountant by trade, Lach holds a PhD in Organization Development from Benedictine University. He is currently CEO of the MetalBoss Family of Companies based in Alberta, Canada. Lach's research interests are in the areas of group dynamics, teams, the dynamics of change, humility, managing innovation, and the use of positive psychology to improve performance. He has published with the *Journal of Leadership, Accountability and Ethics,* the *Journal of Organizational Psychology,* the *Organization Development Journal,* and the *Journal of Leadership Studies.* Lach is also a reviewer with the *Organization Development Journal* and *AUDEM: International Journal of Higher Education & Democracy* and has been elected as Member-at-Large of the AOM–MC Division for the 2013–15 term.

Véronique Zardet is a Professor of Management Sciences at EUGINOV business school, Institut d'Administration des Entreprises, University Jean Moulin Lyon 3, where she is the director of the EUGINOV Center (*École Universitaire de Gestion Innovante*) and director, along with Professor Henri Savall, the founder, of the ISEOR Research Center. She heads the Research in Socio-Economic Management master's program. She holds a PhD in management sciences from the University of Lyon. In 2001, she received with Henri Savall the Rossi Award from the Academy of Moral and Political Sciences (Institute of France) for their work on the integration of social variables into business strategies. Her research is focused on strategic change management and the improvement of socio-economic performance in companies and organizations, particularly in public services and health industry.